Corporate Restructuring

David E. Vance

Corporate Restructuring

From Cause Analysis to Execution

 Springer

Professor David E. Vance
School of Business
Rutgers University
227 Penn Street
Camden, New Jersey 08102
USA
dvance@camden.rutgers.edu

ISBN 978-3-642-01785-8   ISBN 978-3-642-01786-5 (eBook)
DOI 10.1007/978-3-642-01786-5
Springer Heidelberg Dordrecht London New York

Library of Congress Control Number: 2009933286

Cover design: WMXDesign GmbH, Heidelberg

Printed on acid-free paper

Springer is part of Springer Science+Business Media (www.springer.com)

Preface

This book discusses the one concept that can be universally applied to restructure any company, anywhere, at any time and in any industry. It can be used to grow sales, increase net income, improve cash flow, satisfy every customer, save the whales, preserve the rain forest, and make grown men weep. Of course any book that promises all that is silly on its face, but you wouldn't think so by reading the dust jackets of many books.

The truth is that every industry is different, just as every company is different. There is no one formula, concept or magic potion that will fix every problem everywhere. This book is designed to provide an overarching framework for analyzing a company; diagnosing its problems; and providing a new CEO or turnaround consultant with an array of proven tools.

Most failing companies can be saved if prompt aggressive action is taken. But, management often refuses to look the tiger in the eye, meaning they refuse to focus on the real problems. They delay or avoid the drastic change needed. This book helps them to see what needs to be done and the payoff for doing it. The techniques discussed in this book can also be used to transform underperforming companies into top competitors.

This book was written because existing restructuring books either focus on financial engineering or they are CEO memoirs recounting how they did what they did. Neither class of books provides a complete and integrated view of how to restructure a company.

Chapter 1 discusses how to make a sober assessment of a company's performance and prospects. It also provides tools for diagnosing root problems. Chapter 2 discusses how to reverse engineer desired performance goals.

Chapter 3 discusses people issues such as relations between a new CEO or turnaround consultant and the board of directors; building a turnaround team; improving the quality of a company's employees; unions; and layoff law. Chapter 4 discusses how to estimate an optimum staffing level and identify specific targets for headcount reduction. It also discusses labor cost controls that can be implemented without layoffs.

Chapter 5 discusses critical evaluation of divisions, subsidiaries and other businesses. Often a company can make substantial progress by shedding underperforming units. Stop the bleeding is one of the first commands of restructuring.

Chapter 6 is a critical evaluation of products, customers and contracts. Companies often have unprofitable products, customers and facilities, but don't realize it. Refocusing a company on its core products and best customers can transform an underperforming company into an outstanding one.

Chapter 7 discusses revenue growth and new products. A company must grow or die. No company can cost cut its way to success. So this chapter addresses means and methods for growing revenue. New products and services are key growth components for most businesses.

Chapter 8 discusses factors that influence pricing opportunities such as markets, product life cycle and how to apply insights from economics. Chapter 9 discusses customers and service. Unless a company can satisfy customer needs and wants, it has no purpose and no future.

Chapter 10 discusses re-engineering, process mapping, continuous process improvement and outsourcing.

Chapter 11 discusses three strategies for identifying cost savings as well as common targets of opportunity.

Chapter 12 discusses management of information technology. This is an area in which management has abdicated control in many companies and that makes it fertile ground for improvement.

Chapter 13 discusses how to fund a turnaround. When a company gets into trouble it should expect its bank to cut off credit. Fortunately there are many alternatives to banks if one knows where to look. Chapter 14 discusses raising cash internally through improved asset management. Chapter 15 discusses emergency cash management techniques to keep a troubled company alive.

Chapter 16 discusses the offensive and defensive use of bankruptcy to restructure a company. Bankruptcy can be used to reform contracts, leases and labor contracts.

Chapter 17 discusses execution. The techniques discussed in the previous sixteen chapters are useless unless a company can execute its plans. This chapter discusses ways to make sure plans are executed in a timely and efficient manner.

This book is based on research developed while teaching corporate restructuring at Rutgers University School of Business Camden for over a decade. It is also based on real world experience restructuring companies. The questions and comments of my students have made a valuable contribution to the content of this book. The good points are a credit to them, the faults are my own.

Camden, New Jersey   David E. Vance

Contents

Chapter 1
Diagnosing the Problem

Introduction

In three days, payroll for 400 people is due. The company has no cash and the bank has cut off its line of credit. What would you do? As acting CFO for a turnaround client, I was faced with this situation.

If a company does not meet its payroll, its workforce will walk out and the company will collapse. And that would just be the beginning of its problems.

Most states impose an absolute obligation on companies to pay employees within a certain number of days. And whether or not a company pays its employees, state and federal governments expect social security, Medicare, and withholding taxes. Such tax obligations cannot generally be discharged in bankruptcy.

This particular company was privately owned, which meant, among other things, that the company's owners had personally guaranteed an outstanding bank loan, so if the company failed, the bank could seize their personal assets.

This company was in trouble and everybody knew it. But the road to hell is not always apparent. This chapter discusses some diagnostic tests to determine whether a company is simply underperforming or headed for real trouble; suggests ways to find underlying problems so they can be fixed rather than papered over; and discusses the turnaround process.

Not all business failures end in bankruptcy. If a company's value declines to the point where it is worthless, the business has failed from the owners view, whether or not it continues to operate in someone else's hands. Other companies simply wind up their affairs and quietly go out of existence. No matter how failure occurs, it usually results in lost of wealth, jobs and has an adverse impact on the company's employees, customers and suppliers.

Stages of a Troubled Company

Companies rarely go from prosperity to failure in one step. Freddie Reiss, and Theodore Phelps, both CPAs classified the stages of a troubled company as early, intermediate, and late (DiNapoli et al., 1999, pp. 8–11). These stages have diagnostic value. They can help boards, owners, and managers understand the reality

D.E. Vance, *Corporate Restructuring*, DOI 10.1007/978-3-642-01786-5_1,
© Springer-Verlag Berlin Heidelberg 2009

of the situation and help drive the radical action necessary to get a company back on track.

Early Stage

In the early stage of financial distress, isolated inefficiencies in production and distribution become more frequent and form a pattern. Quality slips, and inventory builds. Customer complaints become more frequent. Sales stagnate. Margins erode. Repeat sales decline. Cash becomes tight, but immediate obligations are met. Vendors are paid more slowly, perhaps 15 days over due (DiNapoli et al., 1999, p. 9). Management still believes things will improve in the near future. The crisis is not recognized and no corrective action is taken.

Intermediate Stage

In the intermediate stage, production and distribution problems become acute. Quality continues to slip. Gross margins erode noticeably. Material shortages occur as management attempts to conserve cash by reducing inventory. Collections slow. The line of credit is near its maximum. Vendor payments are 60 days overdue. Venders demand payment prior to shipping materials. The bank becomes concerned and demands that the company produce a plan for recovery. The company is in technical default of bank covenants. Morale is falling. There are rumors about the company's problems. The better people are looking for jobs or have left (DiNapoli et al., 1999, p. 10).

Late Stage

In the late stage of financial distress, management and reporting systems breakdown. Deadlines are not met. Rush orders for demanding customers, and customers that pay promptly create havoc with schedules. Quality control becomes non-existent. Returns and re-work increase. Production efficiency drops because of material shortages and frequent schedule changes. Equipment break-downs become common because maintenance has been deferred and stocks of spare parts depleted (DiNapoli et al., 1999, p. 10).

Collections slow. Customers refuse to pay because of poor service or performance. Accounts receivable decline in value as collateral because of their age. Sales decline. The line of credit is overdrawn. Cash balances are negative and the company plays the float. Vendors demand cash before shipping supplies and raw materials. Juggling funds becomes the full time job of the controller. Financial and operational reports become secondary. Management has no performance measures and is flying blind. The bank has turned its loan over to the work-out department, and is desperately trying to get out from under the loan. At the same time, they are charging the company extra fees for violating bank loan covenants, increasing interest rates and demanding more collateral. Customers are becoming impatient with lost, delayed or incorrect orders and poor quality. They are looking for alternate suppliers and plan to switch as soon as possible. Secured lenders have lost all confidence in management. The best employees leave. Collapse is imminent (DiNapoli et al., 1999, pp. 10–11).

Restructuring Tasks

There are three main tasks in restructuring (i) diagnosing problems, (ii) identifying and implementing solutions and (iii) finding the resources to keep the company going until restructuring takes effect. This chapter will begin the process of diagnosing a company's problems. The real world is complex and diagnosis is more like peeling back the layers of an onion than a one time event. As one set of problems is understood and addressed, others become apparent.

Even the best turnaround takes two things, time and money. Finding the resources that will buy a troubled company enough time to restructure is an art form. While it is important to know where to look for money, it is equally important to realize help may never come. So a company should always do what it can to become self-sufficient; and this means making hard choices. Time can be bought by cutting expenses and increasing cash flows. But unless management can use that time productively the company will never achieve its goals.

Three chapters discuss finding the resources to keep a company alive. Internal Sources of Cash discusses how to squeeze cash from a company's existing assets; Financing the Turnaround discusses non-bank, financing; and Emergency Cash Management, discusses steps to keep the company alive while other measures are being implemented.

The balance of the book addresses the long lead time elements of restructuring which are identifying and implementing solutions. There are no magic bullets for restructuring a company. Restructuring is difficult and can be frustrating. Many techniques must be used, some more than once. Sometimes a company will take two steps forward and one step back. But most companies can be rescued if they start early enough and management is willing to take aggressive action.

Restructuring is not just for distressed companies. It can also be used to transform underperforming companies into superior ones. This book provides a broad array of strategies none of which work all of the time, but all of which work some of the time. The art form is to pick and choose from the strategies offered to get the best results for a particular set of circumstances.

Time Span

How much time it should take to restructure a company? This is the wrong question. The right question is how long does a new CEO or turnaround consultant have? The answer is not long.

Deconstruct a turnaround into two phases. Phase I is to get a company to profitability. Phase II is to get a company to superior performance. A turnaround professional probably has less than a year to get a company to profitability. One reads about multi-year restructuring plans, but honestly, most of these companies are playing at restructuring, or using the term restructuring to paper over the fact that they are lost and trying to find their way home.

The turnaround plan should be to do whatever it takes to make the company profitable in a year within the bounds of law and ethics. This means making bigger and more dramatic changes than if one has a two, three or four year plan. A one year time frame provides a sense of urgency that might otherwise be missing.

Achieving superior performance, Phase II, may take an additional year. Those who waste time waste life.

On the other hand, some companies may not have 90 days. They may be on the brink of extinction when a turnaround consultant or new CEO is hired. Further, the owner, board of directors, or bank might not give you 90 days to produce results. The point is you must hit the ground running.

On the first day you should have a task list for week one, week two and so forth. Among the highest priorities in week one are to introduce yourself to the board of directors and get their approval to hire, fire and restructure the company; find people willing and able to serve on a turnaround committee; meet with as many senior executives and as middle management as possible; and stop the company from bleeding cash or making other resource commitments. By the end of the second week, you should have the nucleus of your turnaround team picked and by the third week you should have a rough timeline as to what you are going to do and when you are going to do it. You should be able to show measurable improvements in 90 days. Time is the enemy in restructuring. There is never enough of it. Appendix A Turnaround Timeline provides suggestions as to restructuring tasks and time frames.

If you cannot turnaround a failing company in a year, or substantially improve an underperforming company in that period of time, you probably won't be able to do it. Restructuring is a game for those with a high level of energy and total commitment. Nowhere is it truer than in restructuring, "victory belongs to the swift."

Diagnosing Problems

Management Dissembling

Diagnosing a company's problems is troublesome for a variety of reasons. The first of which is that clients, management even boards of directors never give you the unvarnished truth. They may be so close to a company's people, operations and tradition they cannot see the truth. They may know what the problems are deep down, but be reluctant to articulate them. They may be protecting their turf or their status or perks or they may want to avoid being blamed for a bad situation by acknowledging it.

Often there is a reluctance to look the tiger in the eye. By this I mean a reluctance to confront the real problems, but rather blame trouble on some imagined or peripheral circumstance. Perhaps they do this to avoid acknowledging any blame they might have for the company's situation and perhaps they want to avoid confrontation. Companies blame their problems on war, recession, regulation, litigation, strikes, competition and a hundred other things they cannot change so they don't have to confront the real problems.

This means to get at the truth about underlying problems and you must talk to management at a lot of levels, customers, workers and suppliers. Then you are going to have to re-interview managers again, perhaps several times. One reason to re-interview and re-re-interview managers is to get them to trust you enough to tell you the truth. Another reason is that when you have more information you can ask more penetrating questions. Finally, this iterative process enables you to probe non-responsive and misleading answers.

Common Types of Problems

If the only tool in your tool kit is a hammer, every problem looks like a nail. So before one can diagnose a company's problems, one must have a broad perspective on why companies get into trouble. Table 1.1 is a list of some of the common reasons

Table 1.1 Reasons companies fail or under-perform

Deteriorating gross margins	Excessive overhead (DiNapoli et al., 2001a, C1)
Over expansion or too rapid expansion	Inadequate cash budgets
Loss of a key client or key clients	Collection problems
Increased competition	Inferior products
Poor customer relations	Poor customer service
Failure to deliver promised goods or services	Obsolete products
Failure to adopt new technology (DiNapoli et al., 2001b, C3)	High product cost
Failure to advertise/failure to create demand	Spending too much money on advertising
Spending money on the wrong advertising	Failure to invest in sales and marketing staff
Failure to forecast demand or downturns (DiNapoli et al., 2001c, C1)	Management inattention
Owners extracting too much in pay and bonuses	Changes in regulations or laws
Excessive sales and marketing expenses	Lack of financial model
Excessive debt load (DiNapoli et al., 2001d, C1)	Loss of key management (DiNapoli et al., 2001d, C1)
Price cutting and costly rebates (DiNapoli et al., 2001d, C2)	Overpaying for goods and services (DiNapoli et al., 2001d, C2)
Failure to invest in product development	Litigation
Failure to bring products to market timely (DiNapoli et al., 2001d, C2).	

A company is rarely in trouble for one reason. Usually, a company in trouble because of several factors work together to create financial distress companies either fail or under-perform targets. A recurring theme in companies that perform poorly is an unwarranted belief that more stores, more advertising, more of some mechanical process will turn the day. More loosing stores will only drain a company's cash more quickly hastening its demise. More ineffective advertising has the same effect.

Cause Versus Effect

Another difficulty in diagnosing a company's problems is to determine whether something is a cause or an effect. Management often confuses the two and it is critical for the turnaround consultant or new CEO to understand the difference. For example, excessive debt can drag a company into bankruptcy. But is excessive debt the cause of the problem? Or is it the result of some other problem? Experience shows that excessive debt is usually the result of over expansion, excessive investment in plant and equipment, acquisitions, loss of customers, collection problems or deteriorating gross margins. If expansion or acquisitions is the problem, they must be stopped. If debt is increasing because of customer loss, management should focus on why customers are being lost.

If fewer customers is identified as the problem, is that the cause of the company's problem or simply an effect of some other problem like poor customer service or obsolete products. If management focuses on getting more customers, but fails to improve products and customer service, there are two likely outcomes, either (i) it will lose new customers after a short period of time or (ii) adverse customer selection will take place. Adverse selection occurs when good customers, those who can pay on a regular basis, deal with vendors that provide good service and state-of-the-art products. Only customers that cannot get credit from "good vendors," will remain with the company.

Slow collections might be the result of poor quality products, rather than poor performance by billing and collections. Failure to get repeat sales, the basis for building any business, might be the result of excessive price, poor deliver time, quality or failure of marketing to follow up. Separating causes from effects is difficult; but critical for a successful turnaround.

Tools for Identifying the Problem

Ratios

One way to zero in on the biggest trouble areas is with ratios. Ratios can be used to compare a company's current performance to its historical performance and to compare a company to its best competitors. Few companies do everything wrong and no company does everything right. Ratios help focus attention where needed and can provide achievable performance goals.

Some ratios are used by outsiders to gauge a company's creditworthiness or the likelihood of bankruptcy. Examples of these ratios include: debt to equity ratio, leverage ratio, current ratio, quick ratio also known as the acid test ratio, and times interest earned. These ratios are important because they help build creditor confidence. But as a practical matter, most of the ratios used to evaluate creditworthiness are derivative in nature and are poor indicators of a company's underlying problems.

Another set of ratios focuses on a company's underlying performance and these ratios are more diagnostic in nature. They help pin point a company's strengths and weaknesses and, when compared to industry norms, can be used to set standards of performance which translate into actionable turnaround goals. Examples of these ratios include: revenue per employee, gross profit, profit margin, return on assets, asset turnover, accounts receivable turnover, days sales outstanding, inventory turnover and days in inventory. These ratios and other analytical techniques will be discussed in detail throughout the book.

How do you know whether a company is doing well or about to crash and burn? How do we know whether a company is headed for trouble or positioning itself for roaring success? Obviously, if a company is unprofitable, or cannot meet payroll it is in trouble. But suppose the company is in no apparent danger? What then? Is its performance satisfactory or is it underperforming its peers. Nothing in the world happens suddenly, neither success nor failure. There are always signs as to which way things are going. The trick is to read the signs.

Seven ratios provide an overall indication of a company's performance.

  (i) Sales growth
 (ii) Cost of goods sold as a percent of sales
(iii) Gross margin
 (iv) Overhead as a percent of sales
  (v) Sales and marketing cost as a percent of sales
 (vi) Other overhead as a percent of sales
(vii) Earnings from operations as a percent of sales

Why isn't profit margin included in these ratios? Profit margin depends on getting the prior seven ratios right plus having the right financing and tax strategy. To fix a company, one must fix the fundamentals first, then everything else will take care of itself. Other diagnostic performance measures will be discussed in subsequent chapters.

Sales Growth

Grow or die is the rule in business. Nothing ever stands still. Sales growth (SG) is therefore critical. Sales is a measure of whether the public is satisfied with a company's products and services. Sales growth represents the net result of a company adding new customers and losing former customers to competitors.

Sales growth is the change in year to year sales divided by the prior year's sales as shown in Eq. (1.1).

$$SG = \frac{\text{Sales Yr2} - \text{Sales Yr1}}{\text{Sales Yr1}} \qquad (1.1)$$

For example, suppose a company has $11.5 M in sales this year and had $10.9 M in sales the prior year.

$$SG = \frac{\$11.5M - \$10.9M}{\$10.9M}$$
$$= 5.5\%$$

Whether 5.5% sales growth is good or bad depends on the sales growth of a company's competitors and on its historical performance. For the newspaper business, 5.5% would be spectacular; for Microsoft it would be dismal.

Cost of Goods Sold as a Percent of Sales

Many companies fail, not because their sales growth is poor, but because the cost to produce its goods or provide its service is too high relative to sales. Cost of goods sold as a percent of sales (COGS%) is one way to determine whether product cost is a problem. COGS% is the percentage of every dollar of sales used to make the product or provide the service. If COGS% is increasing, the company is headed for trouble. If COGS% is decreasing, the company is becoming more efficient. If COGS% is more or less the same from year to year that could also be a trouble sign for two reasons. First, it means the company has not made improving COGS% a goal, which is another way of saying it is not paying attention. Second, competitors are continually striving to reduce their COGS%. If they can reduce it enough, they can cut prices and steal away the company's customers while remaining profitable. Such competition may drive a marginal company into bankruptcy. Cost of goods sold is the same as cost of service or cost of products. The formula for COGS% is given by Eq. (1.2).

$$COGS\% = \frac{COGS}{Sales} \qquad (1.2)$$

Suppose a company has sales of $11.5 million and cost of goods sold of $7.5 million. What is its COGS%?

$$COGS\% = \frac{\$7.5M}{\$11.5M}$$
$$= 65.2\%$$

This means that of every dollar of sales, 65.2% is consumed producing the product.

Gross Margin

Gross margin is the percentage of every dollar of sales that is left over after a company makes its product or provides its service. Gross margin must cover selling and marketing costs, other overhead, financing costs, taxes and profit. The larger the gross margin, the better. Gross margin is the complement of COGS%. Together, Gross margin and COGS% must equal 100%.

If a company's gross margin is too thin, it may not be able to meet is obligations and it will go bankrupt. The computation for Gross margin is given by Eq. (1.3).

$$\text{Gross Margin} = \frac{(\text{Sales–COGS})}{\text{Sales}} \tag{1.3}$$

Suppose a company's sales were $11.5 million and its cost of goods sold were $7.5 million. What would its Gross margin be?

$$\text{Gross Margin} = \frac{(\$11.5 - \$7.5\text{M})}{\$11.5\text{M}}$$

$$= 34.8\%$$

Overhead Percent

Overhead is the great killer of companies. Overhead is sometimes referred to as Selling, General and Administrative expenses (SG&A). In troubled companies, SG&A often rises faster than sales (Whitney, 1996, 92). An Overhead% that is greater than that of similar companies is also a trouble sign. Broadly speaking overhead is any expense on an income statement between gross profit (sales minus cost of goods sold) and earnings before interest and taxes (EBIT). The formula for Overhead as a percentage of sales (Overhead%) is given by Eq. (1.4).

$$\text{Overhead\%} = \frac{\text{Overhead}}{\text{Sales}} \tag{1.4}$$

Suppose a company has sales of $11.5M and overhead of $3M. What is its Overhead%?

$$\text{Overhead\%} = \frac{\$3\text{M}}{\$11.5\text{M}}$$

$$= 26.1\%$$

Selling Cost Percent

A more sophisticated way to analyze overhead is to separate selling and marketing costs from other overhead. Selling and marketing costs include commissions, advertising, promotional materials, fees for product placement and sales and marketing salaries. The reason for separating selling and marketing costs from other overhead is that one can reasonably expect Selling and marketing costs to rise or fall with sales. Overhead should not rise as fast as sales.

Selling and marketing costs as a percentage of sales (Selling cost %) is given by Eq. (1.5). If Selling cost% is rising faster than sales or falling slower than sales during a downturn, a company may be headed for trouble.

$$\text{Selling cost\%} = \frac{\text{Selling and marketing costs}}{\text{Sales}} \qquad (1.5)$$

Suppose for example, a company has selling and marketing costs of $1.2 million and sales of $11.5 M. What is its Selling cost%?

$$\text{Sales cost\%} = \frac{\$1.2M}{\$11.5M}$$

$$= 10.4\%$$

Not every company reports selling and marketing costs, so a comparison to industry norms may not be possible. However, a company can analyze its own Selling cost% trends over time. For example, if Selling cost% is growing while Sales are flat or declining, selling and marketing dollars may not be deployed effectively.

Other Overhead Percent

Other overhead percent (OO%) is overhead less selling and marketing costs divided by sales as shown in Eq. (1.6). Having teased out selling and marketing costs from overhead, the remaining overhead becomes a more sensitive barometer of whether a company is headed in the right direction (lower OO%) or the wrong direction (higher OO%).

$$\text{OO\%} = \frac{(\text{Overhead} - \text{Selling and marketing costs})}{\text{Sales}} \qquad (1.6)$$

Suppose a company has $11.5M in sales, Overhead of $3M and Selling and Marketing Costs of $1.2M.

$$\text{OO\%} = \frac{(\$3M - \$1.2M)}{\$11.5M}$$

$$= 15.7\%$$

Earnings from Operations Percent

This ratio is a measure of the percent of every dollar of sales that a company makes from operations. Most financial statements have a line labeled something like earnings from operations or earnings before interest and taxes (EBIT). Where a company has charges above this line for things like restructuring or other "one-time" charges there is the temptation to eliminate these charges to increase this ratio. Don't do it. Companies in trouble convince themselves that they would have been profitable but for some one-time charge, but they seem to have such a one-time charge year after year. Look at the unvarnished situation. Earnings from operations as a percent of sales (Earnings%) can be computed using Eq. (1.7).

$$\text{Earnings}\% = \frac{\text{EBIT}}{\text{Sales}} \qquad (1.7)$$

Suppose a company has sales of \$11.5 million and EBIT of \$2.6 million. Using Eq. (1.7) its earnings percent would be

$$= \frac{\$2.6\text{M}}{\$11.5\text{M}}$$

$$= 22.6\%$$

Analyzing Ratios

What does analyzing these seven ratios tell us? Consider Table 1.2. By pulling together a company's historical performance in comparison to its best competitors, it's easier to see what is going wrong in a company at a macro level.

Suppose the restructuring target is Rohrer Manufacturing. The first thing to note is that sales growth is weak compared to its competitors. The first rule of business is to grow or die, and this company is getting dangerously close to no growth. And no growth can quickly tip over to declining sales. The second thing to notice is that it costs substantially more for Rohrer to produce its goods and services than its competitors, 10% more than Potomac Systems. A high COGS% means a low gross margin because they must always add up to 100%.

Table 1.2 Comparison of ratios

	Rohrer manufacturing		Alvin electronics		Potomac systems	
	Current year	Prior year	Current year	Prior year	Current year	Prior year
Sales growth%	1.1	1.5	6.0	7.0	6.0	−5.0
COGS%	74.0	71.0	66.0	68.0	64.0	65.0
Gross margin%	26.0	29.0	34.0	32.0	36.0	35.0
Overhead%	35.0	31.0	24.5	25.0	24.0	28.0
Selling cost%	9.0	7.0	5.0	5.0	4.0	3.0
Other overhead%	26.0	24.0	19.5	20.0	20.0	25.0
Earnings%	−9.0	−2.0	9.5	7.0	12.0	7.0

Presenting a company's historical ratios in comparison to its best competitors can help management understand the nature and extent of the problems facing a company and the need for radical change.

Overhead as a percent of sales is also substantially higher at Rohrer than at its two competitors. Breaking down Overhead% into selling and marketing and other overhead costs we see that Rohrer spends a disproportionate amount on selling and marketing. Yet sales are growing at a fraction of competitors sales. That indicates that most selling and marketing expenditures are being wasted. We can also see that other overhead as a percent of sales is rising even as the company sinks deeper in trouble. Other overhead does not make the product or sell the product. Other overhead goes to things like corporate offices and staff salaries. When a company is in trouble, this is the first area that should be cut.

Finally, Earnings% is the overall result of the interaction of the other ratios. To drive Earnings% into positive territory will require substantial cuts in COGS% and Overhead%. And that's not the final word on making the company profitable. Earnings must cover financing costs and taxes.

Other Diagnostic Ratios

Other diagnostic and performance ratios will be discussed throughout the book to help identify specific problems and suggest specific actions to bring a company to profitability, and then to superior performance. For example Return on Assets (ROA) is a measure of the efficiency. If a company has low ROA it could mean either (i) a company has too many assets or (ii) management is not fully utilizing the assets it has.

Ratios like ROA and Asset Turnover, can be used to determine whether a company has too many assets and other ratios help pinpoint where those assets are. Ratios like Revenue per employee, can help determine whether a company is over staffed and the chapter on Labor Cost can help determine where the overstaffing occurs and how much can be saved by reducing staffing. The seven ratios discussed above provide a rough cut of a company's problems. In subsequent chapters we will probe much deeper.

Models

A model is a description of how something works. If you want to improve something, first create a model of it. Then you will have a systematic way to assess the effects of various changes.

An income statement is one form of model, but, there are other useful models. One problem with income statements is that most are cluttered with minutia and are not well formatted for restructuring. Consider the income statement for Pinto Foods shown in Table 1.3 Panel A. What can we say about Pinto? We can say it is going to die.

A company that is not making a profit is unlikely to attract capital in the form of bank loans or investors. And, suppliers will be reluctant to extend credit to a company with dubious prospects.

A zero profit can easily tip over into a loss. If a company is not making a profit, it is unlikely to have money to invest in new product development, advertising,

Table 1.3 Pinto foods income statement

Panel A			Panel B		
		Percentage of revenue			Percentage of revenue
Revenue	**10,000,000**	100.0	Revenue	10,470,000	100.0
Cost of goods sold	5,000,000	**50.0**	Cost of goods sold	4,988,955	47.7
Gross profit	5,000,000	50.0	Gross profit	5,481,045	52.4
Sales and marketing expenses	350,000	3.5	Sales and marketing expenses	366,450	3.5
Other overhead	**4,600,000**	46.0	Other overhead	4,383,800	41.9
Total operating overhead	4,950,000	49.5	Total operating overhead	4,750,250	45.4
Earnings before interest and taxes	50,000	0.5	Earnings before interest and taxes	730,795	7.0
Interest	50,000	0.5	Interest	50,000	0.5
Earnings before tax	0	0.0	Earnings before tax	680,795	6.5
Taxes (assume a 25% rate)	0	0.0	Taxes (assume a 25% rate)	170,199	1.6
Net income	0	0.0	Net income	510,596	4.9

Panel A is the baseline income statement for Pinto Foods showing it has zero profit. Companies with zero profit can easily turn into companies with losses. By changing (i) revenue, (ii) cost of goods sold as a percentage of revenue and (iii) other overhead by as little as 4.7%, Pinto Foods can be transformed, as shown in Panel B, into a company with a respectable net income.

breaking into new markets, improving plant efficiency, or recruiting the best sales-people and engineers from the competition. In fact, just the opposite might happen. Competitors might be tempted to recruit its best people. And if competitors are prof-itable they might simply be able to out spend a company like Pinto Foods which is on life support.

Consider what Pinto Foods would look like if we changed three critical areas (i) sales, (ii) cost of goods sold as a percent of sales and (iii) other overhead. For purposes of this exercise, assume that selling and marketing costs rise in proportion to revenue and that interest cost cannot be changed in the short term. Let us change each critical variable by just 4.7%.

If revenue is increased by 4.7% it will grow to $10,470,000 as shown in Table 1.3 Panel B. What about cutting the cost of goods sold as a percent of revenue (COGS%) by 4.7%? We can see from Panel A that 50% of every dollar of sale goes toward the cost of goods sold (COGS% = 50%). One way to visualize this is to think of a can of beans that Pinto sells for $1.00. The cost of producing each can of beans, the cost of goods sold, is $.50 giving a COGS% of 50% ($.50/$1.00). Now suppose we could find a way to produce that can of beans for 4.7% less. Then each can of beans would cost $.4765 ($.50 × (1–4.7%)) and the COGS% would be 47.65% ($.4765/$1.00). Cut the COGS% on every product and apply that new COGS% to get the projected cost of goods sold. In this case the new cost of goods sold would be $4,988,955 (47.7% new COGS% × $10,470,000 sales.)

For Pinto Foods, making these two fairly modest changes increases gross profit $481,045. Next cut other overhead, that is overhead not directly used for sales and marketing, by 4.7% giving a new other overhead of $4,383,800 ($4,600,000 × (1–4.7%)) as shown in Panel B.

Together these three modest changes result in an earnings before interest and taxes (EBIT) of $730,795 or more than 14 times the previous EBIT of $50,000. The changes made in Panel B produce earnings before tax (EBT) of $680,795. Assuming a tax rate of 25%, net income is about $510,596. While not spectacular for a company with $10.5 million in sales, it is a dramatic improvement. Changing (i) sales, (ii) cost of goods sold as a percent of sales (COGS%) and (iii) Other overhead by even a small amount can result in a dramatic improvement.

The take away lesson from this exercise is that even small changes in the right places can pull a company back from the brink of disaster. The techniques discussed in the following chapters should enable a company to make even bigger improvements.

Ethics

Why Ethics?

Ethics is the pop culture topic of the day. It is all the rage to demand business students take ethics courses while giving a pass to political science and history majors. So what is the point of discussing ethics in the context of restructuring? Is it to fulfill some misguided sense of political correctness? Or is it simply the right thing to do?

In reality, neither of those reasons provide a burning, driving, compelling reason to discuss ethics in the context of restructuring. Ethics is important because when a company is in distress, managers, employees, and owners sometimes think their circumstances give them license to do whatever it takes to make the company profitable. Sometimes executives say: "I don't even want to know what you are doing. Just make it happen." Such words are a receipt for disaster.

It's important to discuss ethics because the cost of unethical behavior is *always* higher than any imagined savings from improper conduct. People who violate ethical standards *always* get caught. Let me repeat that. People *always* get caught violating ethical standards no matter how clever they are. And ethical violations can be costly. They can result in litigation, fines, and other sanctions. So cost alone is a compelling reason to stay on the side of he angels.

Public Relations is another reason. Companies must deal with investors, banks, investment banks, employees, government agencies, and customers. They all want to be confident that they are dealing with a "clean" company. They want a company that can focus on business and not be distracted by an ethical lapse that may derail the company. There is no clearer example of the fate that befalls a company that treads on the edge of an ethical violation than Arthur Andersen. Even before they were convicted of destroying evidence, the company imploded as clients and employees pealed off. While the firm was ultimately exonerated of destroying evidence, the charge contributed to client loss and the demise of the firm.

Managing a turnaround can take 16 hours a day, 7 days a week. The last thing management needs to deal with is irate customers, suppliers, employees, investors or government agencies. Staying on the right side of ethical standards reduces the likelihood management with have to address such distractions. In sum, the objective of an *enforced* ethics policy is to clear the decks so that management can focus on the business of the business.

Sample Ethics Policy

Every company should have an ethics policy and everyone should be expected to know, understand and adhere to that policy. An ethics policy should be clear, simple and to the point. The longer the ethics policy, the less likely it is to be read and remembered. Also, the longer the policy, the greater the likelihood that someone will want to read loop holes into the policy or deliberately misinterpret it. Table 1.4 proves an example of an ethics policy.

It is always good to have an attorney review the policy. However, ask the attorney to limit the policy to one side of one sheet of 8.5" × 11" paper. Anything longer is not likely to be read or understood.

The actions of an individual employee may provoke a lawsuit against the company for discrimination or violation of a government regulation. The best defenses against this are to (i) have a clear, simple ethics policy (ii) make sure everyone has read and acknowledged that they understand it in writing and (iii) promptly discipline anyone that violates the policy.

Managers should be required to re-read and sign off on this ethics policy yearly. This is not burdensome for a one page policy. Such a sign-off may be facilitated through a web based document. Such actions can help the courts distinguish

Table 1.4 Sample ethics policy

1. Neither the company nor its employees will discriminate on the basis of race, creed, ethnicity, gender, handicap or sexual preference
2. The company and its employees will deal fairly with: customers, suppliers, employees and government agencies
3. Sexual or racial harassment will not be tolerated. Anything that tends to make an employee uncomfortable in the work-place may be considered harassment
4. Stealing from the company, its customers or employees will not be tolerated. It is company policy to *criminally prosecute* anyone who steals
5. The company will comply with all city, county, state and federal laws and regulations, including, but not limited to: payment of taxes properly due and owing, labor, wage, and employment laws, and environmental regulations

Violation of any of the above ethics guidelines is grounds for immediate termination.

between the actions of a single, unethical individual, and the policy of the company as a whole. Sometimes this is enough to insulate a company from liability for employee misconduct. Be proactive and invest in prevention.

☞ BUT...☜

An Ethics Policy does not mean that a restructuring team can avoid tough decisions for example the decisions to cut personnel and close plants.

Complexity

Restructuring a corporation is one of the most complicated problems in business. It involves sales and marketing, product development, customer relations, financial analysis, asset management, creditors, shareholders, employee relations, management and a high degree of leadership.

Most business problems are fairly bounded with well-defined, closed-end solutions. Turn the crank enough and you get to a result. On the other hand, corporate restructuring is open-ended and has poorly defined bounds. Consider the following suggestions.

Segmentation

Segment problems to the extent possible. This adds clarity to the definition of the problem and may suggest a range of solutions. On the other hand, be mindful that everything in business is connected to every other thing.

Think Broadly About Problems

Search for techniques, ideas, and solutions, within the company's industry, but also consider solutions from other industries and non-business disciplines.

Boundaries

Look for places a problem can be bounded, if even on one side. For example, do you really care if cash flow exceeds forecast?

Information and Decisions

Expect ambiguity, noise and incomplete information. Decide how to treat information. For example, how much corroboration is necessary to identify a problem or trend? Never wait for complete information to make a decision. It may never come and if complete information were always available, management could be replaced by computers. The art of management is to make good decisions with incomplete information.

Think in an Interdisciplinary Way

Master as many intellectual tools as you can. Accountants need to understand marketing, marketers need to understand quality control, quality control needs to understand customer service, production needs to understand accounting, and everyone needs to understand people. Everything needs to work together.

Conclusion

Companies never go directly from success to failure or well performing to marginal. Companies slip in degrees and an alert executive will be able to read the signs and take corrective action to assure the company's success. However, some executives cannot read the signs, or they do not want to read the signs or they are unwilling to do what is necessary to put the company on the right course.

There are a handful of ratios that can quickly determine whether a company is headed for trouble. These ratios should be compared both to a company's historical performance and to those of its best competitors. Ratios give the big picture view of a company's problems. In subsequent chapters, more detailed diagnostic tools are presented along with suggestions to drive profitability.

While bold and aggressive action is required to transform an underperforming company to one with superior performance, it is important to stay on the side of the angels, both legally and ethically. Everyone on a turnaround team, and all managers should be required to read and sign off on an ethics policy so they know the limits of the action they can take. A turnaround is difficult enough without having to deal with legal or ethical problems.

Notes

1. Overhead reductions failed to materialize after the Mercedes/Chrysler merger for example engineering and finance were still duplicated.
2. Motorola failed to embrace digital technology and lost market share to Nokia.
3. SL Industries and other companies failed to predict the downturn in telecommunications in 2000 and was stuck with all the overhead of excess capacity.
4. Loews theaters filed bankruptcy, having taken on too much debt to build modern multiplexes and failed to close older screens.
5. Cultural differences between the management team that made Chrysler a scrappy, aggressive competitor, and the more staid Daimler-Benz management caused Chryler's key managers to leave depriving Chrysler of the character that made it an attractive merger partner.

References

DiNapoli D, Sigoloff SC, Cushman RF (ed) (1991) Workouts and turnarounds: the handbook
of restructuring and investing in distressed companies. Business One Irvin, Homewood, IL,
pp 8–11

DiNapoli D, Sigoloff SC, Cushman RF (ed) (2001a) Market's shift after Merger Hurt Chrysler's
fortunes. Phila Inq C1, C2, 31 Jan

DiNapoli D, Sigoloff SC, Cushman RF (ed) (2001b) Motorola is full of history, but its future looks
troubled. Phila Inq C3, 11 Mar

DiNapoli D, Sigoloff SC, Cushman RF (ed) (2001c) Telecom industry's woes hit a manufacturer
hard. Phila Inq C1, 20 July

DiNapoli D, Sigoloff SC, Cushman RF (ed) (2001d) Lowews Cineplex Files for chap 11 as part of
a buyout plan. Phila Inq C1, 16 Feb

Whitney JO (1996) Strategic renewal for business units. Harv Bus Rev 84–98, July–Aug

Chapter 2
Setting Restructuring Goals and Reverse Engineering a Company

Introduction

It is easier to reach a goal if you can break it down into a series of well defined sub-goals. Sounds simple enough but a surprising number of people believe the way to make a company profitable is to sell as much as possible and spend as little as possible and hope what is left over is enough. Such a plan, if one can call it that, will result in a lot of frenetic activity and few results.

The first thing a company has to do is to make a realistic assessment of where it is. This is done by comparing a company's performance to that of its best competitors. The company should then make a sober assessment of what its goals should be for three months, six months, a year, two years and three years.

If a company is on the brink of bankruptcy or in bankruptcy, it might seem imprudent to invest time and energy thinking about what the company should look like in a year or three years. But, many companies have gotten in trouble because they have sacrificed long term planning and investments to meet short term goals. So as with everything else in life, the best path is a balance between working short term goals and investing in long term performance.

Business Model

The key to understanding anything at a deep level is to build a model of it. This is true of an economy, a ship, airplane, a building, a political system or a business. A model identifies key elements and their relationship to one another. One advantage of building a model is that it forces one to prune away a lot of detail so the big picture comes into bold relief. Another advantage is that a well thought out model shows how each element impacts every other element. This in turn will help focus limited time and attention on areas where it will have the maximum payoff. A model can be used to avoid false starts and wasted effort. It is far more efficient to try plans in a model to see whether they will work than it is to implement a strategy only to find out it is doomed to failure after the commitment of substantial time, money and material.

D.E. Vance, *Corporate Restructuring*, DOI 10.1007/978-3-642-01786 5_2,
© Springer-Verlag Berlin Heidelberg 2009

Adding Realism to the Model

The most importing thing in any turnaround is to be realistic about the time, money and resources available and to be equally realistic about the goals that can be achieved over the relevant time horizon. How do we know what is reasonable and what is just a fantasy? The answer is to look at the company's best competitors and analyze their models. If the sales of a company's best competitors are not increasing year to year, as for example with most newspapers, it is unrealistic for us to assume we can grow our way to profitability. The company must find some other route to profits. If cost of goods sold is 80% of sales for a company's best competitors, it is unrealistic to assume it can cut cost of goods sold to 60%.

Realistic turnaround goals start with a thorough analysis of competitors' sales, costs and growth trends. Realistic goals do not necessarily mean goals should be set to industry averages. Goals may stretch competitive performance by a reasonable amount.

Reverse Engineering Turnaround Goals

Many of the elements needed to build a realistic business model and reverse engineer a turnaround plan have already been discussed in chapter one. We just have to put them together.

The amount needed to cover overhead, financing costs and profit is essentially a break-even analysis question. When Sergio Marchione was hired to restructure Fiat in 2004 he found that engineers were designing cars on the assumption that they could make and sell 300,000 per year, far more than their actual sales. He insisted that they redesign cars and production methods to be profitable with half that number of sales. In effect he ordered his engineers to cut their break even point in half (Kahn and Power 2006). The traditional break-even formula given in Eq. (2.1) sets profits equal to zero.

$$\text{Profits} = \text{Sales} - \text{Variable Costs} - \text{Fixed Costs} \qquad (2.1)$$

This equation can be adapted to model restructuring goals. For example Other overhead and Financing costs replace fixed costs. Other Overhead is defined as Overhead less selling and marketing costs. Cost of Goods Sold and Selling and marketing costs can be used to estimate variable costs. With these substitutions, and assuming profit equal zero in a break even situation, Eq. (2.1) can be re-written as Eq. (2.2).

$$0 = \text{Sales} \times (\text{Gross margin} - \text{Selling cost\%}) - \text{Other overhead} - \text{Financing costs} \qquad (2.2)$$

Moving the fixed costs to the left of the equal sign gives Eq. (2.3).

$$\text{Other overhead} + \text{Financing costs} = \text{Sales} \times (\text{Gross margin} - \text{Selling cost\%}) \quad (2.3)$$

Dividing both sides by (Gross margin − Selling cost%) gives Eq. (2.4).

$$\text{Sales} = \frac{\text{Other overhead} + \text{Financing costs}}{(\text{Gross Margin} - \text{Selling cost\%})} \qquad (2.4)$$

No company is going to hire a CEO or pay a turnaround consultant to get the company to break even, that is to say zero profit. So we must include a target profit in this model. We can do this by treating profit as another "fixed cost," which it is from the point of view of management or the turnaround team. Therefore we modify Eq. (2.4) to include Target Profit (TP) as another "fixed cost" along with Other overhead (OO) and Financing Costs (FC).

At this point we are going to make one more modification to (2.4). Instead of the equation equaling Sales, we are going to say it equals Required Sales as shown in Eq. (2.5). Required Sales are the sales necessary to cover Other overhead, Financing costs and Target profit given a company's Gross margin (GM) and Sales cost% (SC).

$$\text{Required Sales} = \frac{\text{OO} + \text{FC} + \text{TP}}{(\text{GM} - \text{SC})} \qquad (2.5)$$

For example, suppose Gross margin is 32%, Selling cost% is 6%, Other overhead is $950,000, Financing Costs are $200,000 and the target profit is $100,000. What sales are required sales?

$$\begin{aligned}
\text{Required Sales} &= \frac{\$950,000 + \$200,000 + \$100,000}{(32\% - 6\%)} \\
&= \frac{\$1,250,000}{26\%} \\
&= \$4,807,692
\end{aligned}$$

If Forecast Sales are equal to or greater than $4,807,692 the company should be able to meet its profit target. However, if sales are less than $4,807,692 the company will fail to meet its profit target.

Given Eq. (2.5) it is possible to reverse engineer restructuring goals. The left side of the equation is the sales required to cover all costs considering the relationship of costs to one another. Of all the elements in the equation, sales is the element that is usually the most difficult to predict.

If actual sales fall below the Required Sales, the restructuring will be unsuccessful. So, if we have a good sales forecast, we can figure out what other overhead, financing costs, gross margin and sales cost% have to be to reach the target profit.

Subsequent chapters of the book discuss detailed methods for reaching the other overhead, financing, gross margin and sales cost% goals of this model. The objective of this chapter is to set broad restructuring goals for the turnaround team.

Suppose an honest forecast of sales was $3,828,000. Given the costs, gross margins and sales cost% above, the company would fail to reach its profit target in a significant way because $4,807,692 of sales was required under the current cost structure whereas only $3,828,000 was forecast.

What is the solution? Other overhead is usually the easiest cost to cut because other overhead dollars are not used to make the product or deliver the service and they are not used to sell the product or service. Improving the Gross margin by reducing the cost of goods sold is usually the next easiest thing to do. Selling cost% is often difficult to reduce because one does not want to risk losing sales. Reducing financing costs is usually the most difficult cost to cut in the short run, but it can be done.

So, suppose we set the goal of cutting overhead by 10% from $950,000 to $855,000 and increasing gross margin by 1% from 32 to 33%. Would achieving those goals be sufficient to meet profit targets? Plugging these values back into Eq. (2.5) gives the following.

$$\text{Required sales} = \frac{\$855,000 + \$200,000 + \$100,000}{(33\% - 6\%)}$$
$$= \frac{\$1,155,000}{27\%}$$
$$= \$4,277,778$$

Since required sales of $4,277,778 is still greater than forecast sales of $3,828,000, this first estimate of the restructuring goals are inadequate. Clearly more radical change is required to reduce required sales to less than forecast sales. The answer is to reexamine every aspect of the cost model to see where more cuts should be made.

This process of working the model, reshaping it, and trying various combinations of cuts is critical to setting achievable restructuring goals. One might expect to have to rework the model a half a dozen times until all elements come together to achieve the desired result.

Just to be clear, reducing target profit (TP) is not an option. Target profit is the end game. A CEO or restructuring consultant willing to sacrifice target profit is frankly not needed. The board of directors is likely to yell, "NEXT!"

Goals Must Be Realistic

When a company is in trouble, it is much more important to be realistic than to paint a pretty picture for the board of directors or turnaround committee.

Factors other than sales inform targets for other overhead, gross margin, selling costs and financing costs. Competitor performance is key to setting realistic goals (Whitney, 1996, p. 87). For example, if a company's best competitor has a gross margin of 30%, it is probably unrealistic to set a target gross margin of 40%. Likewise if the Selling cost% of the best competitor is 6%, it is probably unrealistic to set a 4% goal for Selling cost%. For a turnaround plan to work, it must be rooted in reality.

Forecasting Sales

It's always imprudent to assume sales growth will rescue a distressed company. Reasons include: lack of money for selling and marketing expenses and the fact that distress is usually accompanied by production, quality, scheduling and customer service problems.

Most troubled companies fall into the trap of forecasting the sales they need which creates a misleading picture. A better approach is to have sales and marketing create a detailed sales forecast down the hall and around the corner from where the restructuring team works. Sales and marketing should have no information on Required Sales, target profits or costs. A sales forecast should be realistic and independent of what is needed to meet restructuring goals.

Forecasts that are based on facts and detail are more likely to be realistic than forecasts based on wishful thinking and good intentions. Ideally, a sales forecast would identify the number of potential customers in each territory, their names, how much they purchased last year as well as expected future sales. Expected sales should be tempered by information about customers the company has lost or is about to lose as well as objections they have to the company or its products. This sales forecast should also factor in new sales territories and territories that have been abandoned.

Other factors that should be considered when developing a sales forecast include:

  (i)   Whether customers will be reluctant to deal with a troubled company,
 (ii)   The accuracy of prior sales forecasts, and
(iii)   Whether the sales forecast is consistent with historical and industry trends.

A probabilistic sales forecast is better than a forecast that predicts an exact dollar value of sales.

Probabilistic Sales Forecasts

No one can forecast sales with 100% accuracy. Sales forecasts are usually an expected value or a consensus number. Assume sales are normally distributed around the forecast value, which is generally a good assumption absent information to the contrary. That means that there is about a 50% chance that the sales forecast will be exceeded and a 50% chance that actual sales will fall short of the forecast. If the turnaround team designs goals to fit expected sales they have 50% chance that the turnaround will fail.

In reality, it is impossible to design turnaround goals that will be successful 100% of the time. The issue is how much risk the turnaround committee or board of directors is willing to tolerate.

Suppose a company forecast expected sales of $3,828,000 with a standard deviation of $100,000. What sales forecast should be used in planning the turnaround?

Fig. 2.1 Sales distribution

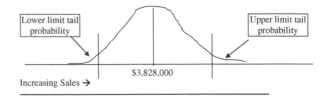

Figure 2.1 is a visual representation of the sales distribution in which $3,828,000, the expected value, is in the middle of the distribution.

Assuming the sales distribution is normal, the upper and lower tails will be symmetrical. We need the turnaround committee to agree on the amount of risk they are willing to tolerate in sales falling short of the plan goal or on the other hand the amount of confidence they want in the plan's sales goal. The amount of risk they are willing to tolerate is represented by the area in the lower limit tail probability. The confidence is 100% of the area under the curve less the amount of risk the turnaround commit is willing to take. Equation (2.6) along with Table 2.1. can be used to determine the sales we should use as Required sales for purposes of the restructuring plan.

$$\text{Low limit of sales} = \text{Expected sales} - Z^*\sigma \qquad (2.6)$$

Z values correspond to the area betwen the upper and lower tail of the distribution as shown in Table 2.1.

Suppose the turnaround committee demands a 90% confidence that the sales target will be met. That means they are willing to tolerate a 10% risk that the sales goal will not be met. To achieve this goal, the area under the left tail of the curve must

Table 2.1 Normal distribution table

Area	Z value
68.3%	$\pm 1.00\,\sigma$
79.9%	$\pm 1.28\,\sigma$
90.1%	$\pm 1.65\,\sigma$
95.0%	$\pm 1.96\,\sigma$
98.0%	$\pm 2.06\,\sigma$
99.0%	$\pm 2.58\,\sigma$

The normal distribution table indicates how many standard deviations plus and minus the expected value are needed to encompass the designated area between the tails of the distribution. The Z-value is the number of standard deviations needed. For example, about 68.3% of the area under the curve will be bracketed by the interval from the expected value − 1.0 standard deviation to the expected value plus 1.0 standard deviation. The total area under the curve is 100%.

contain 10% of the area, which is the same as saying it contains 10% of the total probability. Since we assume a normal distribution, the area in the upper tail is also 10%. The area between the two tails is 80% (100% − 10% − 10%).

The closest estimate for 80% in the above table is Z = ± 1.28. Select the negative Z value to find the boundary between the lower tail limit and the central area of the curve. Putting our values into Eq. (2.6) yields

$$\text{Lower limit} = \$3,828,000 - 1.28 \times \$100,000$$
$$= \$3,828,000 - \$128,000$$
$$= \$3,700,000$$

So given a sales forecast of $3,828,000 a standard deviation of $100,000 and the turnaround committee's risk tolerance of 10%, the restructuring plan should design for sales of $3,700,000. If this is less than Required Sales as defined in Eq. (2.5) the restructuring plan goals must be modified by reducing overhead, financing costs, cost of goods sold and sales and marketing costs until Required Sales are less than $3,700,000.

How Sensitive is the Business Model to Small Changes in Assumptions?

Forecasts are never perfect, so it is only prudent to test the sensitivity of a business model to small changes in assumptions. Assumptions are things like the Gross margin, Selling cost%, Other overhead and Financing costs.

Assume that Gross Margin is 35%, Selling cost is 6%, Other overhead is $750,000 and Financing Costs are $200,000 and the target profit is $100,000. What sales are required to break-even? Applying Eq. (2.10) we find.

$$\text{Required Sales} = \frac{\$750,000 + \$200,000 + \$100,000}{(35\% - 6\%)}$$
$$= \frac{\$1,050,000}{29\%}$$
$$= \$3,620,690$$

If Forecast Sales are $3,700,000 the company should surpass break-even with its existing sales/cost structure. Suppose margins deteriorate by 2%, and Selling Costs increase by 1%, what then?

$$\text{Required Sales} = \frac{\$750,000 + \$200,000 + \$100,000}{(33\% - 7\%)}$$
$$= \frac{\$1,050,000}{26\%}$$
$$= \$4,038,462$$

With Forecast sales of only $3,700,000 the model indicates the company will loose money. So what is the solution to this high level of sensitivity to changes. First, the restructuring team must monitor gross margin and Selling cost% very closely. Second, the restructuring team should design in larger safety margins by planning to cut other overhead, financing costs and selling cost% and increasing gross margin more than needed to drive Required Sales below forecast sales.

Constraints on the Model

Consider again the facts we started this exercise with (Other overhead of $950,000; Financing costs of $200,000, target profit of $100,000, Gross margin of 32%, Selling cost% of 6% and forecast sales of $3,700,000. Suppose, because of contracts and other reasons, other overhead can only be cut to $850,000 in 1 year. How much improvement is needed in Gross margin to meet goals? To answer that question we again use Eq. (2.5) but replace Required sales with Forecast sales to give Eq. (2.7).

$$\text{Forecast sales} = \frac{OO + FC + TP}{(GM - SC)} \tag{2.7}$$

$$\$3,700,000 = \frac{\$850,000 + \$200,000 + \$100,000}{(GM - 6\%)}$$

$$\$3,700,000^*(GM - 6\%) = \$1,150,000$$

$$\$3,700,000^*GM - \$222,000 = \$1,150,000$$

$$\$3,700,000^*GM = \$1,372,000$$

$$GM = \$1,372,000/\$3,700,000$$

$$= 37.1\%$$

Applying algebra, it can be found that Gross margin (GM) must improve to 37.1% which means COGS%, the cost of producing the product or providing the service must be cut from 68% of sales to 62.9% of sales. While this is difficult, it has been done.

A COGS% of 62.9% on sales of $3,700,000 translates into a target production budget of $2,327,300. When assigning goals to turnaround team members, it is easier for them to visualize goals in terms of dollars than as a percent of sales.

Suppose the company's best competitors in its industry have a gross margin of only 36%. Then the company should take another look at Selling cost% and financing costs to see what those goals would have to be in order to make the model work. Equation (2.7) could be used again, but this time one might set Gross margin to 36%, other overhead $850,000, financing costs $200,000, and target profit at $100,000 and solve for a target Selling cost%. If reducing Selling cost% seems unfeasible, the turnaround team should reexamine other elements of the model until there is consensus on goals for various components of the restructuring model. Once those goals are in place the team can start searching for ways to achieve specific goals in earnest. Before they such goals are agreed the turnaround team is flying blind.

Selling and Marketing Costs Not Detailed

Suppose selling and marketing costs are not broken out as a separate line item? As a practical matter, when doing an actual restructuring, you should have access to enough accounting detail to pull together total selling and marketing costs. These costs might be scattered across a dozen different accounts in different departments but it can be done. But if competitors' selling and marketing costs are not broken out, it will be difficult to determine whether the turnaround goal for a Selling cost% is realistic. In that situation, the model can be adapted by treating Overhead as an undifferentiated mass which includes both selling costs and other overhead. This gives Eq. (2.8). All the other variables have their usual meaning.

$$\text{Required Sales} = \frac{\text{OH} + \text{FC} + \text{TP}}{\text{GM}} \qquad (2.8)$$

Suppose, for example, suppose Gross margin (GM) is 33%, Overhead (OH) is $1,032,692, Financing Costs (FC) are $200,000, Target Profit (TP) is $100,000. What are Required Sales?

$$\begin{aligned}
\text{Required Sales} &= \frac{\text{OH} + \text{FC} + \text{TP}}{\text{GM}} \\
&= \frac{\$1,032,692 + \$200,000 + \$100,000}{33\%} \\
&= \$4,038.46
\end{aligned}$$

The methodology for setting restructuring goals would then proceed in the same fashion, setting goals for various cost components and testing their reasonableness before making them restructuring goals.

Applying the Model

Once the turnaround team has a model that meets the profit target, it is in a position to assign responsibility to team members. Some team members will be deployed looking at overhead expenses; others will be deployed looking at the costs of goods or services sold. Some will be deployed to examine financing or selling and marketing costs. The goals of each team member will be to bring their costs in line with the parameters of the turnaround model.

This model can also be used beyond the first year of restructuring to guide the company to superior performance in a disciplined way. A significant advantage of reverse engineering company goals rather than building up budgets to see what profit is left over is that reverse engineering sets expectations managers can work toward. Budget processes tend to start with the departmental needs with profit seen as a residual. Reverse engineering places profit goals in the center of planning and decision making.

Conclusion

A macro level model which considers factors such as sales, gross margin selling and marketing costs, financing costs and overhead can be used to set realistic restructuring goals. Does Required Sales exceed Forecast Sales? If so, the business model must be rethought. Unlike many problems it is not enough to throw a handful of numbers into an equation and turn a crank. The real world is much more complex and solutions usually require multiple iterations to arrive at a realistic solution.

Such a model allows approaches to be tried on paper before resources are committed. Reverse engineer turnaround goals so specific responsibility with specific targets can be assigned. A model also helps define criteria for success and can be applied at the division or subsidiary level to identify divisions or subsidiaries that cannot be saved.

References

Kahn G, Power S (2006) Auto outsider gets fiat going by flouting industry traditions. Wall St J A1 and A12, 26 Oct

Whitney JO (1996) Strategic renewal for business units. Harv Bus Rev 74(4): 84–98, July–Aug

Chapter 3
People

Introduction

It would be great if a company could be restructured just by moving numbers and things around, but that is not realistic. Restructuring means change and few people are comfortable with change, especially the radical change that restructuring requires. Change works best when people understand why the company is being restructured and how (Tichacek, 2006).

Good people can push a company further and faster than anyone can imagine. Bad people can kill a company. Mediocre and even average people can make progress slow and painful. Restructuring involves a balance between getting the best people and managing costs.

People issues go far beyond a company's staff and management to the company's owners, board of directors, bankers, suppliers, financiers, shareholders, and government relations. Labor cost is discussed in a subsequent chapter. This chapter focuses on the people issues that can propel restructuring forward or stop it in its tracks.

Turnaround Committee

Often the people who got a company in trouble are not the right people to restructure it. First, if those running the company had the skill and motivation to restructure the company, they would have already improved the company's performance. Second, those in power during a company's slide have a tendency to defend past actions. Third, those in power are probably so comfortable with the company's current method of operation they will be reluctant to drive significant change if not downright hostile to it.

When a troubled company is acquired by another company, the acquiring company can simply replace management. However, when a new CEO is hired to restructure a company things become trickier. The CEO is hired by the board of directors and the board of directors may be reluctant to endorse change. A consultant hired to spearhead a turnaround has the same problem.

D.E. Vance, *Corporate Restructuring*, DOI 10.1007/978-3-642-01786-5_3,
© Springer-Verlag Berlin Heidelberg 2009

For a new CEO or turnaround consultant, communication is the key to winning board support. But communicating with whole board is cumbersome. If the company has a Board of Directors, a committee of three or four outside directors should be formed to coordinate with the new CEO or turnaround consultant and report to the Board.

The CEO or turnaround consultant should be in constant communication with the turnaround committee. By constant I mean two or three times a week. If there is no Board, then a committee of shareholders or investors should be organized because the turnaround team will need their support.

The problem for a new CEO or turnaround consultant is even trickier if the company is privately held and the owner-entrepreneur got the company in trouble. Many private companies have directors in name only or no directors at all. In that case, the new CEO or turnaround consultant should suggest creating a turnaround committee composed of people the owner-entrepreneur trusts. Ideally the turnaround committee would be composed of the owner-entrepreneur's acquaintances who are corporate executives or CEOs in their own right.

A turnaround committee can have many forms. For example, New Century Financial Corporation, a sub-prime mortgage broker was thrown into financial crisis when banks cut off funding. The outside board chairman Fredric Foster took over operations and used the director of the audit committee, and New Century's public accounting firm as an ad hoc strategy committee that he consulted virtually every day. Jerry Levin was appointed CEO of Sunbeam after disclosure of substantial accounting irregularities. He teleconferenced with board members almost every day to discuss issues of strategy and executive recruitment. The point is that the board may provide a pool of people who can serve as a sounding board for turnaround strategy and they should be consulted frequently, perhaps daily, because things break very rapidly when a company is in crisis. On the other hand, board members may not have the experience or knowledge to help. Some knowledge gaps in specialized areas like bankruptcy can be filled by bringing in outsiders to teach board members basic principals. Some board members may not want to commit the time to advise during a crisis (Lublin and White, 2007). Both of these factors argue for a small, experienced and accessible turnaround committee.

So what are the goals of a turnaround committee? First, facilitate communication between the new CEO or turnaround consultant and the board of directors or owner-entrepreneur. Second, they review and approve the turnaround strategy and goals. Fourth, in the case of a privately held company, they provide a buffer between the new CEO or turnaround professional and people who got the company into trouble in the first place.

Whether the turnaround team is working with a committee of directors, investors or the owner-entrepreneur, it is important that they establish overall, agreed upon goals. We will call these people, however constituted the turnaround committee.

The turnaround committee is an essential element in a quick and relatively smooth restructuring. It is therefore imperative that the new CEO or turnaround consultant get and maintain its confidence. The measures of a company's performance, discussed earlier, provide language to discuss goals. However, the committee should not be involved in day to day turnaround operations.

Setting and achieving reasonable goals is one way to maintain the committee's confidence. Communication is another, and this means communication of bad news as well as good news. The turnaround committee should never be surprised by anything. Finally, the CEO or turnaround professional should be willing to listen to, and accommodate the concerns of the committee. One of the realities of consulting is that one cannot force a client to do anything. Likewise a CEO hired to restructure a company cannot force a board to do something against their best judgment. So sometimes a consultant will have to abandon an idea he or she thinks brilliant, but the committee dislikes.

Incumbent Management

A philosophical question with real consequences is whether the management team that rode, or drove the company into trouble, is the right team to lead a turnaround. Some say that if they had the attributes: skill, energy, perspective, etc. to turn a company around, they wouldn't have let it get into trouble in the first place. Other problems with current management may include a tendency to defend past actions, and a preoccupation with maintaining one's position.

In companies where the owner – entrepreneur has control of the company it may be difficult to convince him or her to relinquish control to a turnaround team. Other problems with using incumbent management include (i) a tendency to second guess, or debate each new action, and (ii) the very real possibility, even probability, that they will use their knowledge of the company to undercut the turnaround team's actions.

One of my clients had far more programming staff than could be justified for their client base. Among my recommendations were that a number of programmers be laid off. The president of the company called in the programmers, and in my presence laid them off. Three weeks later as I was walking among the buildings of the complex and saw several of the programmers. I asked how their job search was going. When confronted, they said the president of the company called them in after our meeting, said they weren't really terminated and he told them to lay low so I wouldn't know they had not been terminated. It's hard to make progress when recommendations are undercut. This is not an argument for wholesale replacement of existing management. Current management has invaluable knowledge of the company. But the old CEO and a handful of top managers may have to be replaced.

Turnaround Team Structure

The job of the turnaround team is to implement change. To do that they must understand the relationship of all elements of the company to each other, to customers and to suppliers. They should also be able transition between problems that need immediate attention and strategic issues.

Employees selected for the turnaround team should be temporarily relieved of other duties so they can devote all their time and energy to the turnaround. Why? To be an effective crisis management team, they must move fast. If they have to manage their current operation as well as analyze company operations for the turnaround, there will be a natural tendency to spend too much time in their old role to the detriment of their role on the turnaround team. This may mean populating the turnaround team, not with department heads, but with their best lieutenants, not with executive vice presidents, but their direct reports. It might also mean that junior people might be temporarily elevated to department head so that some department heads can work on the turnaround team.

The team should include people with experience in all aspects of the company to provide the widest possible view of how things currently work, as well as, how they should work after restructuring. The team should include people who can critically evaluate turnaround proposals and even be contrarians. The point is to bring the best thinking to bear on issues. At the end of the day the new CEO or turnaround team leader must make the hard choices (Whitney, 1996, 95).

There are several key questions when deciding on the composition of the Turnaround Team.

(1) Can present management make the transition to crisis management?
(2) Does present management have the skills and experience necessary to lead the company through a turnaround?
(3) Can they be objective in their decision making?
(4) Have they accepted the need for change and demonstrated a willingness to implement drastic changes?
(5) What skills are needed to supplement present management?
(6) Should outsiders be brought in to round out the management team?

A major, though oft unspoken advantage to using current managers is that they know the company, customers, suppliers, industry and the skeletons in the closet. All this shortens the learning curve. On the other hand, those that cannot embrace change must be let go. When Jack Welsh committed GE to six sigma quality, he evaluated the beliefs of his top executives. Those that were not committed to the process were terminated (Charan, 1999).

Outside professionals are often included on the turnaround team, for example accountants and management consultants specializing in the company's industry, turnaround consultants, and investment bankers. CPA firms can provide a pool of highly qualified individuals to staff a turnaround on a moments notice.

The ideal team is probably a blend of current managers and outside consultants.

Supplementing Management

Placing highly qualified and motivated leaders throughout an organization is one of the keys to success. After reviewing the qualifications of current management, one might find they don't have the skills, experience or attitude necessary to implement the changes identified by the turnaround team. This means hiring from outside to supplement the management team. The turnaround committee and outside advisors can help define the type of individual needed. However, recruiting can be a long and time consuming process. Therefore, it should begin as soon as a need is identified.

Advertising for management talent may bring spotty results, and a mass of unscreened resumes. Consider using an executive recruiter. There are two types of recruiters contingent fee, and retainer fee.

Contingent fee recruiters are paid a percent of the salary of any candidate hired. Fees can range from 25 to 40% of salary. If none of the candidates they put forward is hired, you owe them nothing.

Retainer fee recruiters are paid in advance to find a candidate. Fees range around 30% of projected compensation. Retainer recruiters only work on positions with compensation packages well above $100,000. Retainer fee recruiters are paid whether or not a firm hires one of the candidates they identify. However, many have a strong reputation for finding the right person at the right time. Retainer recruiters spend a lot of time understanding a company's needs. Then they look for someone who is successful in the industry and in the type of position that needs to be filled. For example, if a company wants to recruit a new CEO, the retainer fee recruiter might cold call a division president at some other company and ask them whether they are ready to move up to the big chair. Theoretically, a company's internal recruiters can do this if they have enough pluck. However, because time is of the essence in restructuring, it is probably more cost effective to use a retainer recruiter who is familiar with the firms and executives in the company's indus-try. *The Directory of Executive Recruiters*, published by Kennedy Information Corporation lists both contingent and retainer recruiters and is indexed by industry, type of position and geographic location. It is available in most libraries.

Turnaround Team

A turnaround team needs a strong leader with a strategic view, who can do the critical analyses suggested in this book and who will drive change. The turnaround team should also have specialists in a variety of areas who are capable of looking beyond their specialty to see how their actions impact the company overall.

Sales and Marketing

Most turnarounds involve significant changes in sales and marketing. It is important to find or recruit someone who will:

(1) Re-examine product lines. Which aren't carrying their weight?
(2) Re-examine sales mix
(3) Re-examine pricing
(4) Define markets for new and existing products

(5) Analyze channels of distribution
(6) Upgrade the sales force
(7) Cement customer relations
(8) Integrate the changes necessary to drive new and repeat sales, and improve customer satisfaction.

Operations

Significant operational improvements are needed for most companies in trouble. The team will need someone who can address the following issues:

(1) Identify significant cost reductions
(2) Improve scheduling efficiency and delivery
(3) Improve quality
(4) Rationally consider outsourcing and make the transition to outsourcing where appropriate
(5) Improve time to market for new products and services
(6) Design for flexibility
(7) Improve facility utilization
(8) Improve inventory management
(9) Improve customer service responsiveness

Finance

The turnaround team must have a strong finance person. This person should be a CPA or MBA or both. This individual must:

(1) Make accurate cash flow projections
(2) Identify and implement short-term cash management strategies
(3) Deal with creditors
(4) Generate accurate and insightful analyses of company operations
(5) Continually test the turnaround plan for realism
(6) Measure performance to goal and provide an early warning system for deviations from plan
(7) Resist the temptation to reduce the severity of the turnaround plan once immediate financial pressures abate.

Human Resources

Human resources can make a significant contribution to a restructuring, but only if they have an appreciation of restructuring goals and can move at the pace required.

The roles of Human Resources in a turnaround include

(1) Implement and maintain a headcount management system
(2) Recruit executives for the turnaround team
(3) Prepare for and implement layoffs
(4) Maintain the good will of remaining employees
(5) Evaluate salary structures

Transaction from Restructuring Team to New Management

At some point, there must be a transition from a turnaround team to a permanent management structure. The questions are (i) when should that transition take place and (ii) what should become of those on the team?

Diagnosing the company's problems and identifying opportunities to improve company performance might take three to six months. As proposed solutions to problems are approved by the turnaround committee the implementation phase will begin. Permanent management changes should be in place at this point in time. Those managers who have underperformed should be let go and those who will replace them hired. Temporary restructuring staff hired from CPA and consulting firms should be released to minimize restructuring costs. Those on the restructuring team recruited from within the company should be considered for promotion to areas where they have operational responsibility for implementing restructuring recommendations.

Management Problems

Every company in trouble and most companies that are underperforming have a variety of management problems. These problems must be identified and cleaned up before substantial restructuring can take place.

Uri Bar-Joseph and Zachary Sheaffer wrote a seminal article for the *International Journal of Intelligence and Counter-Intelligence* in which they drew a number of parallels between surprise in the strategic theater and surprise, that is to say crises, in business (Bar-Joseph and Sheafrer, 1998, p. 331). Among their conclusions is that crisis need not mean complete failure. A crisis can arise from (i) significant, unexpected charges to income, (ii) loss of key clients, (iii) violation of bank covenants, (iv) uninvited take over attempts, or (v) a significant violation of state or federal regulations.

They cite a number of major business failures which took many by surprise including Barings Bank, 1995; Metallgezelschaft, 1993; Credit Lyonnais, 1995; Daiwa Bank, 1995 and Orange County, California 1995 (Bar-Joseph and Sheafrer, 1998, p. 331). To this we might add Enron, 2001, Global Crossing 2002, Arthur Andersen 2002, sub-prime mortgage backed securities and Lehman Brothers 2008 and General Motors in 2009.

Their hypothesis is that warning signs of business crisis existed in every instance but were not heeded. They attribute crisis to failure to properly detect, evaluate and act on early warning signs because of an organizational culture created by poor management. Among the behaviors which contribute to a company ignoring signs of trouble are,

(1) limitations on the flow of information,
(2) discounting, ignoring or under reporting failings of key clients, programs and products,
(3) ignoring irregularities in internal controls, and
(4) management bias which becomes incorporated in strategic decision making.

Bar-Joseph and Sheaffer attribute the inability to detect and defuse pending crises to four classes of factors (i) psychological pathogens, (ii) organizational obstacles (iii) political inhibitors and (iv) warning/response factors.

Psychological Pathogens

Psychological pathogens are inappropriate individual behaviors which tend to stifle communications and independent analysis. Examples of psychological pathogens include fear of superiors, lack of skepticism, paranoid-megalomaniac leadership, cognitive dissonance which is a discrepancy between information and beliefs, heuristic judgments which is resorting to shortcuts when faced with complex situations, escalating commitment to a chosen course of action, over confidence, managerial stress, managerial arrogance and egocentric self-image, a tendency for managers to act on personal preferences rather than rationally assessing threats and opportunities, a conflict prone or introverted managerial style and an aversion to discrepant views (Bar-Joseph and Sheafrer, 1998, pp. 336–338).

These factors mask impending trouble and create resistance to change. The solution is not to try to reform inappropriate behaviors, but to eliminate people with these behaviors. Companies should not be in the behavior modification business, they should be in the behavior selection business (Seitz, 2005).

Organizational Obstacles

Organization norms sometimes emphasize inappropriate reliance on methods rather than substance. Organizational atrophy occurs when precedent becomes paramount, means become more important than ends, organizational vision is limited as is participation in decision making, and an organization has a tendency toward conceptual rigidity and authoritarianism. Over reliance on standard operating procedures and reluctance to challenge procedures in changing circumstances is another sign of organizational atrophy. Politicking, which is bickering, and manipulative parochial interests, interpersonal and inter-group conflict, or obstructing action to gain political advantage is corrosive to an organization. A company's culture can be so rigid that data, trends or information that does not fit the company line are ignored. This is sometimes characterized as "group think" in which individuals abdicate their responsibility for independent critical analysis in favor of the low risk go-along to get-along behavior. Compartmentalization, that is sharing information on a "need to know" basis and giving such information to those who are authorized rather than those who need it is another sign of organizational dysfunction (Bar-Joseph and Sheafrer, 1998, pp. 339–340).

The free flow of ideas in information is critical for successful restructuring. Restructuring is about change and obstacles to well thought out change must be eliminated. Restructuring is about more than cutting costs and growing revenue. Restructuring must go to the core values that people bring to the enterprise.

Political Inhibitors

Some executives view the company as a stage to advance their own fortunes rather than a vehicle for creating shareholder wealth. Such people might use scarce information to gain political power, impede cooperation, or reject competent professional assessments. They might also interfere in professional assessments to assure an outcome that supports their predetermined view. They may be dogmatic or monolithic in their approach and spurn the opportunity to get a second opinion on a complex situation (Bar-Joseph and Sheafrer, 1998, pp. 340–341).

This situation is especially harmful when executives pressure accountants to report a certain level of profit whether or not the facts justify it, or marketing to forecast sales in excess of what they realistically project, or to get finance to report a greater return on an acquisition than is realistic. In short, people who politic place their own interest ahead of the interests of the company. Such people should be identified and eliminated. The moral, legal, and ethical duty of every employee is to protect and advance the interests of the shareholders and not their own interests.

Warning/Response Factors

Those intent on advancing their own interests rather than those of the organization use several techniques to gain advantage while obscuring warning signals and the adverse consequences of their actions. For example, they may use disinformation to increase the amount of "noise" making it more difficult to identify real warning signals. They may cry wolf which means repeated warnings about situations which are unlikely to materialize causing policy makers to become callus to warnings. They might also delay or inhibit the dissemination of information so that they can take advantage of the timing of a decision to go, or not go through with their actions (Bar-Joseph and Sheafrer, 1998, pp. 341–342).

   While Bar-Joseph and Sheaffer seem pessimistic, it is important to understand that such obstacles exist; can be identified; and must be eliminated. These kinds of problems need not reach the executive suite for their corrosive effects to be felt. Departments, plants and strategic partners infected with these problems can also cause or create nasty surprises. The restructuring team should be alert for them and work to eliminate them. Some can be changed through directives, backed up by consistently applied examples. Sometimes specific individuals have to be eliminated. One of the reasons for an independent Turnaround Committee is to get beyond these organizational problems.

Bad Attitudes

Whenever change is afoot, some people with resist that change in a thousand subtle ways and even openly. It is just as inevitable that even in the absence of change some people will have a bad attitude about work, management, the company and its customers. Unchecked, negative attitudes are a virus that can spread through an organization. Often the only way to stop the spread of negative attitudes is to let people go. Trying to change attitudes is a waste of time and rarely works. There is an old adage that says, "Never try to teach a pig to sing. It is a waste of time and annoys the pig." If people are unhappy with the company, the best thing you can do for them, and for the company, is to cut them loose.

Culling the Herd

Needless to say, those who steal from the company, have chronic absenteeism, discriminate on the basis of race, sex or sexual preference, are loud and abusive or who act out should be immediately terminated. This should be an on-going process. Bad employees can kill a company, but poor employees can lead it to a slow and painful death.

   Restructuring is an ideal time to cull employees. Slackers, those with bad attitudes and people who are mediocre or simply screw-ups should be identified and eliminated. We are not talking about eliminating the people who have committed an offense. We are talking about eliminating employees who aren't as productive as they should be. It is widely believed that General Electric and other companies systematically "release" a certain percentage of employees who fall in the bottom of their performance categories each year. Systematically culling employees will result in a better performing staff, aware of the consequences of non-performance, and probably grateful they no longer have to work with under performers. Underperformers tend to not do their work, so it gets spread around to those who do, creating an additional burden on good performers.

   While there are few official pronouncements on systematic weeding, perhaps 5–10% of employees are released each year in companies with such programs. One advantage of releasing low performers is that most workers know who the under-performers are so it is easy for them to understand why those particular people were eliminated. A program to systematically weed low performing employees should be used to improve employee quality on an on-going basis.

Blue Chair Employees

Most new employees get right to work as soon as they are hired, but there is a percentage that do not. They may ask for a desk lamp, and when a desk lamp is provided, ask for an electric pencil sharpener. When the electric pencil sharpener is provided, they may ask to move their desk closer to the window. When their desk is closer to the window they may ask for a blue chair. This pattern of conduct indicates the individual is not focused on adding value to the company, but engaging in a little game to see how far they can push the company. This type of employee will never be satisfied, and will always place burdens on his or her supervisor and coworkers. These individuals should be released immediately. The longer they stay, the more the company will have to pay in unemployment benefits and the longer they stay, the more of their work that will get shifted to their coworkers, which is unfair.

Training

Training and retraining staff and management is a critical component in develop-ing the best and most effective management and workforce. Training has a number of payoffs. First, training improves efficiency and productivity by informing peo-ple of the best techniques to achieve specific goals. Second, training provides a forum for discussing company goals and how to implement them. Third, training improves retention and company loyalty because it demonstrates the company is interested in developing its people. Commerce Bank, headquartered in Cherry Hill, New Jersey enjoyed a great reputation for customer service for a number of reasons, and one of the most important is the extensive training given to every employee (Austen, 2007)[1].

Unions

Workers have a right to organize into collective bargaining units (unions) and nego-tiate for wages and benefits. A successful union drive is an indication of the failure of management. Employees organize into unions when they believe management isn't taking care of them.

The first rule of leadership is to take care of your people. If you do, your employ-ees won't want a union. Taking care of your people does not mean throwing bags of money at them. Loyalty cannot be bought. Taking care of them means treating them fairly, with respect, and keeping open channels of communication.

One of the most common places that leadership breaks down is in first line supervision. First line supervisors often do not have the training or experience to understand the elements of leadership, and some are tempted to use supervisory authority to extract personal favors from workers and sometimes they feel entitled to treat workers as inferiors. Senior managers should be alert for friction between workers and first line supervisors because if first line supervisors treat workers improperly, workers will view that as though the whole of management is treating them improperly. Therefore, first line supervisors should be closely monitored, evaluated by their staffs, and thoroughly trained in proper management.

Unions effectively impose another layer of management on a company. Every layer of management adds cost and reduces flexibility. Union contracts are about classifying people and jobs. And when a company needs to out hustle its competitors to grow, or stay in business, lack of flexibility can be deadly (Bhide, 1986, p. 60). Unions also make it difficult to reward outstanding workers and release underperforming workers.

The bottom line is that if a company takes care of its people every day, they will not want a union. Start taking care of workers now, not when union organizers are on the company's doorstep. Then it is too late.

Layoffs

For most people, being laid off is one of the most traumatic things they will experience short of loss of a loved one. Therefore, it's important to handle layoffs in a professional manner and minimize trauma. Among the reasons to treat those laid off in a professional manner are that,

(1) The employees not laid off will watch, very carefully, how the layoff is handled imagining they could be next.
(2) It is a small world, and today's laid off employee might be an employee of your customer or supplier tomorrow.
(3) Angry employees tend to be litigious.

Layoff Notice

Most employees are employees at will. That means absent a contract or some other promise of employment, they can be terminated at any time without a reason. When a reason is given, and it's a *prohibited reason* such as race, sex, age, religion, or sexual preference that reason can become grounds for a successful lawsuit. Therefore, when employees must be laid off, do not give a reason for the layoff. Do not make promises about continued employment or about rehiring. Any such comment might be construed as an oral contract for employment even if there was no intent to make such an oral contract. If the facility in question is unionized, consult a labor lawyer before issuing layoff notices.

Layoff Guidelines

Many restructurings require significant staff reductions. The following suggestions were culled from those who have been through the experience.

(1) Make all staff cuts at once. Do not layoff in stages. That only prolongs the pain and uncertainty of the people to be retained.

(2) Do not insult employees, tell them their performance was inadequate or otherwise criticize them. It isn't necessary and it is a distraction for both the company and the employee. If anything, say layoffs are in response to market forces and no more. Do not elaborate on that statement.

(3) Do not let employees engage you in a discussion of their performance. Emphasize the importance of looking toward the future, and getting the next job.

(4) Provide information as to how then can collect unemployment compensation, the address of the unemployment compensation office, and recommend they file for unemployment *immediately*.

(5) Provide information on COBRA – Continuation of medical benefits, as required by law. Usually an employee can remain on an employer's medical policy for up to 18 months if they pay their own premiums. Medical coverage is a big concern for laid off workers

(6) Compile a packet of job search materials listing:

    a. Websites: for example:

      http://www.jobstar.org – a job search and resume writing guide
      http://www.hrsjobs.com – a web site for searching government jobs
      http://www.monster.com – a site listing 800,000 US jobs
      http://www.jobbankusa.com – a site listing US jobs

    b. Lists of Professional Recruiters

    c. Guidelines for writing resumes and cover letters

    d. Lists of books that can help with job searches: for example:
      What Color Is Your Parachute? by Richard Nelson Bolles, *The Directory of Executive Recruiters* by Kennedy, and *On the Job* by Steve Viscosi

(7) If the budget permits, and the workers need it, make off-site computers, fax machines and mail services available.

Anything the company can do to place laid off employees in new positions will be appreciated by them, watched by those still employed by the company and will reduce the cost of post layoff unemployment taxes.

On the other hand, there are a few examples of headcount reduction that have been poorly handled. Circuit City laid off 3,400 highly compensated workers and announced it would hire lower wage workers to replace them (Haberkorn, 2007). If those who have been loyal employees of the store for years are treated this way, can any employee expect better treatment? Some who have shopped a Circuit City since the layoff complained they couldn't get help from the replacement staff even when they wanted to buy. Circuit City filed for bankruptcy in November of 2008 and ceased operation in March 2009 (Kolker and Erik, 2009). Radio Shack laid off 400 people by email (Kolker and Erik, 2009). This is not the level of professionalism that inspires confidence.

Layoff Law

The federal Worker Adjustment and Retraining Notification Act (WARN) must be considered when reducing headcount. This may be a free country, but we are not free to do what we please. Even when employees are employees at will, the federal government still imposes some requirements on an employer who intends to close a plant or have a substantial layoff.

The Worker Adjustment and Retraining Notification Act[2] (WARN) requires 60 days advanced notice to workers and government officials if there is a "plant closing" (Code of Federal Regulations, 1989).

Covered employers include any company with 100 or more full time employees or 100 or more workers, including full and part time workers that cumulatively work more than 4,000 hours per week excluding overtime. Those on temporary furlough and who reasonably expect to return to their jobs are also counted in determining whether a company must comply with the rule. Contractors and temporary employees are included in determining whether a company is large enough to fall within this regulation, but contractors and temporary workers might not be entitled to notification.

A plant closing can be an individual plant or a facility within a plant in which 50 or more employees suffer an employment loss. A plant is considered "closed" even if a few workers remain at work.

A "mass layoff" which also triggers the notification requirement is defined as loss of employment for 33% of the workforce and at least 50 employees. Managers and supervisors count as employees for purposes of this rule.

Generally, notification is required if employees will lose work for 6 months or more, or work hours will be reduced by 50% or more. For purposes of this rule, the government can look back 90 days or look ahead 90 days to count layoffs.

Notice must be given to:

(1) The local governmental unit to which the company pays the most taxes. This is often the town or city in which the facility is located, but may be the county. Notice must be given to the highest elected official of that governmental unit.
(2) The state representative who administers the Job Partnership Training Act.

(3) The union representative, if workers are represented by a collective bargaining agreement.
(4) Employees who may be laid off.

Notice must include:

(1) The date when the layoff is expected to occur.
(2) Whether the layoff is expected to be permanent or temporary,
(3) Whether seniority "bumping rights" exist.
(4) The name and telephone number of the company official to contact for further information.

There are a few exceptions to WARN provisions such as strike or lock-out, natural disaster, or financial collapse. However, the burden is on the employer to prove it falls within the exception. Since worker protection statutes are often construed in favor of workers, this burden may be difficult to overcome.

Some states have passed their own version of WARN, but state laws often lack the federal exceptions or place additional burdens on employers. The best approach is to contact the state Department of Labor in which the facility is located and obtain guidance from them about state requirements. This may sound like a pain but is always better to be on the side of the angels and scrupulously comply with the law.

The penalty for failure to provide notice is that employees may sue the company for damages reasonably resulting from the failure. Principally, this is a claim for lost wages, but an inventive lawyer can always find additional damages.

The effects of the WARN rule include:

(1) A 60 day delay between the time employees are identified as redundant and the time they can be removed from payroll.
(2) Poor at-work morale of those identified for layoff and interference with the effectiveness of the non-laid off workers if for no other reason than their need to talk about their problems,
(3) The potential for sabotage,
(4) Politicians who may villanize the company and or try to brow-beat the company into withdrawing the layoffs.

While the WARN law may seem burdensome, companies should be thankful it is not as burdensome as the French and some other European rules. For example, a French employee with 10 years service is entitled to 2 years severance pay and an employee with 25 years service is entitled to 4 years severance pay (Code of Federal Regulations, 2006).

If a company is over staffed, it is overstaffed and the fact that a company has to comply with WARN and carry unproductive or under productive employees for 60 days does not change that fact the employees may have to be laid off to save the company.

Employees to be laid off should be separated from those who will remain as soon as practical. There is some ambiguity in the rule as to whether sending employees home with pay constitutes a layoff without the requisite notice.

The strategy should therefore be to send them to a "retraining" program which might just be a room with tables and chairs and a moderator to teach them how to update resumes, conduct a job search, or tap into government retraining programs. Employees should not be forced to go to such programs, but should be given the option to go to them or stay home. If employees are given options along the way, it is much more difficult to argue that they were sent home and that constituted a layoff without the requisite notice. There are a number of "out placement" services that do this professionally.

Conclusion

A company will live or die, not just by its products and services, but by the quality of its people. So an important element of restructuring is to put the right people in the right places and eliminate the wrong people from the organization.

Turning around a company requires dramatic change in a short period of time. To maintain the confidence of the board of directors requires constant communication and a willingness to listen. Communicating with the whole board is cumbersome so a turnaround committee comprised of outside directors should be formed as a liaison to the board and it should be vested with the power to approve most turnaround decisions.

A turnaround team should be formed which includes both inside managers and outside consultants. Inside managers should be relieved of their ongoing duties until the turnaround is well into its implementation phase. The turnaround team should be lead by an individual who is a strategic thinker, supported by specialists in sales and marketing, operations and finance.

Most companies get into trouble because of management. Cultures that favor process over results, limited access to information and tolerate politicking must be changed. Often the only way to do that is to terminate the worst offenders.

The company should constantly strive to improve the quality of its employees at all levels. Individuals with negative attitudes must go. Low performers should be systematically purged each year. New employees who do not focus on work should be eliminated early, and training of staff and management should be on-going.

The first rule of leadership is to take care of your people. A company that violates that rule may find a union knocking on its door. A union represents an additional layer of management which increases cost and reduces flexibility. If employees are treated well they will not need or want a union.

Headcount reduction is an important element in many restructurings. Layoffs are traumatic for employees, their families and even for the employees not laid off. Therefore, it is important to make layoffs in the most professional possible manner. Avoid giving reasons for a layoff; don't engage in a discussion of individual performance; never discuss the possibility of a rehire; never insult or demean the person being terminated and focus the individual being terminated on getting his or her next job.

Layoffs are controlled by the federal WARN statute which among other things requires 60 days notice to laid off employees, the jurisdiction the company pays the most tax to, and others. States may also have WARN acts which impose additional conditions. While complying with this law might seem burdensome, it is always better to follow the letter and spirit of the law than to skirt it.

Notes

1. Commerce Bank was recently acquired by TD Bank. Customers are waiting to see whether service deteriorates from the high levels they have grown to expect.
2. Statutory Authority is found at 29 U.S.C. 2107(a).

References

Austen I (2007) TD bank to acquire commerce. New York Times. Oct 3. Section C, Business/Financial Desk p 1

Bar-Joseph U, Sheafrer Z (1998) Surprise and its causes in business administration and strategic studies. Int J Intell Counter Intell 11(3) 331–349, Fall

Bhide A (1986) Hustle as strategy. Harv Bus Rev 59–65, Sept–Oct

Bar-Joseph and Sheafrer. 1998. "Surprise and its Causes in Business Administration and Strategic Studies," International Journal of Intelligence and Counter Intelligence, Volume 11, No. 3, Fall. p.331.

Charan R (1999) Why CEOs fail. Fortune 139(12), 21 June. Cvr

Code of Federal Regulations (CFR) (1989) Title 20, Chap 20, Part 639. Source 54 FR 16064, 20 Apr

Code of Federal Regulations (CFR) (2006) *French Labor Law*, Chap 2, Invest in France Agency, www.investinfrance.org. Also see French Labor Code Article L122

Haberkorn J (2007) Circuit city to lay off 3,400. Wash Times. Business and Financial News, Article No. 20070329-WT-CIRCUIT-CITY-20070329. 29 Mar

Kolker C, Larson E (2006) Radioshack layoff notices are sent by e-mail. New York Times. 31 Aug

Kolker C, Larson E (2009) Circuit city liquidation sale will end sooner than it expected. Bloomberg News Service. www.bloomberg.com/apps/news?pid=20601103&sid=afkqKVyLPxP4&refer=us#. Accessed 6 Mar

http://www.nytimes.com/2006/08/31/business/31radio.html?ex=1314676800&en=0ddfbac764da4440&ei=5088&partner=rssnyt&emc=rss

Lublin JS, White E (2007) More outside directors taking lead in crisis. Wall St J B1 and B3, 19 Mar

Seitz D (2005) Leadership development lecture at Rutgers University. 15 Apr. Mr. Seitz is the President of NWL Transformers

Tichacek RL (2006) Root causes: six reasons for change. AACE Int Trans, published by AACE International. PM.07.1–PM 07.5

Whitney JO (1996) Strategic renewal for business units. Harv Bus Rev 84–98, July–Aug

Chapter 4
Labor Cost

Introduction

Salaries, wages and employee benefits are among the most significant costs any company faces. Attracting and retaining the most talented individuals is expensive, so restructuring involves a balance between getting the best people and managing labor costs. Strategies include (i) set and achieve headcount targets, (ii) compensate fairly and (iii) focus on factors that can inflate labor costs such as overtime, turnover, unemployment taxes and workers compensation insurance.

The difference between superior financial performance and a company struggling to survive is often attention to details that can save a few percent of costs across a wide range of areas. In this regard labor costs are a fruitful target.

Headcount Management

No leader, no entrepreneur, no CEO or consultant, no matter how brilliant can run a company without people to support her or him. The principal that flows from that concept is that no one can restructure a company and lead it to greatness through layoffs. One of the major drawbacks to headcount reduction is that employees have knowledge about the company, its clients, customers, suppliers and operations (Scarlett, 2006). Some of this will be difficult to replicate in the short term. On the other hand, many under performing companies are over staffed.

Work tends to expand to fill the time available and people not stretched every day use the extra time to socialize reducing the productivity of their colleagues. Excess management and staff create layers of procedures that limit a company's flexibility to respond to customers and market forces in a timely manner. Fiat, for example, was on the point of collapse in 2004 when its fifth CEO in three years Sergio Marchionne, was brought in to restructure it. While he used a broad range of techniques, one of the things he did was to cut middle management by 30% and shed a layer of 700 managers whose sole job was to monitor car and truck sales (Kahn and Stephen, 2006).

D.E. Vance, *Corporate Restructuring*, DOI 10.1007/978-3-642-01786-5_4,
© Springer-Verlag Berlin Heidelberg 2009

Overstaffing can be an enormous drain on a company not just for salaries, but for employee benefits such as healthcare, retirement plans, vacations and sick leave which can be 25–35% of wages for a typical, well established company. There are other significant costs to being overstaffed as well. Costs include 6.2% for FICA and 1.45% for Medicare, unemployment compensation which can run from 4 to 6% of wages and workers compensation which can run from 1.5 to 10% of wages depending on a company's industry, state, and claims experience. So the first step in managing labor costs is to manage headcount.

How does one know whether a company is overstaffed? How does one know what the right staffing level is? The best ways to know is to look at successful competitors. Since companies come in all shapes and sizes, the only practical way to make comparisons among companies is by using ratios. One of the most straightforward ratios is Revenue per Employee (RPE) which is a company's revenue divided by its number of employees as shown in Eq. (4.1). For most non-financial companies the terms revenue and sales can be used interchangeably.

$$RPE = Revenue/Number\ of\ Employees \qquad (4.1)$$

Suppose a company has sales of $120,000,000 and 786 employees.

$$RPE = \$120,000,000/786$$
$$= \$152,672$$

The higher a company's RPE, the more revenue each employee generates. While the CEO or a salesperson may close a million dollar deal, it is unlikely someone on the factory floor or a janitor will close deals or make sales. But, the issue isn't who is generating sales. It is the number of people needed to earn the revenue that flows from that sale. By averaging the RPE for a company's best competitors, a company can get a sense of what its RPE should be as shown in Eq. (4.2).

$$Industry\ Average\ RPE = \left(\sum_{1}^{n} (Revenue_i/Employees_i) \right) \Big/ n \qquad (4.2)$$

Where $Revenue_i$ is the revenue of the ith competitor, $Employees_i$ is the number of employees in the ith competitor and n is the number of competitors being considered. Table 4.1 provides an example of this computation.

If a company's RPE is lower than competitors it might mean its people are not doing productive work or there are too many people for the work it has. A consequence of lean staffing is that people find and eliminate unproductive work.

A target number of employees can be estimated by dividing revenue by the industry average RPE as shown in Eq. (4.3).

$$Target\ Number\ of\ Employees = Revenue/Industry\ Average\ RPE \qquad (4.3)$$

Suppose a company has $120 million in sales and the industry average RPE is $176,658.

$$\text{Target Number of Employees} = \$120,000,000/\$176,633$$
$$= 679$$

Table 4.1 Revenue per employee (RPE) and headcount goals

Company	Revenue	Employees	Company RPE	RPE Rank
B	$180,000,000	1,000	$180,000	3
C	$90,000,000	563	$159,858	5
D	$80,000,000	356	$224,719	1
E	$75,000,000	516	$145,349	6
F	$75,000,000	395	$189,873	2
G	$64,000,000	400	$160,000	4
Total RPEs of companies B through G			$1,059,799	
Divided by the number of companies			6	
Industry average RPE			$176,633	

Target number of employees using industry average RPE is 679 as shown above.

Better Goals for RPE

a. Have an RPE in the top three. That means company A's RPE must be at least $180,001.

New Target Number of Employees   =$120,000,000/$180,001
$$= 666$$

b. Be half way between the average and the best performer in the industry. That would mean company A's RPE would have to be $200,689 ($224,719 + $176,633)/2.

New Target Number of Employees = $120,000,000/$200,676
$$= 598$$

c. Have an RPE 10% better than the industry average. That means company A's RPE would have to be $194,315 ($176,650 × 110%).

New Target Number of Employees = $120,000,000/$194,296
$$= 618$$

As employees are eliminated, a company's RPE will rise. But reaching the industry average RPE should not be the final goal even as average profitability should only be an interim goal. A company should strive to do better than average. The question is how much better? The answer can be framed in a number of ways. For example, a company might say it wants to be in the top three, or it might say somewhere between average and the best performer in the industry, or it might say it wants to outperform the average by some percent. The point is that goals have to be reasonable; otherwise people will shut down, rather than trying harder. An exploration of the effect of adopting various goals is demonstrated in Table 4.1.

There are other ways of estimating the target number of employee. One is to use gross profit per employee. Gross profit is sales less cost of goods sold. The another way to estimate the target number of employees is to use operating income per employee. Both methods compare the target company to industry norms.

Having set a target headcount, the next question is how to reach the target. Some companies cut every department across the board by a certain percent. This can have a negative impact as key knowledge is lost, morale sinks, and the company may end up having to rehire in certain areas. Assuming for the moment a company has more staff than necessary, several steps should be taken while people are identified for elimination. First, there should be a hiring freeze. It is pointless to hire people just to lay them off or hire new people while laying off current employees. Churning employees is bad for morale. Across the board head count reductions may leave shortages in critical areas whereas in areas that contribute little may be untouched. A more engineered approach to headcount management is necessary.

A Perfect Organization

Often companies fall into the trap of improving the organization they have rather than asking what an ideal organization would look like. Marvin Davis, a renowned turnaround expert suggests that a company design the ideal organization with no names on the organization chart. For each position on the chart, write a brief description of job duties and only after this ideal organization is created, determine whether any of the incumbent management has the requisite qualifications. The result might be to bring middle and lower level managers forward to more significant leadership positions, to reassign senior managers, to highlight gaps in management skills, or to indicate that some managers no longer fit into the organization. Davis calls this the "green field" approach (Davis, 2008).

Low Performing Employees

Table 4.1 analyzes a company which, compared to the industry average, was overstaffed by 107 people (786 employees –679 target number of employees). If the bottom 10% of performers were eliminated, that would be 79 or almost three quarters of the people needed to reach industry averages. One advantage of releasing underperformers is that most people know who the underperformers are, so it is easy to understand why particular people were eliminated. The exact percentage of low performers to be eliminated is a matter of management discretion, but pruning should be constant, not just during a restructuring. Identifying low performers, or ranking performance generally, might be distasteful to managers who take the position that all his or her employees are equally valuable. But, to manage is to choose.

A manager incapable of ranking his or her employees is probably not capable of making other important choices.

Staff Functions

Another highly productive place to eliminate people is in staff functions. Identify those who make the product or provide the service, sell the product or service, provide customer service and count the money. Pretty much everyone else is in some kind of staff function. When a company is in trouble, large staffs are a luxury it can ill afford. When a staff function is absolutely necessary, challenge the head of that unit to cut staff by a third to a half. If the function isn't absolutely necessary, eliminate it. Sometimes a staff position is a way to reward a particularly valuable employee. Do not keep a whole staff function just to have a place for that employee. Throw them into the mix making the product, selling the product, servicing customers or counting the money. For the company discussed in Table 4.1, if just 4% of employees were in staff positions, then the company would have about 32 people on staff. Cutting this in half would eliminate 16 people which is about 15% of the way toward the goal of eliminating 107 positions.

Span of Control

How much management is enough? How much is too much? Span of control is a measure of the average number of people each manager supervises. For example, if a company has 25 workers, and there are 5 first line managers to supervise them and one second line manger manages the first line managers, the span of control is 5.

Increasing the span of control reduces the number of middle managers. The question is how wide a span of control is appropriate. Management texts say span of control in most organizations ranges from 3 to 30 (Bobbitt et al., 1974; Gulich and Urwick, 1937; Davis, 1951). The more standardized the task the easier it is to increase the span of control. Suppose the span of control of the company in Table 4.1 is 7. That means that for every 7 workers there is one first line manager and for every seven first line managers there is one second line manager and so forth.

It would be tempting to simply divide the number of employees, 786, by 7 to get the number of first line managers. However, this process would overstate the number of middle managers because the middle managers are included in the headcount of 786. A better way to begin the process is to subtract the number of first line managers from the total number of employees (E) to estimate the number of workers (W) as shown in Eq. (4.4). The number of first line managers can be estimated as the number of employees divided by the span of control, S.

$$W = E - E/S \qquad (4.4)$$

Suppose one does not know a company's span of control? The best way to find the span of control is to use a company's headcount management system to find the span of control by actually counting how many people "report to" any given position. If a company does not have a headcount management system, span of control can be estimated by solving Eq. (4.4) for S the span of control to get Eq. (4.5).

$$S = \frac{E}{(E - W)} \tag{4.5}$$

The quantity $(E - W)$ is just the number of managers. If one can count the number of managers that quantity can be substituted into (4.5) to get (4.6) an estimate of the span of control.

$$S = \frac{E}{M} \tag{4.6}$$

When analyzing a company's actual organization it is very likely that some layers of management will have a span of control greater than this estimate and some less. Where the span is greater than the target span, leave the greater span and move on. However, where the span is less than the target, that represents an opportunity to cut costs.

Using data from Table 4.1 the number of workers can be estimated at about 674 (786 total employees – 786/7). However, if 79 unproductive workers and 16 staffers are eliminated as previously discussed then the actual number of employees on which the span of control of analysis should be based is 691 (786 initial total workers – 79 underperforming employees – 16 staff employees). Using formula (4.4) the new estimated number of workers is 593 (691 – 691/7).

As a convention, when a calculation results in a fractional person round up to the next whole number. Table 4.2 illustrates the effect of changing span of control from 7 to 10. The salaries for each level of management are only meant to be illustrative and are not based on real data.

The second convention when applying a span of control analysis is that the person at the top of the organization is never eliminated. This is so because his or her

Table 4.2 Span of control analysis

Job description	(1) Salary per person	(2) Span of Control = 7	(3) Span of Control = 10	(4) Excess managers (2) – (3)	(5) Excess salary (4) × (1)
President	$140,000	1	1		
Vice Presidents	$90,000	2		2	$180,000
Directors	$75,000	13	6	7	$525,000
Managers	$50,000	85	60	25	$1,250,000
Workers	$30,000	593	593		
Totals		691	660	34	$1,955,000

cooperation is needed to achieve the savings indicated by increasing the span of control. A third convention is to assume all other workers are productively employed. As processes are improved, fewer workers may be needed and the span of control analysis can be applied to the reduced workforce.

As shown in Table 4.2, this technique would eliminate another 34 positions. So in our example, the application of three techniques: (i) identification and elimination of the low 10% of performers, (ii) cutting or eliminating staff positions, and (iii) increasing span of control provides a systematic means of eliminating 129 positions (79 + 16 + 34) which is more than the initial target of 107 without closing a plant which might disrupt the continuity of production and customer service. Depending on the circumstances, one might use this model to estimate the impact of eliminating fewer low performers or retaining more staff in areas like product development. Also note that for every dollar of salary saved by adjusting span of control or through some other headcount adjustment the company saves an additional 15–60% depending on a company's industry and benefits package.

Headcount Management System

A headcount management system is an indispensable tool for a rational headcount reduction program. Some companies have fairly sophisticated personnel systems which can serve as a headcount management system. CISCO, and other high performing companies constantly monitor headcount (Mankins and Steele, 2005, p. 70). However, in all probability, an underperforming company will have to develop one. Most companies have payroll systems which include employee name, location and department code. Additional information that should be collected or developed includes position number, position description, the type of position, the position number of every employee's boss, and an employee's relative value to his or her immediate organization. Position numbers are an important control because no one should be able to create a position and put a person on the payroll without an approved position number.

Position type is a characterization of the nature of the position. Some people make the product or manage those who do. Some sell the product or manage those who do. Some count the money or manage those that do. Others service the customer or manage those that do. A few have profit and loss responsibility. Everyone else is staff.

Without indicators to identify top performers it is difficult to determine who should go and who should stay (Bhide, 1986, p. 62). All the employees in every unit should be ranked as to value at least annually and preferably quarterly during a restructuring. Ranking does not mean filling out long tedious personnel evaluations. Ranking should simply be a list of the names of people in a unit ranked from most valuable to least valuable in terms of the unit's mission.

Constructing a workable headcount management system need not be a year long programming exercise. Export a list of names, departments, location codes and salaries to an Excel file from the payroll system. Create columns in the spreadsheet for the data elements described above. Assign a unique number to every individual. Don't worry about a fancy numbering system that reflects the organization. The organization will change and keeping the fancy system in tact takes time and money. Identify those reporting to the CEO and put the CEO's position number in the "Reports to" column. The CEO reports to the Board of Directors give them position number 00000. Give each of the CEOs direct reports a copy of the file without the salary information and ask them to identify their direct reports and so forth. At each level positions should be classified as to type. All management should be notified by the CEO that this database is being created. Personnel should walk this analysis through the company manager by manager until every person has been assigned, typed and rated.

Unit managers who delay, dissemble, argue or take the position that all employees are equally valuable are either being uncooperative or not exercising the kind of judgment needed to push the company forward. Their ranking should be reduced.

The whole process should take no longer than three weeks if one is serious and diligent. Table 4.3 is an example of Headcount Management Data. Once the data are gathered, it can be sorted and subtotaled by "Reporting to" position number to estimate span of control. Staff positions can be counted and better identified and low performers can also be identified.

Consultants and Temporary Workers

Many companies hide their real headcount by using consultants and temporary employees. While consultants and temporary employees can be useful for short term projects, they often become a permanent fixture. Consultants and temporary employees are also expensive. If they have been working for the company for 60 days or more they should be included in the headcount analysis. Including them might make revenue per employee drop dramatically. But, the objective is not to have good statistics. The objective is to understand where a company is and what must be done to restructure it.

Be careful not to target highly compensated employees for elimination simply because they are highly compensated. This may be seen as age discrimination since salaries tend to rise with seniority. Those targeted for layoffs should be selected for poor to mediocre performance, or because a job category or department is no longer needed.

Compensation

The first rule of leadership is to take care of your people. That means that once headcount goals have been achieved, the remaining personnel should be competitively compensated.

Table 4.3 Headcount management data

Position No.	Type	Description	Name	Salary	Reports to	Rank
100000	P&L	CEO	Smith	140000	000000	1/1
200000	Make	VP Manufacturing	Jones	90000	100000	6/7
210000	Make	Dir. Purchasing	Auburey	75000	200000	5/7
220000	Make	VP Production ATL	Barbara	80000	200000	1/7
230000	Make	VP Production PHL	Conway	75000	200000	2/7
240000	Make	VP Production NJ	Douglas	70000	200000	7/7
250000	Make	VP Production LA	Edwards	80000	200000	3/7
270000	Sell	VP Sales & Marketing	Crenshaw	95000	200000	2/7
231000	Make	Mgr. Warehousing	Gallagher	55000	220000	.
232000	Make	Mgr. Day Shift	Houseman	60000	220000	.
233000	Make	Mgr. Maintenance	Ingersol	55000	220000	.
234000	Make	Mgr. Night Shift	Jenkings	55000	220000	.
235000	Staff	Mgr. Personnel	Katz	50000	220000	.
235000	Count	Mgr. Accounting	Lyons	55000	220000	.
235100	Staff	Asst. Pers Mgr.	Montenez	40000	235000	2/5
235050	Staff	Personnel Clerk	Oscar	30000	235000	1/5
235060	Staff	Personnel Clerk	Peterson	30000	235000	4/5
235070	Staff	Mgr. Secretary	Qustein	25000	235000	3/5
235070	Staff	Receptionist	Rodriquez	25000	235000	5/5
232100	Make	Day Supvsr. 1	Simmons	40000	232000	3/6
232200	Make	Day Supvsr. 2	Travis	40000	232000	4/6
232300	Make	Day Supvsr. 3	Unger	40000	232000	5/6
232400	Make	Day Supvsr. 4	Valentine	40000	232000	1/6
232500	Make	Day Supvsr. 5	Wassinger	40000	232000	6/6
232600	Make	Day Supvsr. 6	Xavier	40000	232000	2/6
232110	Make	Worker 1	A	25000	231000	1/7
232111	Make	Worker 2	B	25000	231000	2/7
232112	Make	Worker 3	C	25000	231000	3/7
232113	Make	Worker 4	D	25000	231000	7/7
232114	Make	Worker 5	E	25000	231000	6/7
232115	Make	Worker 6	F	25000	231000	5/7
232116	Make	Worker 7	G	25000	231000	4/7

The CEO of the company reports to the Board of Directors Position No. 00000. Every position should be classified as Make, those who make the product or service the customer or manage people who do; Sell, those who sell the product or service or manage those who do; Count, those who count the money or bill the customers or manage those who do; P&L are those who have profit and loss responsibility; and Staff, are everyone else.

Salary surveys are of enormous value in determining whether people are fairly compensated. The company's objective should not be to pay the most. Nor should it be to pay below average. Competitive salaries are above average salaries. Why above average? A company's objective should be to attract and retain the best people. A company cannot do that if their compensation plan is merely average. If labor costs are "too high" the solutions are to reduce headcount, or apply automation and outsource, not underpay employees. On the other hand, if compensation is well above industry norms, then reducing compensation should be considered.

However, reducing compensation can have a deleterious affect on morale. The best strategy for reducing compensation is to limit annual increases until compensation comes in line with target salaries.

Wage Give Backs

Restructuring is about saving the company and sometimes a company cannot survive at the level of compensation being paid to workers. Under extraordinary circumstances, such as those facing the legacy airlines wage concessions were probably appropriate. However, this should probably be one of the last tools used to restructure a company. In the last several years, many industries have demanded and received wage give backs, particularly airlines, auto workers and auto parts suppliers.

A company should only ask for wage concessions when wage rates are significantly higher than those paid in competing companies. Labor should be provided with information on how much higher their wages are than industry standards. Salary and wage concessions are more likely to be accepted if executives and top management make wage concessions as well.

The easiest way to get labor to digest these roll backs are to (i) apply them to newly hired individuals or (ii) limit annual increases until wages fall more in line with industry norms. Suppose a company starts labor at $14 per hour and the labor rate rises to $20 per hour with 10 years seniority. If the prevailing starting wage were $10 per hour, a company might say that all those hired after a certain date would start at $11 per hour and would reach $20 per hour after 15 years. It does no good to set the starting wage below the prevailing rate because that will only attract below average workers.

Labor Leverage

While controlling headcount is important, it is also important to measure whether a company is getting value for the salaries wages and benefits it pays. One measure of value is labor leverage which is the revenue divided by the total dollars spent on salaries, wages and benefits as shown in Eq. (4.7)

$$LL = R/(S + W + B) \qquad (4.7)$$

Where LL is labor leverage, R is revenue and S, W and B are salaries wages and benefits respectively. If labor leverage is decreasing as compared to the company's historical performance that can mean it either has too many employees or too much is being spent on salaries, wages and benefits. This measure is particularly sensitive to disproportionate increases in executive wages and benefits.

Boards of directors concerned that management might be enriching themselves at the expense of shareholders should track labor leverage. Acquirers, private equity firms, and investment banks might also use labor leverage to determine whether there is excess compensation which can be trimmed.

Termination and Severance Pay

Generally, a company is under no obligation to provide termination or severance pay. One notable exception is for employees who have a contract with the company. Individual contracts are rare, except for executives. Where there are executive contracts, they specify termination payments. Another exception is when workers are covered by a union contract. The contract itself may specify termination and severance pay.

Worker rights to non-contract compensation will come in three forms. First, a company will have to compensate an employee for earned vacation which has not been taken. Second, if an employee comes within the WARN statute, described previously, he or she may be entitled to 60 days notice of the layoff which means, in effect, the employee is entitled to 60 days of pay beyond the point in time at which a company identifies the individual for layoff. Finally, laid off employees will generally be entitled to up to 6 months of unemployment compensation which will ultimately will be paid by the company through future unemployment compensation taxes.

When a company has trouble meeting payroll and executives are taking substantial, though temporary salary cuts, it should probably not offer termination pay. Such offers create additional cash demand and a burden that may push the company past the tipping point of collapse.

At the other end of the spectrum are companies that are in no jeopardy of becoming insolvent, but are simply underperforming their peers and are trying to shed costs to improve profitability. In those circumstances, termination or severance pay is probably appropriate. Reasons include (i) supporting the morale of the remaining workers who will look to those laid off as an indicator of how the company will treat them, (ii) laid off workers may become employed by customers or suppliers tomorrow, so their goodwill is important and (iii) termination pay reduces the risk of employee litigation. At one time General Motors gave white collar workers a severance package of 1 month's pay for every year of service up to a maximum of 15 months (Durbin). A number of years ago, Westinghouse turbine division only provided a year's severance pay to an employees with twenty of service. Both these packages were considered extremely generous and are probably unrealistic for a company in trouble.

Benefits

Benefits are a touchy area for reform. Health care costs rise without end, pension funding is expensive and uncertain, and vacation and sick leave can add substantially to labor costs.

Pensions

Many companies, for example IBM, Verizon, General Motors and others are terminating defined benefit plans (Hoffman, 2006). Defined benefit plan termination should be high on a list of company reforms. Of the nation's 100 largest companies only 31 offer traditional, defined benefit plans down from 89 out of 100 in 1985 (Powell, 2007). Companies should provide for employee retirement. But the rules governing defined benefit plans coupled with the uncertainty in actuarial assumptions and return on plan assets mean that a company's annual pension obligation can fluctuate wildly from year to year.

The alternative is a defined contribution plan in which the company contributes an amount equal to a percent of an employee's salary to a pension account in the name of the employee. Defined contribution plans have the virtue of predictability. Defined contribution plan assets are also more portable than defined benefit plan assets and if an employee quits or is terminated he or she can take his or her plan balance with them.

If a company decides to terminate a defined benefit pension plan, it should consult a lawyer regarding the exact steps for doing so. Among the issues to consider will be notice to current plan participants, computation of the present value of vested and unvested benefits, treatment of plan surplus or shortage, and the nature of the defined contribution replacement benefits.

Health Benefits

Every company should provide some health care insurance for its employees and their families, even if the plan has high deductibles and limited benefits. A more comprehensive plan is better if a company can afford it. Why? The objective is to get the best employees. To get the best employees, people must feel safe working for the company. The two things that say safety to employees are a stable, profitable company and a decent health care plan.

Other Labor Cost Management Strategies

At some level restructuring is a game of finding and harvesting half a percent of savings here and a half a percent of savings there. All these saving mount up and can make the difference between a company struggling to survive and one which is the best in its field. There are many opportunities to reduce labor costs without reducing headcount or cutting pay or benefits.

Executive Compensation

Executive compensation should be the subject of scrutiny as well as the compensation and benefits of the rank and file. Leadership by example will make it easier for lower ranking employees to swallow any sacrifices they may have to make.

Normalize the Compensation of Top Executives

The compensation of the top third of a company's managers should be compared to the compensation of their industry peers. If a company is struggling for survival and an individual's compensation is above industry norms, he or she should be asked to take cuts to those norms. If a company is merely underperforming, less drastic steps can be taken. The important thing is for people to see that management is sacrificing for the good of the company, and the burden is not being solely carried by labor.

End Executive Bonuses Until Superior Performance Returns

Performance bonuses are an anathema in an underperforming company. Bonuses should only be paid for superior performance, not just survival.

Bonuses are often given in the form of stock options. Stock options are problematic for several reasons, including valuation and the fact that the public, investors, and employees do not understand how executives can harvest millions in compensation when a company is doing poorly.

Stock options, if awarded at all, should be set using a strike price that implies at least a 15% return on shareholder equity. Equation (4.8) provides an estimate of the target strike price.

$$\text{Strike price} = \text{Market price} \times (1 + \text{Return})^n \qquad (4.8)$$

Where Market price is the market price at the time options are granted, Return is the rate of return to shareholders assuming no dividends and n is the number of years before options vest. Option holders would have to grow the company faster than the target rate of return for the options to be "in the money."

Suppose a share of the company's stock is selling for $10 and a company wanted to award options that vested in 2 years. Assume management's target return to investors is 15%. The strike price would have to be at least $13.23 per share.

$$\text{Strike price} = \$10 \times (1 + 15\%)^2$$
$$= \$10 \times 1.3225$$
$$= \$13.23$$

If stock options are awarded based on achieving certain targets, and those targets are not met, management should not reset the targets. Changing performance targets sends the signal that management won't be held accountable for their failures.

Overtime

Overtime, that is premium pay for non-exempt employees working more than 40 hours per week, can radically alter a company's cost structure. Suppose a service

Table 4.4 Analysis of overtime

	Straight time In-house service	Overtime In-house service	Subcontract service
Revenue per hour:	$21	$21	$21
Costs per hour			
Subcontractor		$16	
Labor	$10	$15	
Other variable costs	$3	$3	
	$13	$18	$16
Contribution per hour	$8	$3	$5
Contribution margin (%)	38	14	24

Contribution is revenue less variable costs. Contribution margin is contribution divided by revenue.

company can bill its customers $21 per hour and it can either use its own labor or subcontract out the work to another company for $16 per hour. Suppose further that the company's wage rate is $10 per hour and there is another $3 per hour of variable costs associated with servicing customers. What is the impact of (i) using overtime to service customers, (ii) hiring more employees to do the work at straight time or (iii) subcontracting out the work? Table 4.4 shows the relative impact of using straight time, overtime or in the alternative subcontracting out work on a company's contribution margin and economic model.

In this example we see that overtime dramatically erodes contribution margin. Most companies consider the premium part of overtime compensation, that is, the differential over and above straight time pay as waste. When overtime is used on an on-going basis, people come to rely on it as part of their base compensation. To protect what they perceive as an entitlement they may slow production so there is always plenty of work left to generate overtime.

The payroll department should analyze data on the amount of overtime by facility, department, supervisor and individual. Overtime reports should routinely be provided to several levels of management and overtime management should be a component of manager evaluations.

Turnover Costs

Turnover is a hidden cost of labor. Few employees are 100% productive from the day they are hired. For employees to be fully productive they must know how their department works and how their work affects departments down stream from them, as well as how to get what they need from other departments. Acquiring customer knowledge and developing relationships with customers also takes time. Well developed employee-customer relations can assure the follow-on sale. Lack of employee-customer relations can result in the permanent loss of a customer.

One of my clients was a telemarketing company that measured everything. Few telemarketing companies attract natural born salespeople. Yet analyses showed that anyone who stuck with the job would improve their sales rate. Measured from the first month of work to their fourth month of work, sales productivity increased by a factor of about four after which it reached a plateau.

This means is that in their first month, the company was paying them full wages, but receiving only 25% productivity. In the second month, the company was paying full wages and receiving about 50% productivity and in the third month the company was paying full wages and receiving abut 75% productivity. In other words, the company got one and a half months of work for three months of wages.

The time that it takes an employee to become fully productive varies from industry to industry and job to job. The real cost of turnover comes from having to reinvest in this start-up cost over and over again. In telemarketing, retailing and some other industries turnover can reach 400%. That means that most people quit jobs before they become fully productive. The high cost of turnover is not limited to low wage jobs. Engineering companies, law firms, accounting firms and software companies face similar problems.

Define turnover as the number of new hires divided by the average head count as shown in Eq. (4.9). Why new hires and why not terminations? The reason is that new employees are less efficient until they learn their jobs.

$$TO = NH/((E1 + E2)/2) \qquad (4.9)$$

Where TO is turnover, E1 is the number of employees at the beginning of the year and E2 is the number of employees at the end of the year and NH is the number of new hires. Suppose a company has 150 technicians at the beginning of a year and 180 technicians at the end of the year and hires 100 technicians during the year. In this case turnover is

$$TO = 100/((150 + 180)/2)$$
$$= 100/165$$
$$= 60.6\%$$

Lost productivity can be estimated by considering the difference between an employee at full productivity and his or her starting productivity, the individual's salary and benefits as shown in Eq. (4.10).

$$LP = (((FP - IP)/2) \times T \times SB) \times (NH - (E2 - E1)) \qquad (4.10)$$

Where LP is lost productivity, FP is full productivity, IP is initial productivity, T is the time it takes a person to become fully productive in months, and SB is the salary and benefits paid over a month, NH is the number of new hires, E2 is total number of employees at the end of the year and E1 is the total number of employees at the beginning of the year. This equation automatically adjusts for the fact that a company may be growing or shrinking in size.

Employee productivity is measured using factors like production, billable hours, bill rate, degree of supervision and other factors. Each company must apply the facts and circumstances of its situation to measure productivity. This estimate of lost productivity should tell a company as to whether this is a high priority problem.

Suppose a company pays its service technicians $3,000 per month. In the first month, they accompany more senior technicians. In the second through 12th months they work independently, but often have to call upon more senior technicians to help them out. After a year on the job, most need little help or coaching. Over the course of a year, the company hired 100 technicians and the company's workforce increased from 150 to 180 technicians. Suppose productivity was 40% when hired rising to 100% over the course of a year. What is their lost productivity due to turnover? Applying the facts to Eq. (4.10) gives

$$
\begin{aligned}
LP &= (((100\%-40\%)/2) \times 12 \times \$3{,}000) \times (100-(180-150)) \\
&= 30\% \times 12 \times \$3{,}000 \times (100-30) \\
&= \$10{,}800 \times 70 \\
&= \$756{,}000
\end{aligned}
$$

In this example, with a turnover of 60.6%, lost productivity cost about $756,000. Suppose turnover could be cut in half to about 30.3%. Rearranging Eq. (4.9) we get Eq. (4.11).

$$
\begin{aligned}
NH &= TO \times (E1 + E2)/2 \\
&= 30.3\% \times (150 + 180)/2 \\
&= 30.3\% \times 165 \\
&= 50 \text{ new hires.}
\end{aligned}
\tag{4.11}
$$

The lost productivity on 50 new hires would be

$$
\begin{aligned}
LP &= (((100\%-40\%)/2) \times 12 \times \$3{,}000 \times (50-(180-150)) \\
&= 30\% \times 12 \times \$3{,}000 \times 20 \\
&= \$216{,}000
\end{aligned}
$$

While it is impossible to eliminate turnover, reducing it by half in this example saves about $540,000 ($756,000 – $216,000). These savings represent hard dollar savings which can be confirmed by measuring productivity. The extra time it takes new hires to do work is often reflected in aggregate overtime, the cost of mistakes, and reduced productivity for those who train, coach and assist new hires.

Putting these savings into perspective, total technician salaries for the year with an average of 165 technicians is about $5,940,000. So the savings of $540,000 is about 9.1% of wages ($540,000/(165 × $3,000 × 12)).

The Hudson Institute, a private, not-for-profit research organization located in Indianapolis estimates the cost of turnover can be 150% of the departing worker's salary. Turnover for all US industries is about 15%, but it is 50% for bank tellers,

100% for retail, and 120% for fast food. They estimate most employees are apprentices, and not fully productive for 8–12 weeks.[1,2]

If employee turnover as measured by Eq. (4.6) is more than about 40%, it might be a high payoff area for restructuring. On the other hand, if turnover is less than 20%, restructuring should probably focus on other areas.

Workers Compensation

Workers compensation insurance it required in most states. It provides coverage for the medical expenses and wages of workers injured on the job. Workers need not show their employer was at fault in order to gain coverage under workers compensation. However, in exchange for employers giving up the right to deny liability, statute generally limits the benefits workers receive. Workers compensation disputes, if any, bypass the regular court system for special workers compensation courts.

Workers compensation policies are experience rated which means that the more claims there are, the higher the premiums a company must pay. The most important way to reduce workers compensation premiums is to implement an aggressive safety program.

Experience rating considers several factors among them are whether there is a pattern of accidents which indicates that management is not safety conscious.[3] A company's claims history is rolled into a variable called an experience modification factor. If this factor is 1.0 it means the company has about average claims for its industry and it should be charged standard rates. However, if a company's claims experience is worse than the industry average the modification factor will be greater than one, which means the company will pay more than standard rates. If the experience modification factor is less than one, the company will pay less than standard rates. The experience modification factor is based on a three year claims history.[4] Reducing claims reduces insurance premiums.

Another thing a company can do is make sure policies are properly rated. Rates are quoted per hundred dollars of salary and vary by job function. For example, the rate for an office worker might be $0.28 per hundred dollars of salary, whereas the rate for a machinist might be $3.47 per hundred. Do not rely on the workers compensation insurance agent to properly classify workers. Verify their work.

Overtime can artificially boost pay because of the overtime premium. Since the risk to an insurance company is the same no matter whether a person is on straight time or overtime, only the straight time portion of overtime should go into the calculation for policy rating purposes.

Suppose Murray Co has a $5 million annual payroll allocated between Office Workers and Machinists. Further, suppose they had more accidents than the average machine shop so their experience modification factor is 1.20. Their Workers Compensation Premiums would be computed as shown in Table 4.5.[5]

Table 4.5 Workers compensation premium computation

Job Classifications	Salary Dollars	Units of Salary	Standard Rate	Standard Premium
Office workers	$300,000	3,000	$.28	$840
Machinist	$4,700,000	47,000	$3.47	$163,090
	Insurance premium at standard rates			$163,930
	Company experience modification factor:			× 1.20
	Total premium:			$196,716

Suppose Murray Co has been accident free for three years and its experience modification factor has dropped to .90. How much will it save because of its improved safety record? Assuming workers salaries and Standard Rates remain the same, they will save: $49,179 ($196,716 old premium − $163,930 standard rate × .90 new experience modification factor) or about a 25% reduction in insurance premiums. Placed in the broader context of total labor costs, this is a savings of about 1% of salary ($49,197/$5,000,000).

Unemployment Compensation Taxes

Unemployment compensation taxes, like workers compensation, are also experienced rated. Unemployment is a fund which pays individuals, usually for 26 weeks, if they become unemployed through no fault of their own.

Schemes for taxing employers to provide unemployment compensation vary from stated to state. In New Jersey, for example, rates are based both on an individual employer's claims experience and on the state's overall claims experience.

Each year, the state computes an Employer Reserve Ratio. This ratio is the sum of all the unemployment taxes an employer pays, minus the sum of all claims against the employer for the year, divided by the employer's average wages for the last three years. The Employer Reserve Ratio is used to find an employer's tax rate in the table the state is using for any particular year.[6]

Individuals who made as little as $8,700 in wages from a company can claim up to $12,350 in unemployment benefits. So in a sense, terminating an employee is like writing a check for $12,350.[7] Never the less, unemployment taxes are manageable costs. Strategies include terminating new hires sooner rather than later. If an employee earns less than $8,700, their total benefit (claim) will be severely limited.

If a worker is terminated for cause, he or she may be ineligible for unemployment compensation. Cause includes absenteeism, excessive tardiness, fighting, theft, or insubordination. Keep detailed records of attendance, and employee discipline. Further, employees who simply quit are almost never eligible for unemployment compensation.

Example: Mandy Industries has an annual unemployment taxable payroll of $6 million. About a year ago, the new controller noticed that a large percentage of new hires were just walking off the job and filing for unemployment. She began keeping detailed records and as a result, unemployment claims were denied for a substantial number of individuals. Since claims were down, the state reduced Mandy's unemployment tax rate from 5.8 to 4.1%. Mandy wanted to know how much the controller saved the company.

$$
\begin{array}{lll}
\text{Old unemployment tax} & 5.8\% \times \$6{,}000{,}000 = & \$348{,}000 \\
\text{New unemployment tex} & 4.1\% \times \$6{,}000{,}000 = & \underline{\$246{,}000} \\
& \text{Savings:} & \$102{,}000
\end{array}
$$

This is a savings of about 1.7% of payroll ($102,000/$6,000,000).

Conclusion

Labor is one of the most significant costs faced by companies. Many underperforming companies have excess employees. Controlling headcount is critical to managing labor cost. By comparing a company's revenue per employee to that of its best competitors, it can estimate the number of employees it should have. Approaches for getting down to a target headcount in an orderly way include constructing an ideal organization rather than trying to modify an existing one, culling the low performing 5–10% of employees, reducing the number of employees in staff positions and reducing middle management by increasing the span of control. By reducing headcount, a company saves salary dollars, employer taxes, benefit costs and a variety of other labor costs that can total 15–60% of direct salary dollars.

Companies also have substantial opportunities to save labor costs without laying off people. Reducing overtime and employee turnover can save several percent of a company's labor cost. Improving safety to reduce workers compensation claims and auditing workers compensation insurance bills for accuracy can save a few percent of labor costs. Terminating new hires that are not working out sooner rather than later, and denying unemployment claims for employees that quit or are terminated for cause, can also reduce labor costs by a few percent. The key to these savings is a human resources department that pays attention to details.

Notes

1. "Hidden Costs of Turnover Cut Profits," Philadelphia Inquirer, February 11, 2001 p G1.
2. Ibid. p G3.
3. *Exploring Experience Rating*, State of New Jersey Compensation, Rating and Inspection Bureau, Department of Banking and Insurance, Newark, New Jersey, 1998. p 2.
4. Ibid. p 7.
5. *Exploring the Cost of a Workers Compensation Insurance Policy*, State of New Jersey Compensation, Rating and Inspection Bureau, Department of Banking and Insurance, Newark, New Jersey, 1999. p 9.
6. Ibid. p 24.
7. This changes from year to year. The local Unemployment Office will have this information.

References

Bhide A (1986) Hustle as strategy. Harv Bus Rev 59–65, Sept–Oct

Bobbitt RH Jr, Breinhold RH, Doktor RH, McNaul JP (1974) Organizational behavior – under-
    standing and prediction. Prentiss-Hall, Englewood Cliffs, NJ, pp 36–37

Davis MA (2008) Take no prisoners. AMACOM American Management Association, New York,
    pp 49–50

Davis RC (1951) The fundamentals of top management. Harper, New York, pp 272–280

Durbin, D. Ann (2006) GM cuts white collar jobs. Phila Inq D2, 29 Mar

Gulich L, Urwick L (1937) Papers in the science of administration. Institute of Public
    Administration, New York, pp 183–187

Hoffman E (2006) Is your pension plan retiring before you? Bus Week Online. http://www.
    businessweek.com/investor/content/apr2006/pi20060421_275355.htm. Accessed 21 Apr

Kahn G, Power S (2004) Keeping control: 2004 workforce norms: Schonfeld releases new bench-
    marks for sales & gross margin per employee. The Controller's Report. pub. Institute of
    Management & Administration, pp 16–20, Sept

Kahn G, Power S (2006) Auto outsider gets fiat going by flouting industry traditions. Wall St J A1
    and A12, 26 Oct

Mankins MC, Steele R (2005) Turning great strategy into great performance. Harv Bus Rev 65–72,
    July–Aug

Powell EA (2007) Fewer large firms offering traditional pension plans. Phila Inq D2, 12 May

Scarlett B (2006)Organisational management and information systems. Financ Manage 39–
    41, Nov

Chapter 5
Evaluation of Businesses, Divisions, Facilities, and Dealerships

Introduction

One of the main reasons companies under perform is that they lose focus. Companies evolve over time. Products, services and business units tend to grow in number. What made sense at one point in time might not make sense now, but people and companies tend to do the same thing over and over again without questioning why they are doing what they are doing or whether it still makes sense. Often it takes an outsider, a new CEO, turnaround consultant, investor, or board member to take a critical look at a company.

It is rare when any two businesses, divisions, facilities, or dealerships are equally profitable; some are probably very profitable, and some unprofitable. The unprofitable, when averaged in with the profitable can make the overall company look bad. Identification and elimination of losing businesses and facilities can dramatically improve profitability and enhance a company's chances for survival. One way to think of this is cutting out the cancer, the money losing, and the marginal. Then management time and attention can focus on improving the profitability and performance of its core business (Whitney, 1996, 85).

Businesses

Companies successful in one business to assume they can be succeed in any business. The reality is quite different. Businesses often under perform because they lack focus. This happens at a number of levels:

(1) The company has no clear direction. What does it want to be or do?
(2) The company is performing unnecessary, repetitive or unproductive tasks
(3) The company is servicing an unprofitable market
(4) Non-core businesses drain management time and company resources
(5) The company is trying to deliver products or services which it is not good at, and which do not fit into its overall business or market strategy

D.E. Vance, *Corporate Restructuring*, DOI 10.1007/978-3-642-01786-5_5,
© Springer-Verlag Berlin Heidelberg 2009

(6) The company has business units that are under performing, but the company does not have the expertise to drive those businesses to success and does not have the time and resources to learn those businesses.
(7) The company does not systematically measure performance.

Analyzing Divisions, Subsidiaries and Business Units

Re-specialization

Companies with cash often acquire other businesses without any real goal as to what they want the company to look like in the long run. As a result, they become large and diverse, with management expertise spread thin. This makes the overall company less efficient. To regain efficiency and shed debt companies should sell off peripheral businesses, for example Alcoa is getting out of the plastic wrap business, Newmont Mining is getting out of investment banking, and Anglo American is getting out of the road resurfacing business. By sliming down to their core businesses, and only making acquisitions in core businesses, companies hope to drive efficiency (Matthews, 2007). Both diversification and re-specialization should be considered as strategies. But, if diversification is pursued, each new business must earn its keep and not burden profits, capital or management expertise.

In every company, some divisions, subsidiaries or business units do better than others. To simplify the discussion we will call all these components of a company divisions, Sometimes a major step toward revitalizing the whole company is to shed underperforming divisions. Dell, for example, will not tolerate a business that doesn't make money (Stewart and O'Brien, 2005).

There are at least four dimensions along which divisions should be evaluated (i) operating profits, (ii) revenue and cost trends, (iii) return on invested capital, and (iv) market position.

Operating Profits

Operating profit by division consists of its revenue less costs of goods sold and operating expenses specifically related to that division. The allocation of corporate overhead, financing costs and taxes should be removed from this analysis. What is left is a picture of how well each division compares to other divisions.

As an example, consider Table 5.1. The Chemical and Government Systems divisions are clearly profitable, Electronic Components is somewhat profitable, Farm Machinery is breaking even, and Ceramics and Tile is losing money. If the only thing the company did was to eliminate the Ceramics and Tile division, Income from Operations would increase by $6 million or about 10%.

Table 5.1 Collin industries division analysis

Dollars in thousands	Chemicals division	%	Government systems	%	Farm machinery	%	Electronic components	%	Ceramics and tile	%	Totals
Sales	100,000	100.0	200,000	100.0	30,000	100.0	40,000	100.0	50,000	100.0	420,000
Cost of goods sold	45,000	45.0	160,000	80.0	23,000	76.7	22,000	55.0	42,000	84.0	292,000
Gross profit	55,000	55.0	40,000	20.0	7,000	23.3	18,000	45.0	8,000	16.0	128,000
Sales and marketing expenses	3,000	3.0	2,000	1.0	1,000	3.3	2,000	5.0	4,000	8.0	12,000
Facilities	12,000	12.0	5,000	2.5	3,000	10.0	4,000	10.0	5,000	10.0	29,000
Depreciation	3,000	3.0	1,000	0.5	1,000	3.3	2,000	5.0	2,000	4.0	9,000
Research and development	3,000	3.0	500	0.3	500	1.7	6,000	15.0	0	0.0	10,000
Other administrative costs	2,000	2.0	1,500	0.8	1,500	5.0	1,000	2.5	3,000	6.0	9,000
Operating expenses	23,000	23.0	10,000	5.0	7,000	23.3	15,000	37.5	14,000	28.0	69,000
Income from operations	32,000	32.0	30,000	15.0	0	0.0	3,000	7.5	−6,000	−12.0	59,000
Corporate expenses											29,000
EBIT											30,000
Interest expense											15,000
EBT											15,000
Income taxes											4,500
Net income											10,500
Average division assets	100,000		120,000		35,000		30,000		30,000		315,000
Return on division assets (%)	32		25		0		10		−20		

Revenue and Cost Trends

Simply looking at the operating income of a division for a single year is one dimensional. Consideration should also be given to revenue and cost tends. A profitable division can be on the path to unprofitability and an unprofitable division may be on a path to profits, so trends are important.

Since most ratios build on revenue, revenue growth is a key profit driver. If revenue for a division is flat or declining year after year, the company should consider shedding it. Why? The rule in business is grow or die. A division that is not growing is already beginning to die. To make sure the revenue slow down is not just a one time occurrence, for example, due to loss of a single contract or client, revenue growth should be examined over two, three and five years.

A division with flat or declining sales might have obsolete products, poor service or bad management all of which can be fixed, but the division might also be in a declining industry, in which case the division should be sold off before it loses all value.

Sometimes it is important to act before trends show up in the numbers. Seigle's Inc. a regional home center business with 60% of its sales to retail customers and 40% to builders decided in the 1990's that it couldn't competed with Home Depot. It closed its home stores and focused its energy on becoming a premier supplier to large home builders. Home builders want suppliers who can both supply and install windows, doors and roof trusses and guarantee the work. This shift helped Seigle's move from increasingly competitive retailing, and low margin wholesaling, to higher margin, service and installation (Bailey, 2003).

Trends in gross margin are a critical barometer of a division's future prospects. If gross margin is decreasing, it doesn't matter whether revenue is growing. At some point, gross margin will become so thin that gross profit will not cover selling and marketing expenses, other overhead, and financing costs.

Gross margin could shrink because the cost of goods sold keeps increasing in a market where price increases are limited by competition. Often, unfavorable trends in gross margin can be reversed by restructuring the production and distribution process. However, sometimes costs are driven by factors outside a company's control such as raw material prices, regulations, and labor unions.

Trends in research and development expenditures are another important dimension of whether to keep or shed a division. Some industries require a consistent, high level of investment in research and development to maintain market share, for example video games, semi-conductors and pharmaceuticals. Companies for which sales growth is low, gross margin is low and research and development expenditures are high are headed for trouble.

Some divisions would be profitable if their other overhead where lower. Other overhead, which is overhead less selling and marketing costs, can almost always be cut. So if revenue growth is good, gross margins are adequate, and research and development expenditures are reasonable a division should probably not be eliminated simply because other overhead is excessive. Increasing other overhead as a percent of revenue is probably a sign of poor management rather than some intrinsic flaw in the division or its products.

In the example of Table 5.1, cutting other overhead by 15%, would not make the Ceramics and Tile Division profitable. Cutting other overhead 15% for the Electronics Division would add $1,950 to operating income (15% × (Facilities $4,000 + Depreciation $2,000 + Research and Development $6,000 + Other administrative expenses $1,000)), and would increase division operating income by about 65% which is about 12.4% of sales.

A 15% reduction in other overhead for the Farm Machinery Division would only add $900 to operating income (15% × (Facilities $3,000 + Depreciation $1,000 + Research and development $500 + Other administrative costs $1,500)). So even with fairly deep cuts in other overhead, the operating income of the Farm Machinery Division would still only be 3% of sales. This is so close to zero that operating income could easily tip over into a loss. So this factor coupled with relatively low gross margin makes this division another candidate for disposition.

Return on Division Assets

Return on assets (ROA), as shown in Eq. (5.1) is usually computed at the company level, but it can also be computed at the division level.

$$\text{ROA} = \frac{\text{Net income} + \text{Interest} \times (1 - \text{Tax rate})}{\text{Average assets}} \qquad (5.1)$$

Since interest and taxes are usually a corporate expenses, not a division expenses, the return on assets for a division collapses Eq. (5.1) to Eq. (5.2).

$$\text{ROAD} = \text{Operating income/Average assets} \qquad (5.2)$$

ROA for a division (ROAD) is comparable among the divisions within a company, and it is comparable for divisions on a year to year basis. However, it is not directly comparable to ROA of other companies or to industry ROA. The difference is that ROA reflects the after tax productivity of assets, whereas, ROAD reflects the pre-tax, pre-financing productivity of assets. For Collin Industries, Table 5.1 ROAD is 32% for the Chemical Division ($32,000/$100,000); 25% for Government Systems ($30,000/$200,000); and 0%, 10% and –20% for Farm Machinery, Electronic Components and Ceramics and Tile divisions respectively.

While a ROAD close to zero or negative is bad. The question is what constitutes an acceptable norm for performance. To compare ratios against other companies, it is necessary to see what each division would look like if it were a free standing company.

Comparing Divisions to Industry Norms

Many companies have businesses in different industries, so to analyze company performance in the aggregate is misleading. Consider the example in Table 5.1 Collin Industries Division Analysis. The Chemical Division clearly has a different economic model than the Government Systems Division; Farm Machinery is different from Electronic Components and so forth.

Whether a company's ratio for gross margin, return on assets, or accounts receivable turnover is good or bad depends on how it compares to industry norms. So to make an analysis of Collin Industries meaningful, it must be treated like a series of free standing companies, each of which can be compared to its own industry. For Collin Industries, the income statement provides detail about revenue and expenses by division. The only costs that have to be allocated are corporate overhead, interest expense and income taxes.

Allocation of Corporate Overhead

No allocation scheme is perfect; however, absent any specific information to the contrary, corporate overhead expense should be allocated based on each division's share of revenue as shown in Eq. (5.3).

$$\text{Division overhead} = \frac{\text{Division revenue}}{\text{Total Revenue}} \times \text{Corporate overhead} \qquad (5.3)$$

So, for Collin Industries, $6.9 million of overhead should be allocated to the Chemical Division (($100 million/$420 million) ×$29 million) and $13.8 million should be allocated to Government Systems Division (($200 million/$420 million) ×$29 million), and so forth.

Allocation of Interest Expense

Interest expense allocation should be based on the average assets supporting each division as shown in Eq. (5.4). Average assets can be estimated by adding beginning and ending assets and dividing by 2.

$$\text{Company interest expense} = \frac{\text{Average Division Assets}}{\text{Total Average Division Assets}} \times \text{Interest expense}$$
$$(5.4)$$

So if the Chemical Division had 32% of total assets, 32% of the interest expense or $4.8 million (($100 million/$315 million) × $15 million) would be allocated to that division; $5.7 million of interest would be allocated to Government Systems (($120 million/$315 million) × $15 million.

Unfortunately, it is not always clear how many dollars of assets are dedicated to each division. In that case, interest might be allocated based on cost of goods sold as shown in Eq. (5.5).

$$\text{Division interest expense} = \frac{\text{Division COGS}}{\text{Total COGS}} \times \text{Interest expense} \qquad (5.5)$$

The reasoning is that some of the factors that make cost of goods sold high also mean there is a large investment in assets. For example, high equipment costs tend to push up cost of goods sold and high equipment costs come from large investments in equipment. Expensive materials tend to push up cost of goods sold and that may be reflected in high values of raw material, work in process and finished goods inventory. So for the Collin Industries example, interest expense of $2.3 million would be allocated to the Chemical Division (($45 million/$292 million) × $15 million) and $8.2 million would be allocated to the Government Systems Division (($160 million/$292 million) × $15 million).

Allocation of Income Tax Expense

Income taxes should be allocated based on adjusted division income. This allocation is complicated by divisions with operating losses. In that case they shelter income taxes that other divisions would have to pay. So to allocate taxes, one must first find the corporate tax rate then allocate it to division operating income after a burden is added for each division's overhead and interest allocation. The effective tax rate is given in Eq. (5.6).

$$\text{Effective tax rate} = \frac{\text{Corporate income tax expense}}{\text{Corporate earnings before taxes}} \qquad (5.6)$$

Collin Industries has an Effective tax rate of about 30% ($4.5 million/$15 million). The effective tax rate is then applied to each division using Eq. (5.7).

$$\text{Division tax} = \text{Effective tax rate} \times (\text{Division operating income} - \text{Allocated}$$
$$\text{corporate overhead} - \text{Allocated interest expense})$$
$$(5.7)$$

The income tax allocation for Chemical division would be about $6.1 million (30% × ($32 million – $6.9 million – $4.8 million)).

Having allocated all costs to all divisions, each can then be treated as a free standing company for purposes of comparison to companies in their particular industry as shown in Table 5.3 Collin Industries Divisions as Stand Alone Businesses.

Comparable Companies

While a new CEO or turnaround consultant should have access to detailed information on accounts receivable, inventory and other assets by division, such detailed information is not always available for competitors. If a company's key competitors have divisions which span a number of industries, those divisions must be deconstructed into stand alone companies before meaningful comparisons can be made. The aforementioned allocation methods can be used to put competitor's divisions on a comparable footing with the target company's divisions.

Franchises

Companies that franchise present a special analytical problem because they often own some facilities and franchise others. For example part of Denny's revenue and income is generated from company owned restaurants and part comes from franchise fees. To lump the two revenue and cost streams together makes any analysis of the whole company meaningless. So such companies must be deconstructed into two divisions, "owned stores" and "franchised stores."

Corporate overhead can be allocated based on revenue. Cost of goods sold can be used to allocate assets and interest expense should follow assets. Income tax expense can also be allocated by applying the effective tax rate to operating income less corporate overhead and interest expense. So, for example, if Denny's were compared to IHOP, the financials of both companies would have to be deconstructed into "owned stores" and "franchise stores" so that separate ratios could be constructed for each.

Market Position

Not every company can be the biggest and best in its field. Likewise divisions may not be the biggest or best in their field. A strategic question is whether a company has enough market presence to distinguish itself, or is it an "also ran"? Can a division find a niche wherein it has a unique product or even a niche were it is one of the top three companies? For smaller companies the question is whether it can grow into a top three company? Or, stepping back from that, can it become a top three regional player?

If a division cannot distinguish itself in some way, if it cannot establish brand equity, that is the perception that it provides safe, reliable goods or services at a fair price, then there is a substantial question as to its viability. Why? If a company or division cannot distinguish itself, its goods and services will be perceived as commodities.

Commodity pricing is driven by pure competition. That means a company will not be able to raise its prices because its customers can buy similar goods elsewhere.

Table 5.2 Collin industries divisions as stand alone businesses

	Chemicals division	%	Government systems	%	Farm machinery	%	Electronic components	%	Ceramics and tile	%	Totals	%
Sales	100,000	100.0	200,000	100.0	30,000	100.0	40,000	100.0	50,000	100.0	420,000	100.0
Cost of goods sold	45,000	45.0	160,000	80.0	23,000	76.7	22,000	55.0	42,000	84.0	292,000	84.0
Gross profit	55,000	55.0	40,000	20.0	7,000	23.3	18,000	45.0	8,000	16.0	128,000	16.0
Sales and marketing Expenses	3,000	3.0	2,000	1.0	1,000	3.3	2,000	5.0	4,000	8.0	12,000	8.0
Facilities	12,000	12.0	5,000	2.5	3,000	10.0	4,000	10.0	5,000	10.0	29,000	10.0
Depreciation	3,000	3.0	1,000	0.5	1,000	3.3	2,000	5.0	2,000	4.0	9,000	4.0
Research and development	3,000	3.0	500	0.3	500	1.7	6,000	15.0	0	0.0	10,000	0.0
Other administrative costs	2,000	2.0	1,500	0.8	1,500	5.0	1,000	2.5	3,000	6.0	9,000	6.0
Allocated corporate overhead	6,905	6.9	13,810	6.9	2,071	6.9	2,762	6.9	3,452	6.9	29,000	6.9
EBIT	25,095	25.1	16,190	8.1	−2,071	−6.9	238	0.6	−9,452	−18.9	30,000	−18.9
Allocated interest expense	4,762	4.7	5,714	2.9	1,667	2.9	1,429	3.6	1,429	2.9	15,000	2.9
EBT	20,333		10,476		−3,738		−1,190		−10,081		15,000	
Income taxes or tax benefit	6,100	6.1	3,121	1.6	−1,121	−3.7	−357	−3.7	−3,264	−6.5	4,500	4.5
Net income	14,233	14.3	7,355	3.7	−2,617	−8.7	−833	−0.9	−7,617	−15.2	10,500	10.5
Allocation of assets												
Average division assets	100,000		120,000		35,000		30,000		30,000		315,000	
Corporate assets	4,000		8,000		1,200		1,600		2,000		16,800	
Allocated assets	104,000		128,000		36,200		31,600		32,000		331,800	

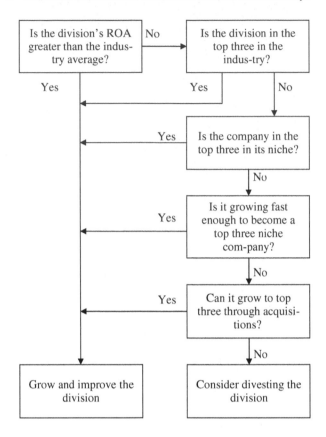

Fig. 5.1 Division market position analysis

Competition inevitably drives price lower. That means that the only way a company can survive is to be the low cost producer. Economies of scale are usually needed to become a low price producer. But if a company isn't in the top three in its market, the odds of it becoming a low cost producer through economies of scale diminish rapidly. So if a division is not in the top ranks of its niche, it may find itself in an intractable situation.

If a division is growing and profitable there is no need to shed it; being a small player is not fatal. But, it may indicate trouble ahead.

What should a division too small to dominate its niche do? If a company can grow faster than its market, one might project when it will be in, or close to the top three. If that is a reasonable point in time, organic growth might be the solution. If its growth rate is insufficient, and the return on investment of the division is high, acquisitions might provide a path to market dominance. However, if the division is small, marginally profitable, not growing as fast as the market and there are no feasible acquisitions, consider divesting the division. Figure 5.1 provides a guide for deciding whether to keep or divest a division.

Disposition of Underperforming Divisions, Subsidiaries and Business Units

How does one eliminate the Ceramics and Tile division without taking a charge for closing the division? The best alternative is to package the division for sale. Among other things this means having free standing accounting and information systems. The company should also make the division as profitable as possible prior to sale. If it can be nudged into profitability, it is more likely to sell for more than book value.

Another possibility is to set up the division as a free standing corporation and spin off shares of that company to the shareholders. Campbell Soup did this when it spun off Vlasic (Bloomberg, 1997; Collins, 1997). Such a spin-off would probably be classified as a dividend in kind and dividends in kind must be recorded at their fair market value. The difference between the book value of the spun off corporation and its fair market value must be recorded as a gain or loss. The fair value will depend on many things including the amount of the corporation's overall debt allocated to the spun off division. So by varying the debt load, one can vary the fair market value. The optimum debt load is one which makes the fair market value of the spun off company just slightly greater than the book value of its assets.

Break-Up Value

A question that often arises when a company is in trouble is whether it would be more valuable if it were broken up and the parts sold off. This is a different question than whether weak divisions should be sold off to restore the health of the core. A break-up involves splitting the company up and giving shareholders a proportionate interest in the newly split off companies or selling all of a company's divisions.

Before one can address whether break-up value is more than the value of a company as a whole, one must ask several questions. First, why would the parts of a company be worth more than the whole? Second, worth more to whom? Third, how might one estimate whether it is worthwhile to break up a company?

The parts of a company can be worth more than the whole for a number of reasons. Companies that try to do a lot of things rarely do them all well. A company that is split up into specialized companies is more likely to be efficient and focused. Another reason the parts can be worth more than the whole is that a company which spans several industries is hard to value. Valuation difficulty creates risk which will manifest itself in a wide dispersion of possible firm values. Buyers are likely to extract a risk premium for this uncertainty by pricing the firm at the low end of the range of possible values.

Valuation often turns on who is valuing a company. A holding company might buy almost any company with above average cash flow. This sets a pretty high bar and companies in trouble or that are underperforming are unlikely to reach that bar, at least pre-restructuring.

On the other hand, companies that are trying to dominate a market, or buy technology or patents in their industry are likely to pay a premium, but only for companies in their industry. They generally aren't interested in buying a company just to capture the division in their industry.

To get a rough idea of the break-up value of a company, recast all divisions as stand alone companies. Then value each of these companies. It is beyond the scope of this text to discuss valuation methods. However, methods are discussed in detail in several other books. See *Raising Capital* Chap. 9 (Vance, 2005) or *Corporate Valuation: A Guide for Managers and Investors* (Daves et al., 2004).

Facility Analysis

Some companies have large numbers of facilities with common characteristics. Examples include hotel chains, retailers, restaurant chains, and banks. Just as divisions never perform equally, facilities never perform equally. Bad facilities drain resources as well as management time and talent from good locations and may ultimately drag an entire enterprise down with them.

Facilities should be measured by profitability, sales and cost trends, and return on investment. While the goal is to increase the sales and profitability of every facility, management should not shrink from identification and elimination of the worst facilities. Where facilities are relatively homogeneous, progress toward improving performance can be monitored using metrics.

Metrics also called key performance indicators are industry specific performance measures that often include non-financial data. To measure the performance of facilities, one must understand an industry in detail. This may involve considerable industry specific research. Trade associations and trade magazines are an important source of information on metrics.

Retail stores are measured on year over year sales, sales per square foot, cost per square foot, and the ratio of sales per square foot to cost per square foot. Other retail metrics include things like the number of people visiting a facility, and conversion rate which is the percentage of visitors who purchase something. Average sale and contribution per sale are additional metrics. Metrics like sales by day of the week and time of day are used to minimize staffing during slack times and make sure there is enough staff to properly service customers during busy times.

Metrics take global goals like sales and break them down into components that are easier to operationalize. Sales growth per store is a breakdown of company sales growth. Average sale is a breakdown of store sales. Conversion rate translates visits to sales. The number of visits times conversion rate times the average sale gives store sales. By breaking down each large goal into smaller sub-goals it is easier to find and implement strategies to optimize the metric and thereby optimize the overall results.

Cable and phone companies use metrics like revenue per subscriber and contribution per subscriber. Hotels use occupancy rates to measure performance and airlines use metrics to determine the percentage of seats filled on every flight. Realtors use vacancy rate to measure the performance of commercial office space.

In restructuring a company it is important to identify and measure the specific metrics for the company's industry. It might also be necessary to create new metrics to drive and measure company performance.

The best facilities should be studied to determine what makes them the best. Is it location, facility condition, advertising, management, staff training, or customer service? The characteristics that make the top ten facilities the best should be analyzed and rolled out to other facilities.

Some facilities, perhaps the bottom 5–10% may be so far below target levels that they are candidates for closure. Eliminating poorly performing facilities makes substantial progress toward profitability. Companies striving for excellence should have an on-going program to identify and eliminate underperforming facilities.

Table 5.3 is of the kind of study a company might prepare to decide whether to close, restructure or refurbish facilities. Panel A analyzes sales, sales growth and profitability. Panel B analyzes Return on Assets (ROA) and cost trends.

The analysis shows a company with operating profit of $10,173,000 on sales of $136,800,000. On the surface this does not seem bad. However, operating profit must cover corporate overhead, financing costs and taxes. Even if the company was debt free and in the 30% tax bracket, the return to investors would only be about 5.2% of sales ((operating income of $10,173,000 – taxes of $3,051,900)/Sales of $136,800,000)) which is nothing to brag about.

Thinking in terms of the 80–20 rule, eliminating the worst performing 20% of facilities would increase operating income by $1,605,500. Eliminating all nine facilities with operating losses would increase operating profit by $1,913,000. While the worst facilities should be closed as soon as possible to stop the bleeding, it is difficult to cut one's way to success.

Attention should be given to why some facilities work brilliantly and others are so abysmal. Is it, for example, the location? The most profitable facilities in Table 5.3 seem to be placed in very desirable neighborhoods. Is it the per-capita income in the neighborhoods where the restaurants are placed? Those who earn more spend disproportionate amounts on dining. Is it the quality of restaurant management or management training? Is it the quality of the wait staff or the cooks? This information is critical for decisions on closing, improving and siting future facilities.

Consider trends. For example, the Wilmington, North Carolina and the Mt. Laurel, New Jersey facilities are both loosing money, but they are growing steadily, most recently at 6% per year and their costs of goods sold as a percentage of sales (COGS%) is declining. The difficulty seems to be that their other overhead at 26.7 and 26.4% respectively, is greater than the company wide average of 21.4%. If other overhead could be brought in line with company averages, operating profit of Wilmington would increase by $159,000 ((Wilmington OO% of 26.7% – company average of 21.4%) × Wilmington sales of $3,000,000) and Mt. Laurel would increase by $175,000 ((Mt. Laurel OO% of 26.4% – company average of 21.4%) ×

Table 5.3 Facility analysis

Panel A Sales, growth and profits

Facility	Owned or lease term	Sales	Sales rank	Sales growth (%)	Growth rank	3 year avg. growth (%)	3 year growth rank	Operating profit	Profit rank
Los Angeles, Beverly Blvd.	Owned	12,000,000	1	12.50	1	11.60	1	2,590,000	1
Los Angeles, Sunset Ave.	Owned	10,000,000	2	11.00	2	10.60	2	1,800,000	2
Los Angeles, Pacific Blvd.	Owned	8,000,000	3	9.50	3	8.60	3	1,350,000	3
New York, Fifth Avenue	3/31/2014	8,000,000	4	8.00	4	7.60	4	1,170,000	4
Wilmington, DE DuPont Way	Owned	8,000,000	5	8.00	5	7.60	5	1,154,000	5
Wash, DC, Pennsylvania Blvd	8/31/2015	7,000,000	6	3.00	17	2.10	17	750,000	6
Los Angeles, Braxton Place	Owned	6,000,000	7	8.00	6	7.10	6	730,000	7
New York, Park Place	9/30/2015	6,000,000	8	3.00	18	2.10	18	670,000	8
Marlton, Prominade	5/31/2020	6,000,000	9	6.00	10	5.10	11	550,000	9
New York, Battery Street	4/15/2012	5,000,000	12	7.50	7	7.10	7	400,000	10
Pasadana, Walker Terrace	Owned	5,000,000	13	7.00	8	6.60	8	350,000	11
Falls Church, River Road	9/15/2020	4,000,000	15	7.00	9	6.10	9	270,000	12
Washington, E Street	Owned	6,000,000	10	-8.00	23	-8.40	23	90,000	13
Arlington, 7th Street	Owned	4,000,000	16	5.00	13	4.10	14	70,000	14
Washington M Street	Owned	5,900,000	11	-10.00	25	-10.40	25	17,000	15
Chicago, Wacker Drive	7/31/2015	3,500,000	19	-6.00	21	-6.90	21	15,000	16
Pittsburg, Steel Plaza	12/31/2012	3,800,000	18	-2.00	19	-2.40	19	10,000	17
Wilmington, NC Carolina Pl.	8/31/2012	3,000,000	23	6.00	12	5.10	12	-20,000	18
Mt. Laurel, NJ Route 70	Owned	3,500,000	20	6.00	11	5.60	10	-67,500	19
Chicago, West Side Ave.	Owned	4,000,000	17	-10.00	26	-10.90	26	-110,000	21
Atlantic City, Bally's	6/30/2012	3,200,000	22	5.00	15	4.60	13	-110,000	20
Reading, Mulbury Drive	Owned	4,500,000	14	-9.00	24	-9.40	24	-187,500	22
Pittsburg, Mellon Avenue	Owned	3,500,000	21	5.00	14	4.10	15	-265,000	23
Pittsburg, Waterfront Street	6/30/2020	2,000,000	25	4.00	16	3.60	16	-310,000	24
New York, West 42nd St.	4/30/2016	2,900,000	24	-7.00	22	-7.40	22	-373,000	25
Vienna, Va. Lexington Ave.	Owned	2,000,000	26	-3.00	20	-3.40	20	-470,000	26
		136,800,000						10,173,000	

Table 5.3 (continued)

Panel B Return on assets and cost trends

Facility	COGS%	GOGS% rank	3 year average COGS%	3 year COGS% rank	OO%	OO% rank	ROA (%)	ROA rank
Los Angeles, Beverly Blvd.	67.00	1	66.80	1	10.40	1	36.30	7
Los Angeles, Sunset Ave.	68.50	2	69.10	2	12.50	2	25.70	8
Los Angeles, Pacific Blvd.	69.00	3	69.40	3	13.10	3	23.00	10
New York, Fifth Avenue	70.00	4	70.90	6	14.40	6	136.00	1
Wilmington, DE DuPont Way	70.20	5	70.40	4	14.40	5	23.70	9
Wash, DC, Pennsylvania Blvd	74.00	13	76.70	17	14.30	4	94.90	2
Los Angeles, Braxton Place	71.00	6	71.10	7	15.80	7	15.50	11
New York, Park Place	72.00	9	73.40	12	15.80	8	93.10	3
Marlton, Prominade	74.00	14	74.10	13	15.80	9	76.40	4
New York, Battery Street	71.00	7	71.40	8	20.00	12	61.50	5
Pasadana, Walker Terrace	72.00	10	72.40	9	20.00	13	7.50	12
Falls Church, River Road	71.00	8	70.70	5	21.30	14	46.60	6
Washington, E Street	80.00	20	83.60	23	17.50	10	1.90	14
Arlington, 7th Street	76.00	19	78.20	19	21.30	15	1.70	16
Washington M Street	81.00	23	84.20	25	17.70	11	0.40	17
Chicago, Wacker Drive	75.00	18	77.10	18	23.60	18	2.80	13
Pittsburg, Steel Plaza	74.00	15	75.90	16	24.70	20	1.80	15
Wilmington, NC Carolina Place	73.00	12	73.20	11	26.70	22	-3.90	20
Mt. Laurel, NJ Route 70	74.50	17	75.30	14	26.40	21	-2.20	18
Chicago, West Side Avenue	80.50	22	82.40	21	21.30	16	-3.30	19
Atlantic City, Bally's	74.00	16	75.60	15	28.40	23	-21.00	24
Reading, Mulbury Drive	81.50	25	84.30	26	21.70	17	-7.20	21
Pittsburg, Mellon Avenue	83.00	26	79.90	20	23.60	19	-7.50	22
Pittsburg, Waterfront Street	72.00	11	72.90	10	42.50	25	-70.50	25
New York, West 42nd St.	81.00	24	83.60	24	30.90	24	-74.20	26
Vienna, Va. Lexington Ave.	80.00	21	82.60	22	42.50	26	-13.70	23

Mt. Laurel sales of $3,500,000) respectively. This would turn Wilmington's loss of $20,000 into a profit of $139,000 and it would turn Mt. Laurel's loss of $67,500 into a profit of $107,500.

On the other hand, there may be facilities that cannot be saved no matter how much effort is applied to them. So the strategy is to close the worst of the worst and then examine the next tier of underperformers to see whether they can be restructured. However, there is never enough time when restructuring so the decision as to which to close and which to save should be made with all deliberate thoroughness and speed.

Disposition of Underperforming Facilities

The approach used to dispose of an underperforming facility can have a financial impact. In a perfect world, one could close a facility at no cost simply by turning out the lights. The real world is more complicated.

There may be costs for severance pay, pay for a winding up the operations, and costs associated with increased unemployment taxes. There is also likely to be a write-off of inventory, furniture, fixtures and leasehold improvements. These costs are unavoidable so they should not factor into the decision to close a facility. Be sure to comply with the Worker Adjustment and Retraining Notification Act (WARN) discussed elsewhere in this book.

One of the biggest costs involves real estate. If a facility is leased, early termination of the lease is bound to involve significant penalties. Many commercial leases run 5 years or more and if such a lease is terminated early, the landlord is going to want rent to the end of the lease even though the facility is no longer generating income for the company. Costs for future lease payments must be recognized when the facility closes and will drive losses deeper. So for a leased facility, the question is whether the company should close it as soon as it is identified as an underperforming facility or wait until the lease ends. If the facility is generating positive cash flow, then waiting is an option. However, if the facility has a negative cash flow, the present value of the negative cash flow should be compared to the present value of the lease termination penalty. If the lease termination penalty is greater, then perhaps the facility should be operated until the present value of the negative cash flow exceeds the early termination penalty. This may mean operating the facility until near lease end.

Sometimes, a landlord will accept a lump sum penalty to terminate a lease. For this to be worthwhile, the penalty must be much less than the remaining balance on the lease. An additional consideration is how the lease is structured. If the lease is triple net, meaning the lessee must pay property taxes, maintenance and insurance in addition to lease payments to the landlord, payment of an early termination penalty looks better because such an agreement will terminate the lessee's obligation for taxes, insurance and maintenance.

If the facility is owned, a company has more flexibility and an underperforming facility can be closed at once. The sooner it is, the sooner the company can liquidate the facility and raise cash for the restructuring.

Dealerships

Chrysler closed underperforming dealerships because they squeeze prices of more successful dealerships. Reducing competition among stores selling the same brand will enable successful dealerships to strengthen prices and ultimately make it easier for Chrysler to pass price increases on to dealers. The metric Chrysler is looking at is the number of dealers it takes to generate 1% of sales in the US auto market. For GM, Ford and Chrysler it takes 300, 280 and 270 dealerships respectively to sell 1% of the market. In contrast it only takes 90 Toyota dealerships to sell 1% of the US market (Boudette, 2007). This gives Toyota dealers advantages of scale as well as reduced competition.

John Deere, the farm equipment and tractor manufacturer, is consolidating its dealerships for a variety of reasons. One is that farming has become a highly sophisticated, technology driven business and customers demand products and services that can help them compete. For example, satellites are used to track the location of seeds; instruments measure soil temperature and control fertilizer spreading. Tractors can even steer themselves to make sure that no spot is plowed twice. This places exceptional demands on the dealers who sell and service Deere equipment. Dealers which are too small cannot keep current with developments in farming technology and cannot afford to hire sophisticated sales managers or enough highly trained technicians, nor can they afford the equipment necessary to service such sophisticated machines. When dealers cannot meet customer demands for sales and service, customers tend to go to other manufacturers. Other factors driving Deere's dealership consolidation include the administrative savings of dealing with fewer dealerships and the time saved chasing bad debts from marginal dealerships. In addition, fewer dealerships with larger territories reduces the risk of price wars (Brat and Aeppel, 2007).

Conclusion

Management must critically evaluate businesses, divisions and facilities and cut those that are draining company resources and management time. Each must be quantitatively analyzed and compared to internal and external norms and goals. With data in hand, some will be clearly identified as winners, some as losers and management judgment will be required to determine which of those in the middle can be saved and which cannot. This is corporate triage.

Among the reasons to promptly identify and cut out underperforming businesses, divisions, subsidiaries, facilities, and dealerships is that restructuring must take place in a limited time, if it is to take place at all. Further, underperforming business elements burn cash and consume a disproportionate amount of management time and attention.

Since the iron rule of business is grow or die, those with little or no sales growth should be critically evaluated to determine whether sales can be improved quickly or whether competition and market trends are going to doom them to be minor players in their market.

Those with good sales growth, but declining margins are prime candidates for restructuring. Internal costs can almost always be improved and even the cost of raw materials can be reduced through improved utilization efficiency or by substituting other, less costly materials.

Facilities must be continuously evaluated. Sometimes a quick road to profitability is to shed facilities with losses or which are underperforming. However, it is impossible to build a business simply by lopping off parts. Top performing facilities should be studied to determine why they are top performers and lessons learned should be applied to other facilities.

Bad divisions, subsidiaries, business units, and facilities are like rocks weighing down a company's performance. Identification and elimination of poorly performing elements of a company can speed its way to superior profits.

References

Bailey J (2003) Shift in customer base transforms a company. Wall St J B5, 6 May

Bloomberg (1997) Campbell may spin off slow-growing businesses. The Financial Post. Sec.1. News, p 13

Boudette NE (2007) Chrysler looks to reduce dealer ranks. Wall St J A10, 25 July

Brat I, Thimothy A (2007) Why Deere is weeding out dealers even as farms boom. Wall St J A1 and A10

Collins G (1997) Seeking status as blue chip, Campbell Sets 7-Unit Spinoff. New York Times, D1, 10 Sept

Daves PR, MC Ehrhardt, RE Shrives (2004) Corporate valuation: a guide for managers and investors. Thompson Southwestern, Mason, OH

Matthews RG (2007) Why firms are returning to their roots. Wall St J A2, 22 Oct

Stewart TA, L O'Brien (2005) Execution without excuses. Harv Bus Rev 102–111, Mar

Vance DE (2005) Raising capital. Springer, New York, pp 165–176

Whitney JO (1996) Strategic renewal for business units. Harv Bus Rev, 84–98, July–Aug

Chapter 6
Evaluation Products, Customers and Contracts

Introduction

Stop the bleeding is often one of the first commands in restructuring. It is rare when any two products, customers, services or contracts are equally profitable; some are probably very profitable and some unprofitable. The unprofitable, when averaged in with the profitable can make the overall company look bad. Identification and elimination of losing products, customers, services and contracts can dramatically improve profitability. This is corporate triage at a more detailed level. Those elements of a business that drain resources, and distract management time and attention should be eliminated. When they are, management can focus on improving the profitability and performance of its core business.

Customers and Products

Customers and products are intimately entwined. Just as a business has no purpose unless it satisfies customer needs, products have no purpose unless they satisfy customer needs. So analyzing products without customer context provides an incomplete and perhaps misleading view of the best course of action.

Analyzing Customers

The notion of analyzing customers derives directly from the question: "Who do you want to be your customers?" Customers should be strategic, significant and profitable. Strategic customers are those that really appreciate a company's core competence and reward that competence with purchases at profitable prices. However, strategic importance goes beyond sales and profits. A customer has strategic importance if it provides entry into a new and more profitable market, or it can help a company grow its expertise in a new technology. For example a customer's research and development might translate into an improved method for providing goods to that customer (Whitney, 1996, p. 98). A flagship customer can have strategic importance as well. A flagship customer is one that is well known. Flagship customers provide an implied seal of approval for a company's goods or services.

D.E. Vance, *Corporate Restructuring*, DOI 10.1007/978-3-642-01786-5_6,
© Springer-Verlag Berlin Heidelberg 2009

Flagship customers build confidence in quality and performance. Overall, strategic customers are those that can help a company grow.

The issue of which customers are strategic is not always obvious. A sales manager might say all customers are strategic, production managers might say customers that purchase large volumes of standardized goods are strategic and research and development or accounting might have a completely different view of which customers are strategic. Evaluation of whether customers are strategic can be facilitated by (i) establishing three or four criteria for strategic importance, (ii) a no holds barred discussion of a customer's strategic importance by representatives across departments, to bring the best thinking to bear on the issue, and (iii) a final decision maker which is usually the general manager, division president or CEO. It is also useful if criteria for strategic importance are ranked and a composite value for strategic importance developed. Out of a hundred, a thousand or ten thousand customers, a company might find that only a handful of strategic customers.

The next level of customer analysis is sales volume. Sort customer sales year to date (YTD) for this year and last year, and rank sales by current YTD sales. If the analysis is being done in the first 6 months of the year, use prior year's sales for the ranking. Print annualized year to year increases or decreases by customer.

Subtotal sales by quintile and in all probability, about 80% of sales will come from the top 20% of customers. Even if 60% of sales come from the top 20% of customers the point is that some customers are more valuable than others in terms of sales and growth.

The next level question is which customers are profitable. Strange as it may seem, small customers require almost as much customer care as large customers for sales calls, order entry, scheduling, shipping and customer service. Is it more expensive to take an order for a thousand electric motors than it is for one? Does it take more time to invoice for a thousand electric motors than for one? If a single electric motor is being shipped via some commercial service like UPS or FedEx Ground, it will be more expensive, per unit, than if a truck load of electric motors is shipped (Whitney, 1996, p. 86). Set up time is another factor that makes small orders relatively more expensive to process than large orders.

Some companies are designed to handle sales of one, two or ten items at a time. Their strategy is to target low volume customers. Retailers and catalogue companies are in this category. If the company's whole strategy is to serve these customers, do it. But, such a strategy won't work for most industrial firms.

An estimate should be made of the profitability of each customer. This need not be a precise allocation of seven layers of overhead. It just needs to be a reasonable estimate of the costs associated with each customer. Depending on the level of detail available in company records, one might be able to estimate the contribution or gross profit on customer orders as well as order entry, scheduling, set-up time, special engineering or customization, special material orders, picking, shipping and collections, management time and attention, systems and capital costs by order. These can be rolled up to find customer profitability. Few companies really know the actual cost to service individual customers and as a consequence, continue to service unprofitable customers (Whitney, 1996, p. 86).

If a company has multiple distribution strategies, for example retail, web, direct mail, and wholesale, the company might want to analyze sales in each channel of distribution separately because different channels have different cost and pricing characteristics. Table 6.1 is an example of how a customer analysis might be organized.

In this example, less than a quarter of customers had strategic value defined as 3.5 or above. Without strategic value, a customer must make a substantial contribution to sales or profit otherwise they simply dissipate management focus.

Customer Profitability Analysis

Traditional accounting systems don't provide a clear picture of which customers are profitable and which are not because they don't trace period costs to customers. Someone should be assigned early in the restructuring process to compute the gross margin and contribution margin of individual products and services. Customer profitability builds on this by considering period costs associated with customers. Examples of period costs are (i) order entry and tracking, (ii) shipping, (iii) special services, and (iv) billing and collections.

Order Entry and Tracking Costs

Order entry and tracking is a function of the number of orders placed. A customer that places one large order is likely to use less of this service than a customer that places twenty smaller orders even if the total sales to each customer is the same. A rough estimate as to the cost of order entry and tracking is to divide the cost of the order entry and customer service departments by the total number of orders processed each year. Customer service costs should include the cost for expediters. This will provide an order cost as shown in Eq. (6.1).

$$\text{Order Cost} = \frac{(\text{Order Entry} + \text{Customer Service Cost})}{\text{Annual Orders Processed}} \quad (6.1)$$

Suppose there are two order entry specialists making $40,000 each; three customer service/expediters making $50,000 each; other order entry and customer service costs of $98,950 and the company processes 774 orders per year. What does it cost to process one order?

$$\text{Order Cost} = \frac{(2 \times \$40,000 + 3 \times 50,000 + \$98,950)}{774}$$
$$= \$328,950/774$$
$$= 425$$

Table 6.1 Customer analysis

Customer	V	G	F	N	Strategic	Industry	Sales	Grth (%)	Contr.	Orders	Avg $ order	Order cost	Billing cost	Slow pay	Account Maint.	Profit
Allied Signal	4	5	5	1	3.75	Electronics	11,000	5.5	4,400	16	687.5	6.80	4.80	0.00	4.00	4,384
General Dynamics	3	4	5	1	3.25	Electronics	9,000	5.5	3,600	12	750.0	5.10	3.60	0.00	4.00	3,587
Lancaster Engineering	5	4	1	3	3.25	Electronics	6,000	22.0	2,400	12	500.0	5.10	3.60	6.45	4.00	2,381
General Electric	3	4	5	2	3.50	Electronics	4,000	8.0	1,600	8	500.0	3.40	2.40	0.00	4.00	1,590
Electronic Components	3	2	1	1	1.75	Electronics	3,000	15.0	1,200	28	107.1	11.90	8.40	0.00	4.00	1,176
Conshohocken Eng.	4	3	1	2	2.50	Electronics	2,000	25.0	800	16	125.0	6.80	4.80	6.45	4.00	778
Phillips	3	4	5	3	3.75	Electronics	2,000	6.0	800	16	125.0	6.80	4.80	0.00	4.00	784
Enterprise Robotics	4	4	1	4	3.25	Electronics	1,500	12.0	600	32	46.9	13.60	9.60	0.00	4.00	573
Berlin Automation, Inc.	4	4	1	4	3.25	Electronics	500	15.0	200	36	13.9	15.30	10.80	6.45	4.00	163
Castle Pharmaceuticals	3	4	3	4	3.50	Biomedical	400	100.0	160	24	16.7	10.20	7.20	0.00	4.00	139
Rutgers Medical Inc.	3	5	2	5	3.75	Biomedical	300	50.0	120	16	18.8	6.80	4.80	6.45	4.00	98
Pennsauken Industries	2	1	1	1	1.25	Electronics	300	9.0	120	64	4.7	27.20	19.20	0.00	4.00	70
Voorhees Biotech	2	4	1	5	3.00	Biomedical	250	150.0	100	16	15.6	6.80	4.80	0.00	4.00	84
Lester Systems	3	1	1	1	1.50	Electronics	200	9.0	80	16	12.5	6.80	4.80	6.45	4.00	58
Lancaster Biotech	3	3	3	5	3.50	Biomedical	180	80.0	72	18	10.0	7.65	5.40	0.00	4.00	55
Ronco Manufacturing	2	1	2	1	1.50	Electronics	70	−20.0	28	80	0.9	34.00	24.00	0.00	4.00	−34
Peoria Engineering	4	3	1	2	2.50	Electronics	60	20.0	24	44	1.4	18.70	13.20	0.00	4.00	−12
Rupert Biotech	3	4	1	5	3.25	Biomedical	40	100.0	16	8	5.0	3.40	2.40	6.45	4.00	0
Asco Communications	3	2	2	2	2.00	Electronics	30	−11.0	12	4	7.5	1.70	1.20	6.45	4.00	−1
Brinkley Telecom	2	2	1	2	1.75	Electronics	25	−15.0	10	72	0.3	30.60	21.60	0.00	4.00	−46
Sharper Image	3	1	2	2	2.00	Electronics	20	−30.0	8	64	0.3	27.20	19.20	6.45	4.00	−49
Yale Technologies	2	1	1	1	1.25	Computer	15	20.0	6	44	0.3	18.70	13.20	0.00	4.00	−30
Camden Manufacturing	2	1	1	1	1.25	Electronics	15	2.0	6	64	0.2	27.20	19.20	6.45	4.00	−51
Electronic Arts	1	1	3	1	1.50	Computer	12	−30.0	5	60	0.2	25.50	18.00	0.00	4.00	−43
Jensen Steel	2	1	1	1	1.25	Electronics	7	NA	3	4	1.8	1.70	1.20	0.00	4.00	−4
							40,924			774						15,650

Strategic importance factors are measured on a scale of 1–5 where 1 is the lowest and 5 the highest. V is how much a customer values the company. G is whether the company can help grow the company's expertise, N is whether a customer can help the company enter a new market. Contr. is Contribution. Dollars in thousands.

Shipping Charges

The relevance of shipping charges depends on whether shipping is FOB shipping point or FOB destination. If the terms are FOB shipping point, the customer must pay for shipping so the only issue is whether the company is capturing and charging the customer for shipping. However, if the terms are FOB destination that means the company is paying to ship it goods and services out of its own pocket. If that is the case then shipping charges by customer should be captured and totaled. These shipping charges will factor into whether the customer is profitable.

Special Services

Some customers are needier than others and demand special services. For example, Wal-Mart insists all shipments contain RFID chips that electronically identify the contents, shipper and other information. Other customers want their goods painted blue when the standard model of a good is red. Whether or not price is increased to cover special services, these costs should be tracked by customer so that customer profitability can be gauged.

Billing and Collections

Ordinarily, one order would result in one billing and collection process. However, there are always those customers who are slow pay, or need repeated follow up calls before they remit payment. On a spreadsheet of customers, have billing and collections put a 1 in a column next to slow payers and leave that column blank for all other customers. Add up this column to see how many slow payers the company has. Collecting from slow-payers costs much more than collecting from customers that pay promptly. Suppose 20% of billing and collection costs are due to the extra work involved in collecting from slow-pay customers and 80% is associated with routine billing and collections. That means in evaluating customers we will have one charge based on the number of orders a customer makes and one charge based on whether it is a slow-pay customer. The equation for the routine billing and collection charge per order is given in Eq. (6.2) and the slow pay charge is given in Eq. (6.3).

$$\text{Order Billing} = \frac{80\% \times \text{Billing and Collection Costs}}{\text{Annual Orders Processed}} \tag{6.2}$$

$$\text{Slow-pay} = \frac{20\% \times \text{Billing and Collection Costs}}{\text{Number of Slow-pay Customers}} \tag{6.3}$$

The purpose of this exercise is not to bill slow pay customers for paying slowly. The purpose is to fairly estimate the profitability of customers when their peculiar characteristics are taken into account. Slow-pay is an important characteristic.

Suppose for example, billing and collections has three collectors earning $45,000 each; a supervisor earning $60,000 and other billing and collection expenses are

$95,250. Further suppose 774 orders are processed annually and there are 9 slow-pay customers.

$$\text{Order Billing} = \frac{80\% \times (3 \times \$45,000 + \$60,000 + \$95,250)}{774}$$

$$= 80\% \times \$290,250/774$$

$$= \$300.00$$

$$\text{Slow-pay} = 20\% \times (3 \times \$45,000 + \$60,000 + \$95,250)$$

$$= 20\% \times \$290,250/9$$

$$= \$6,450$$

While every customer should be allocated a cost for every order they place, slow-pay costs will be allocated to customers only once per year.

Customer Account Maintenance

It is expensive to maintain an active customer. Costs can include the cost of catalogues, brochures and other mailings, salesperson visits, phone calls and responding to bids and queries. When customers require bids, which are common for industrial sales and in construction, costs can include the costs of estimators as well as sales and marketing people. This cost should be allocated to customers using Eq. (6.4).

$$\text{Customer Account Maintenance} = \frac{\text{Costs of Customer Maintenance}}{\text{Number of Customers}} \qquad (6.4)$$

Example: Suppose a company has 25 customers; sales person visits, catalogues, mailings, and phone calls cost $85,000; bids and responses to requests for proposal cost $15,000. What is the cost of Customer Account Maintenance?

$$\text{Customer Account Maintenance} = \frac{\$85,000 + \$15,000}{25} = \$4,000$$

Analyzing Customer Profitability

A profitability analysis should capture customer sales, contribution margin, number of orders, shipping charges, if born by the company and not the customer, special services if not billed back to the customer, billing and collection charges, a slow-pay charge if appropriate and customer account maintenance.

Table 6.1 pulls this information together. Sorting customers by sales, we see that the top 20% of customers contributed 80.6% of sales and 83.8% of profit. The top 40% of customers contributed 96.3% of sales and 99.4% of profit. The remaining 7 profitable customers contributed little to no, yet they probably required almost as much time and attention as more profitable customers; time and attention which have been invested in growing the top tier customers or finding more customers of the same size and industry as the top tier customers. Fewer customers also means the number of order takers, customer service and billing and collections people can be reduced.

A more sophisticated analysis might forecast whether customers are growing fast enough to become significant and profitable in a year or 2 years. For example, growth rates of biomedical companies are significantly higher than those in electronics and computers even though they do not significantly contribute to current sales or profits. Two cautions are advised. First, 1 year's growth rate is not the best indicator of long term growth trends and second, a company cannot hold onto an underperforming customer because it might, at some time in the distant future become a major customer. Based on the data in this example, it might be reasonable to expect the biomedical sector to contribute most of the company's growth in the next few years.

Analyzing Products and Services

Products or services rarely have the same profitability. Just as it makes sense to shed underperforming facilities, it makes sense to shed underperforming products and services. At one point, Nestle, the international food maker, found it had 130,000 products world wide and 30% were not making money (Ball, 2007). A major glass producer reduced its SKUs to 1,700 from 4,000 to improve profitability (Whitney, 1996, p. 86).

A related problem is that similar products erode each other's market share, consume management time and attention, devour product development dollars and make it difficult to achieve economies of scale. General Motors had the Chevrolet, Pontiac, Buick, Cadillac, Saab, GMC and Hummer Brands each of which have overlapping products and overlapping target markets. Ford Motor Company had Ford, Mercury, Lincoln, Mazda, Jaguar, Volvo, Aston Martin and Range Rover brands which to some extent overlap both as to product type and target market. Toyota, on the other hand, has three "brands" the hip, new, edgy offerings like Scion, the reliable, value-for-the-money, no hassle brand Toyota, and the aspirational brand Lexus. BMW has a similar brand strategy with the Mini as the hip, new brand, the BMW 3 series as the value for the money brand and the 5 and 7 series as the aspirational brands (Womack, 2006). Ford took a step toward brand rationalization by selling Jaguar and Range Rover (Thomas, 2008). General Motors shed brands in bankruptcy.

Measurement

There are at least five financial measures of performance for products and services. No one measure presents a complete picture. These are (i) unit gross margin, (ii) contribution margin, (iii) sales and cost trends which include research and development costs, (iv) incremental invested capital and (v) profitability considering total costs including factors like set-up costs, information technology and product associated period costs such as advertising.

Gross margin per unit (GMU) is similar to gross margin as computed for an entire company except that price is substituted for revenue and full absorption cost is substituted for cost of goods sold as shown in Eq. (6.5). Full absorption costs includes direct material, direct labor, variable factory overhead and fixed factory overhead.

$$\text{GMU} = \frac{\text{Price} - \text{Unit Cost}}{\text{Price}} \tag{6.5}$$

Gross margin for a company is the weighted average of the gross margin for all products. High GMU products will tend to drive a company's overall gross margin up. Low GMU products will tend to drag a company's gross margin down. In the chapter on reverse engineering we saw that meeting target profits is extremely sensitive to gross margin. So the strategy should be to sell more high GMU products and fewer low GMU products. Where high and low GMU products compete with each other for the same customer dollars, eliminate the low GMU products. Products with very low GMU or negative GMU should be eliminated as quickly as possible.

Contribution margin is another way to analyze product performance. Contribution margin (CM) focuses on the incremental costs of producing an additional unit of a product and ignores fixed costs because it is assumed that over the short run, fixed costs cannot be changed. Contribution margin represents the percentage of every dollar that is available to cover fixed manufacturing and administrative costs, financing costs, taxes and profit after variable costs are covered.

Contribution margin can be computed at the company level or at the product level. Here we will concentrate on contribution margin at the product level. The equation for contribution margin is given in Eq. (6.6). Variable costs include direct labor, direct materials, variable factory overhead and any variable selling or administrative costs. One common variable selling cost is commissions.

$$\text{CM} = \frac{\text{Price} - \text{Variable Costs}}{\text{Price}} \tag{6.6}$$

Many would argue that contribution margin is a more sensible way to decide whether to keep a product than gross margin because fixed costs are sunk costs. Contribution margin is a particularly good discriminator between good and bad products and services for low volume or custom orders. For example, if a customer orders 1,000 custom build transformers, the question is should the company accept the order and if so at what price? In this example, any engineering time invested in designing the transformers would be included as direct labor and if specialized test equipment had to be bought for the order the test equipment would be classified as direct material. The president of one electronics firm told me that since he started using contribution margin to evaluate new orders his profitability has increased substantially (Seitz, 2005).

Hidden Costs

Just as companies rarely know which customers are profitable because they don't consider all the costs in servicing a customer, companies rarely know which products are profitable because they don't consider hidden product costs. Hidden costs include set-up costs, costs to keep products and labels in compliance with safety codes; the incremental costs of classifying, warehousing and picking small volume items; the cost of capital invested in slow moving inventory as well as the cost of insurance and inventory taxes; costs for catalogues and websites to advertise products and; the costs of information technology to track low volume items.

Price and Cost Trends

Financial accounting is about the past, but management is about shaping the future. In evaluating whether to keep, expand, or discontinue a product or service one must look at the trends. Sales growth is a threshold test. If sales are flat or declining the product or service is going to die. The only question is whether it can be milked as a cash cow for some period of time before discontinuance.

Within the envelop of sales, one must look at price trends. If sales are going up, but unit price is declining, then the only way to keep the product profitable is to reduce unit cost faster than unit prices decline. This is the story with computers and consumer electronics. Prices have been declining over a long period of time. The companies that have prospered are the ones that found ways to cut costs faster than prices drop.

When considering cost trends, look beyond direct material, direct labor, variable factory overhead, fixed factory overhead and variable administrative costs. For many products on-going research and development is required to keep products competitive. So the relevant comparison is to determine whether sales are growing faster than cost of goods sold plus research and development. If research and development eats up substantially all of a product's gross profit, it should be eliminated.

Complementary Goods and Services

Often a company sells goods or services that complement their primary good or service. In an economic sense, a complementary good is one that increases the satisfaction of having another good. For example, a company's primary product might be a machine that opens payment envelops, reads the enclosed check and remittance advice, stores an image of the check and advice in a database and credits customers' account for the payment. The machine just described is a real machine that processes upwards of forty thousand checks an hour. Companies that process such volumes cannot afford for these machines to be down. The complementary good for the check processing machine is a service contract.

The issue is how complementary goods are going to be viewed. A telemarketing company I consulted to was asked by a customer to track its inventory in customer's hands so that automatic reorders could be shipped. The company did the customer tracking as a favor to the client. The tracking consumed the full time work of three high paid programmers and when errors arose in the course of providing this free tracking service, the client demanded its telemarketing bill be reduced.

The difference between these two companies is that the first company recognized that prompt maintenance, had a high value to the customer and priced it as such which generated hansom profits for the company. The second company did not recognize the value of a predictive inventory order system and offered it as a no cost service to its client. As a result, the company tried to provide this service at minimal cost, generating code and maintaining the inventory database on the fly. The result was that the telemarketer incurred costs it shouldn't have, and the customer was never happy.

The solution is to determine the value of every complementary good or service to the customer and price it accordingly. If the price is not high enough to provide a profit, the company should not offer the complementary good. However, if the company can get an adequate price, the complementary goods or services might evolve into a substantial new revenue stream for the company.

Product Fit and Consistency

Some companies want to be all things to all people. It cannot be done. A company must pick and choose where its expertise lies and be the very best it can be in that area. Unfortunately, many businesses, successful and otherwise, find themselves with products that do not fit with their principal product line. A company that makes socks should not also make hats even though they are both apparel because this dual tracking tells retailers they don't know what they want to be when they grow up and they never intend to be the best at anything. On the other hand, a company that makes outerwear might make hats as an extension of their outdoor line and a company that makes gym socks might make sweat pants and sweat shirts as an extension of its sports line.

When a company finds it has products that are not in the same niche, not sold to the same customers, and not used by the same individuals it should consider shedding some of those products to sharpen its brand image as well as focus its marketing, product development and technological excellence.

In an ideal world, a company will be able to segregate a product line that does not fit and sell it off. If the product has substantial sales or is a recognized brand, this sale may generate cash for the restructuring. Most well respected product lines can be sold. However, if a product is inferior, generates many customer complaints, has high warranty costs, or employs obsolete technology, it may be difficult to sell and a company should consider abandoning it and selling off its assets to generate cash.

Product Revitalization

Companies make decisions to add or drop products all the time. Such decisions turn on both sales volume and profitability. Products become less profitable over time as a natural consequence of product maturity. Companies should consider four methods of improving performance before a product is abandoned.

Cutting Costs

Profitability may be restored by cutting costs through product redesign, simplification, and improvements in the production process. The strategy is to set a cost target that would make a product profitable at current and projected prices and challenge the production and engineering departments to meet that cost.

Subcontracting

Sometimes there is no way to reduce internal costs enough to make a product profitable. One solution is to subcontract out all production, shifting company operations to sales, distribution and service.

Advertising

Sometimes a product loses market share and can no longer command a premium price because its brand image has languished. With a sufficient investment in advertising, sales, and marketing it may be possible to reposition the brand and take market share from competitors.

Reinvent the Product

Sometimes a product can be reinvented by adding enough new features so that the market will perceive it as new and reward that newness with increased pricing tolerance. Cell phones are an excellent example of a product that is continually being reinvented. Cameras, text messaging, music and video downloads, web surfing, GPS, television, and touch screen technology have all been added to cell phones to reinvent them. These features have allowed manufacturers to maintain and increase the price of the underlying product.

Terminating a Product

If these four approaches cannot restore a product to a target level of profitability, it may have to be terminated. This raises a series of questions as to what is the threshold for terminating a product. For example, how much profit is enough?

This question is informed by a company's target margins. Remember, in a turnaround, we are using the company's business model to reverse engineer profitability goals. If a product has a 15% margin when the company's target is 40%, it is a candidate for elimination. But what if that product accounts for a significant percent of sales, and that 15% margin contributes a significant amount toward covering overhead and financing costs? Then the decision becomes more complex. One strategy is to strip the contribution of this particular product or product line out of the business model, and then reverse engineer to find the new target overhead that would be needed without the contribution of the low margin product. Another approach would be to set this product or product line up as a separate subsidiary as a step toward (i) selling it or (ii) spinning it off to the shareholders.

Why would a company want to close or sell a product line that is contributing some gross profit, even if its margins fall below target? First, the underperforming product is tying up valuable assets and working capital. Second, the underperforming product is probably consuming a significant fraction of management time and attention which could better be focused elsewhere. Third, underperforming products can easily tip over into losing products absorbing precious capital and making it even harder to turn a company around.

Customers and Products

Once the profitability of customers and products has been evaluated individually, those evaluations can be brought together to identify a company's core profitability. Conceptually, one could plot customers along the top of a grid from most profitable to least profitable and products down the grid from most profitable to least profitable. For most companies this would represent an enormous grid. So as a practical matter, one might consider a grid which ranks customers and products by quintile as shown in Fig. 6.1.

Companies should keep the top 40% of profitable customers and the top 40% of profitable products, shown as the white squares in Fig. 6.1. Companies should get rid of the 40% of least profitable customers and products as show by the heavily shaded squares in Fig. 6.1.

If a company wants to transform itself from an underperforming to a top performing firm, it must take radical action. And though the action is radical, we have seen that the change in a firm's revenue and profits is minimal. Eliminating a company's losing customers and products will boost profits and free an enormous amount of management time and energy to pursue profitable customers.

The difficulty is in deciding whether to keep or eliminate the mid profitability customers and products as shown by the light gray squares in Fig. 6.1. Important factors to consider when evaluating mid-profitability customers are (i) strategic importance, (ii) sales growth and (iii) whether product contribution can be improved. For example brisk sales might indicate an opportunity to raise price.

In the Table 6.1 sales to biomedical companies was growing faster than sales to either the electronics or computer companies. Resources freed up by eliminating unproductive customers and products should be focused on finding every significant biomedical company and determining whether they are new potential customers.

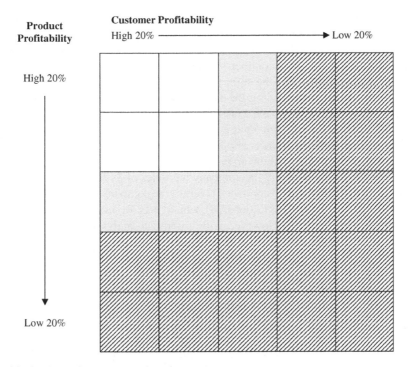

Fig. 6.1 Analysis of customers and products

Liberated resources can also be used to expand sales to existing customers. For example, service and quality can be improved. For customers that do not use the company as a sole source or preferred supplier, the company can ask what it needs to do to become a sole source or preferred provider and after shedding unproductive customers and products it will have the resources to do it. In addition, larger and more profitable accounts can be pursued in core customer industries such as electronics.

Analyzing Contracts

Just as customers and products should be analyzed for profitability, contracts should be analyzed for profitability. Every contract should be profitable. This is one of the few rules of restructuring for which there is no exception. If a company accepts a contract at a loss to secure a new customer, it creates an expectation in the new customer that it will accept contracts on similar terms in the future. Worse, if other customers learn a company is accepting contracts at low prices, they will expect those same terms.

The bigger problem is not that companies intentionally accept contracts at a loss, but that they do not measure the profitability of every contract. Instead of providing exceptional service to a select group of profitable customers, firms who fail to measure profits tend to offer mediocre service to all (Bhide, 1986).

Systems should be in place to scrutinize every contract for profitability. Reports should include the customer, contract, salesperson, price, cost, contribution and contribution margin. Often it is the sales person who quotes the price for specialized goods and services, so including the salesperson' name in the profitability report maintains accountability. Table 6.2 provides an example of what such a report might look like. Contracts for commercial goods such as engineering, custom manufactured items and service contracts are often sent out to bid. Sales people must have pricing discipline or there will be no profits.

In the example in Table 6.2 the company has sales of $17,666,000 and a contribution of $1,678,725 from 23 contracts. Overall, the company's contribution margin is about 9.5% ($1,678,725/$17,666,000) which may or may not be satisfactory depending on the industry. However, with a contract analysis report, it is easy to see that the company accepted several contracts that radically reduced their contribution. For example, the worst four contracts lost a total of $268,875. Identify losing contracts as early as possible to figure out why the bids for these contracts were low, or the costs were high, so corrective action can be taken. Avoiding the four losing contracts would have reduced sales by $3,060,000 to $14,606,000, but it would have increased contribution by $268,875 to $1,947,600 and would have increased contribution margin to 13.3% ($1,947,600/$14,606,000).

Contracts with very low, but positive contribution margin such as the Fine contract for $500,000 which only contributed $3,600, tie up working capital for materials, labor and variable overhead as well as management time and attention. A contract that is barely profitable today can quickly tip over into an unprofitable contract tomorrow. Never play near the edge of the cliff.

Profit Ladder Analysis

Companies often mask a losing contract, product or service by assigning low cost resources to it while allocating high cost resources to contracts, products or services that command a relatively high price. The result is that everything looks profitable when, in reality, the poorly performing contracts are a drag on profitability. The idea behind profit ladder analysis is to match the highest revenue generating activities with the least cost resources to identify activities which are a drag on profitability (Vance, 2003).

Many companies make use of subcontractors and each subcontractor may charge a different rate. Assume subcontractor performance is interchangeable, as it often is when providing a standardized good or service. Likewise, a company may charge different rates to different customers for virtually identical services.

Suppose a company supplies contract programmers and it can bill one client $100 per hour, another $90 per hour, another $75 per hour and the fourth customer $60 per hour. Call these clients I, II, III and IV respectively. Suppose further that the

Table 6.2 Contract analysis

Customer	Contract	Salesperson	Price	Materials	Labor	Var.OH	Comm.	Contrib.	Margin
CT Highway Dept.	A200	Christen, A	2,000,000	750,000	750,000	112,500	38,750	348,750	17.4%
CT Highway Dept.	A203	Christen, A	1,500,000	620,000	550,000	82,500	24,750	222,750	14.9%
MA Dept of Highways	A802	Fine, L	1,100,000	400,000	420,000	63,000	21,700	195,300	17.8%
Boston Construction	A242	Schwartz, S	900,000	300,000	350,000	52,500	19,750	177,750	19.8%
MA Dept of Highways	A807	Fine, L	900,000	350,000	350,000	52,500	14,750	132,750	14.8%
Boston Construction	A240	Schwartz, S	1,000,000	410,000	390,000	58,500	14,150	127,350	12.7%
CT Highway Dept.	A250	Christen, A	1,000,000	400,000	420,000	63,000	11,700	105,300	10.5%
MA Dept of Highways	A808	Fine, L	1,200,000	540,000	480,000	72,000	10,800	97,200	8.1%
MA Dept of Highways	A799	Fine, L	980,000	400,000	420,000	63,000	9,700	87,300	8.9%
Boston Construction	A204	Schwartz, S	550,000	230,000	195,000	29,250	9,575	86,175	15.7%
MA Dept of Highways	A800	Fine, L	740,000	300,000	310,000	46,500	8,350	75,150	10.2%
Boston Construction	A244	Schwartz, S	500,000	210,000	180,000	27,000	8,300	74,700	14.9%
CT Highway Dept.	A201	Christen, A	400,000	150,000	160,000	24,000	6,600	59,400	14.9%
CT Highway Dept.	A202	Christen, A	320,000	110,000	130,000	19,500	6,050	54,450	17.0%
Boston Construction	A215	Schwartz, S	480,000	220,000	190,000	28,500	4,150	37,350	7.8%
Boston Construction	A248	Schwartz, S	400,000	180,000	160,000	24,000	3,600	32,400	8.1%
Stevenson Engineering	A214	Christen, A	72,000	26,000	22,000	3,300	2,070	18,630	25.9%
Stevenson Engineering	A302	Christen, A	64,000	25,000	23,000	3,450	1,255	11,295	17.6%
MA Dept of Highways	A801	Fine, L	500,000	220,000	240,000	36,000	400	3,600	0.7%
Stevenson Engineering	A301	Christen, A	190,000	100,000	105,000	15,750	-3,075	-27,675	-14.6%
MA Dept of Highways	A802	Fine, L	870,000	430,000	420,000	63,000	-4,300	-38,700	-4.4%
Boston Construction	A205	Schwartz, S	1,200,000	550,000	660,000	99,000	-10,900	-98,100	-8.2%
Boston Construction	A233	Schwartz, S	800,000	410,000	440,000	66,000	-11,600	-104,400	-13.1%
			17,666,000					1,678,725	

Var.OH is the variable overhead associated with each contract, Comm. is the commission on the contract. Sales compensation is reduced when salesmen bring in losing contracts. Contrib. is the contribution to company profits. Margin is contribution margin.

Table 6.3 Contract analysis

	I	II	III	IV
Billable rate/hours:	$100	$90	$75	$60
Subcontract rate/hours.	$75	$70	$60	$50
Gross profit/hours.	$25	$20	$15	$10
Gross profit/Contract:	$25,000	$20,000	$15,000	$10,000
Total gross profit: $70,000 per month				

subcontract programmers used for the first contract cost $75 per hour, and subcontract programmers used for the second, third and fourth contracts cost $70, $60 and $50 per hour. To simplify the illustration, assume all clients contract for 1,000 hours of programming per month. These data can be summarized in Table 6.3.

The company might think that it is doing very well because it is making a profit on every contract. The question, however, is whether the company is optimizing its profits. Consider Table 6.4 which pairs the highest priced contract with the lowest cost subcontractor.

By rearranging the allocation of subcontractors to contracts, neither total revenue, total expenses, nor total gross profit changed. However, it is obvious that contract IV, at $60 per hour is unprofitable. By terminating contract IV, the company is increasing gross profit by $15,000 per month or $180,000 per year.

With minor modifications, profit ladder analysis can be used to match planes to routes, trucks to routes, production equipment to products and so forth. The key elements of profit ladder analysis are:

1. List output (contracts, products, routes, etc.) from highest revenue to lowest revenue.
2. List production capacity from least costly to most costly.
3. Match the least costly production method that will do the job to the highest revenue output.

Table 6.4 Profit ladder analysis

	I	II	III	IV
Billable rate/hours.:	$100	$90	$75	$60
Subcontract rate/hours	$50	$60	$70	$75
Gross profit/hours:	$50	$30	$5	–$15
Gross profit/contract:	$50,000	$30,000	$5,000	–$15,000
Total gross profit:	$70,000 per month			

Profit ladder analysis pairs the contract or activity which generates the highest revenue with the lowest cost resource necessary to satisfy customer needs.

4. If low revenue output would be unprofitable using the high cost production method, eliminate the low revenue contract, product or route.
5. Eliminate the high cost production method used to produce the low revenue output.

Conclusion

Sometimes management must prune customers and products to re-invigorate a company. This requires a realistic, quantitative analysis of the contribution of each to profitability. With data in hand, it is usually easy to see that the top 40% of customers and products provide most of the profit, and the bottom 40% of products and customer contribute relatively little toward performance and may even be a drain on company resources.

Customers and products with above average sales growth and profitability are keepers. Since the iron rule of business is grow or die, those with little or no sales growth should be evaluated to determine whether sales can be improved or whether they should be eliminated. Customers, products and contracts should be constantly evaluated to determine whether costs and prices are appropriate.

Contracts with losses or with substandard contribution margins should be promptly identified and analyzed. There is always a reason why a contract under performs. Once that reason is identified controls can be implemented to avoid under performance in the future.

Profit ladder analysis can be used to identify contracts and products which look profitable on the surface, but are actually loosing money. Profit ladder analysis pairs the highest revenue generating contracts, products, or routes with the least cost method of production. It identifies products which only appear profitable because low cost means of production are used for them. Identification and elimination of poorly performing customers, products and contracts can speed a company toward superior performance.

References

Ball D (2007) After buying binge, nestle goes on a diet. Wall St J A1 and A13, 23 July

Bhide A (1986) Hustle as strategy. Harv Bus Rev 59–65, Sept–Oct

Seitz D (2005) Leadership development lecture at Rutgers University. Mr. Seitz is the President of NWL Transformers, 15 Apr

Thomas H (2008) Ford sells land Rover and Jaguar to Tata. New York Times NYTimes.com. http://www.nytimes.com/2008/03/26/business/worldbusiness/26cnd-auto.html. Accessed 26 Mar

Vance D (2003) Financial analysis and decision making. McGraw-Hill, New York, pp 303–306

Whitney JO (1996) Strategic renewal for business units. Harv Bus Rev 84–98, July–Aug

Womack JP (2006) Why Toyota won. Wall St J A16, 13 Feb

Chapter 7
Revenue Growth and New Products

Introduction

Grow or die is an immutable law of business. A company that is not focused on growth is going to have its customers stolen, technology bypassed, best employees lured away and opportunities missed. Ultimately it is going to die. There is no way to stand still in business. Even a business in trouble must find a way to grow. The problem is that companies in trouble or that are under-performing their peers, have limited resources to devote to growth. But the most serious impediment to growth may be what a company is willing to do. In this chapter we will discuss a number of strategies for growth including (i) driving customers, (ii) defining new market spaces, and (iii) new product development.

Driving Customers

A lot of businesses open their doors and expect customers to appear. This strategy might work for Wal-Mart or McDonalds, but for most companies this strategy will not work. Getting new customers is expensive. Repeat sales to existing customers are always less expensive. With new sales, a business must find a customer, let them know where the business can be found, and induce the customer to try the good or service. These are high cost activities. On the other hand, with a repeat sale, the customer has been found and knows how to contact the company, and it has already "tested" the product or service. One of the keys to repeat sales is to make sure the customer perceives the price, product, quality, and satisfaction as superior to that of competing firms.

MBNA the credit card company and America Online (AOL) are two examples of companies that built businesses through relentless target marketing. MBNA was a small regional credit card processor when it launched its affinity marketing program. With affinity marketing, an organization with a name and address list provides that list to a business in return for which the business issues organization branded merchandise and pays the organization a fee. MBNA's first affinity organization was Georgetown University and at the time of its sale to Bank of America for $35 billion,

D.E. Vance, *Corporate Restructuring*, DOI 10.1007/978-3-642-01786-5_7,
© Springer-Verlag Berlin Heidelberg 2009

MBNA had over 5,000 organizations in their affinity network including colleges and universities, the NFL, Merrill Lynch and other financial clients. MBNA harvested customers through relentless direct mail and telemarketing sales. The lessons from MBNA are to narrowly focus on specific customers, drive sales through continuous solicitation, and tap into the ego structure and identity of the customer. In the case of Georgetown alumni, affinity credit cards allowed them to tout their affiliation with one of the country's leading universities each time they made a purchase[1,2]

America Online is another excellent example of relentless marketing. AOL was just one of many internet service providers (ISPs) when it was formed in 1990. To most people, the internet was a vague, technical concept. AOL developed a simple to use front end which eliminated the need for technical knowledge. They also reduced the cost of trying the product by giving away large blocks of free service. Finally, they distributed these free offers through thousands of retailers across the country. The AOL customer based boomed and that gave them the market capitalization to merge with Time Warner, an old line media company, which gave AOL shareholders a 55% ownership of the combined company. The lessons from AOL are to make the product or service easy to use, reduce the cost of trying the product, and market, market, market.[3]

Advertising

Companies in trouble tend to be schizophrenic about advertising. Some companies think that the answer to slack sales is to throw endless amounts of money at advertising. This never works. Others slash advertising budgets when a company is in trouble. While cost reduction is generally a good thing, mindlessly cutting advertising and or other marketing expenses can be counter productive. This schizophrenia is fueled by an old adage: Half of all advertising dollars are wasted, but it is impossible to find out which half (Steinberg 2005).

As with all the restructuring issues we start with the question: Why Advertise? There are a number of reasons,

(1) To let people know about the features of your product
(2) To let people know how to find your company, store, website or 800#
(3) To educate people as to how the product can be used, and
(4) To educate people as to how it will make their life, job, or processes easier or better.

Most advertising dollars miss their mark because they focus on entertainment to the detriment of conveying information which is going to help people make a purchase decision. Information should be the main focus of advertising, entertainment is just the salt and pepper to make it taste better. So, the first principal of advertising is to design a campaign with some specific informational goals in mind.

Measure everything. The only way to know whether advertising money is well spent is if you track results. So the second principal of advertising is to design campaigns with measurement in mind. How will you know that someone is visiting your store or calling your company because of a particular ad? One way is to offer discounts based on coupons that can be traced back to particular media buys. Another way to track the return on advertising is to give discounts if customers know a particular keyword. Yet another way is to ask people how they heard about the company. This last method gives uneven results because people often base decisions on multiple sources of information. However, uneven results are better than no results and with enough data patterns will emerge.

Interpublic Group, an advertising holding company, has set up a special unit to tract the results advertisers get for their money. Some of Interpublic's rivals are also setting up performance measurement units. This performance data should help companies get a better return on their investment in advertising. However, one should never take the data at face value. Ask how it was collected, from whom, how often, and whether any data were omitted from the analysis. It's hard for people to be objective regarding their own performance. So, when an advertising agency tells you its ads are highly effective, be cautious even if they show you data (Steinberg 2005).

Traditional mass media television, radio, and print is very expensive and results are uncertain. So think about alternatives. Direct mail and telemarketing are right for some kinds of products and telemarketing, provides instant feedback. Web based marketing was once considered fringe, and is now considered mainstream.

There are a number of books and articles that provide a rich source of ideas for non-traditional marketing and advertising. Network marketing is an example of a powerful, but sometimes illusive marketing method. Some call non-traditional advertising guerrilla marketing (Levinson 1993). The bottom line is that advertising alone will never save a company although it may useful to drive revenue growth.

Understanding Customers Needs

Most of my MBA students are either corporate executives or own their own company. One of them owned a company that sold packing material for windows such as foam corners, sheets, and blocks. I asked him what he was selling and he said "foam corners, sheets and blocks." The student's business was drifting along, doing all right, but not brilliant and not growing at a competitive rate. But does anyone really want foam corners, sheets and blocks? Of course, not. They are buying protection for their product, improved quality at the point of consumption, and fewer returns and warranty claims. By better understanding customer needs he should be able to position his products more appropriately and anticipate other needs his customers might have which will increase sales.

Solving Problems

If a company thinks about its products and services from the customer's point of view, it will have a much better chance of driving break-out sales. Among the first questions it should ask is, "What problem is the customer trying to solve?" The follow on question is, "How well do our products and services solve the problem?" Once these questions are answered, the company can anticipate customer needs and place sales people and offers in front of the customer at the time and place the customer needs them which will increase the likelihood of closing a sale.

A company's products and services must also create value for a customer. Creating value involves reducing the cost to achieve the customer's goals, saving time, improving quality or improving the customer's experience.

To place oneself in the customer's point of view, one must know how customers actually use a product or service. This is not a trivial issue because customers frequently use products in surprising ways and for surprising purposes. They may use the product for a purpose never conceived of by the company. Another element of putting oneself in the customer experience is to ask how a product or service can be made simpler and easier to use. Fifty years ago, only a trained technician could operate a computer, and now 4 year olds use computers. Companies that made computers easier to use have been highly successful.

Understanding customer needs helps focus marketing because, once a company understands how, where and why its products are being used, it can focus marketing effort on times and places where a customer is likely to buy.

Value Proposition

To grow, a company must constantly look at its value proposition. At one point McDonald's invested $4–$5 billion in new stores over 4 years without any proportional increase in operating income. They stepped back from a growth model based on more stores and instead decided to focus on existing stores by improving the value in each store. They asked, "What do customers want?" The answer was more speed, tastier food, better selection, cleaner stores, friendlier service and a comfortable and inviting experience. The value proposition wasn't driven by massive capital investments but by listening to customers, improved training, new food formulations, and improved store environments. As a result of improving the value proposition McDonalds increased the number of daily customers by 4 million a day to 50 million. And with increased customer traffic, it increased profits (Adamy 2007).

Quick Response Advantage

Low overseas labor costs have decimated the American textile industry, so Abseson Mills decided to compete on customer service and quick delivery time. On average they can fill an order in 14 days down from their previous average of 28 days which is significantly better than the 10–12 weeks it takes to fill an order produced in China. They reduced turnaround time by half through the process of lean manufacturing which cuts out unnecessary steps and simplifies workflow (Holcomb 2007).

Leasing companies enjoy a competitive advantage over banks because most leasing companies can respond to a request for financing in a day or two whereas it often takes banks weeks to decide whether to fund a lease. Cannon Financial Services, Inc. has a service standard in which most leases are approved in 4 to 24 hours.

Federal Express has built a whole business model around prompt response. Organizing a company around responding to customer needs faster than the competition provides a company with an enormous competitive advantage which can help drive sales.

New Products

Customers get bored with even the best products and competitors are always improving their products. So, the company that does not innovate is going to be left behind. A Europe wide survey found the average growth rate for companies focused on product and process innovation was 9% per year as compared 3% per year for companies that were satisfied with their products and services and saw no need to innovate (Lowe 2004).

It may seem foolish to invest in new products and services when a company is in trouble. But, new product development is critical to revitalizing a company and pushing it to peak performance. Remember the first rule of business is grow or die. And new products and services are needed to grow. It is impossible to cost cut one's way to growth. Sometimes a company can improve revenue from existing products by adding new features.

Complacency Kills

Some companies do so well for a while that they get complacent. But competitors, like gravity, never sleep. In the 1990's legacy phone companies were fat and happy when people started getting second phone lines so that they could log onto the internet. Bell Labs figured out how to provide broad band service over conventional phone lines, a technology called DSL, but were complacent about bringing it to market until cable companies offered broad band internet service and people started canceling their second line. They were also late to realize that many young households were either canceling their land lines in favor of cell phones or never got a land line in the first place. One investment house estimates the number of land lines to people's homes will drop by about 8% per year. This trend will continue as Voice Over Internet Protocol (VOIP) takes hold and cell phone usage accelerates. Legacy phone companies could have blunted inroads by cable and cell phone companies if they had introduced new products in a more timely fashion (Young and Peter 2003). Instead they were complacent. This is a story repeated over and over again in every industry. Motorola was a leading cell phone manufacturer, but instead of introducing digital phones, stuck with analogue models and lost market dominance to Nokia (Young and Peter 2001).

Product Pipeline

New products are often needed to drive growth, but new products must be introduced every year, not sporadically. Nissan, introduced a range of new models in 2005 to hit its goal of increasing sales by one million units per year, but introduced no new products in 2006. As a result, 2006 sales were down 12–18% in some markets (Sapsford 2006). Pharmaceutical companies have similar problems because as patents expire, generics enter the market at substantially lower prices devastating profitability.

To offset slower growth in their core business, Cisco Systems, set up an organization to foster internal start-ups. One of the first things they did was to launch an in-house website where employees could suggest new businesses. In 3 years they got 135 substantial ideas and venture capitalists have been brought in to assess the best of them. So far, Cisco has launched three new products from this process. Their strategy is not just to get ideas for new products, but to develop a model for bringing these products to market. In this way, they plan to systematically develop a new product pipeline (White 2007).

The point is that companies should focus a substantial portion of their resources and strategic analysis on (i) filling the new product pipeline and (ii) timing the release of new products for sustainable growth. Some companies aspire to generate 20–30% of each year's revenue from new products.

Killer App.

Sometimes a company has to find a "killer app." The term "killer app." refers to an application that is so great or unique that it blows away the competition.

Staples and OfficeMax provide such a comprehensive array of office products that they eliminated much of the competition from local stationary stores. EBay is a "killer app." Its concept and execution was so great that it overwhelmed the competition and became an instant hit. Amazon.com is a killer app. Google is a killer app, but Yahoo keeps chasing it. The killer app. for Hughes Tool and Die was a roller cone drill head that enabled oil drillers to cut through hard rock (White 1980). Other examples of killer apps include Sony's Walkman and Apple's iPod. It's not easy to come up with a killer app. but it is something management should talk about and think about every day. But no killer app. can dominate a market forever, so companies must always be on the look-out for the next killer app.

New Market Spaces

An old product or service updated and introduced into a new market space can become a new product. One way to think about new products is to think small. Backhoes and front end loaders have been used in construction for four generations. But a few enterprising companies looked at this equipment, so useful on large construction jobs and said, "Can we make smaller versions of these machines for landscaping?" By placing a proven product in a new market space, a new product line and revenue source was created.

A half a century ago, computers weighed tons and filled large rooms. They were also incredibly expensive, the smallest costing the better half of a million dollars. Entrepreneurs in computer engineering saw the need for computers that medium size businesses could afford and mini-computers were born. As the mid-size market niche filled, companies started looking at micro computers which soon evolved into personal computers. Thinking large is another strategy for developing new products. Powerful electric motors, ubiquitous in everyday life, started as motors in toy trains. With a little research and imagination, one can find a number of new market niches for any product or service.

A related idea is to find new uses for old products. Kleenex was introduced in 1924 as a convenient way to remove make-up. In the 1930's it was repositioned as a as a disposable handkerchief. Now the company plans to add a combination of citric acid and sodium lauryl sulfate to tissues, kill viruses, and market them as a way to prevent the spread of colds and flu (Byron 2007). This improvement should help differentiate them in the market and command a premium price.

Thiokol was a company known for making polysulfide sealants, essentially industrial strength caulk used to seal concrete storm drains. The company noticed that the University of Utah was buying two or three barrels of sealant per month and sent a scientist to investigate. He found the University was using it as a binder for solid rocket fuel. Thiokol seized on this discovery and launched a business to make solid rocket engines for the military and eventually landed the contract for the space shuttle boosters, a multi-billion dollar business.

New products and services can come from anywhere, but if one has a systematic framework for finding new products and services, it is more likely they will be found, more quickly and at lower cost.

Complementary Goods

Complementary goods are goods which, when used with other goods increase the user's satisfaction (McConnell and Stanley 2002). Examples are bacon and eggs, peanut butter and jelly, cars and gasoline. Often a company makes or sells a product, but does not sell the complementary goods a customer requires to fill its needs.

For example, when a company contracts with a telemarketer, does it just want a company that can place phone calls, or does it want a company that can support its marketing efforts more broadly. The complementary services for telemarketing might include data mining, direct mail and measuring advertising effectiveness.

Creating and Harvesting Value

It is often the case that a company's product is one of a chain of products and services that satisfy a customer's needs. For example, suppose the customer is a saw mill. It will need saws and blades and de-barking machinery to convert raw logs to finished lumber. Suppose the mill buys saw blades from Able Company for $500 each and when they get dull, rather than buying new saw blades, the mill sends them to Baker Company for straightening and sharpening which it does for $200. The value Baker is creating is about $300 which is the difference between a new blade and a sharpened one.

Each time a blade is sharpened by Baker Company, Able Company theoretically loses a sale. Now further suppose that each blade can be sharpened five times before there is not enough left to sharpen. Able is potentially losing $2,500 in sales for five blades and Baker is making $1,000.

If Able is sophisticated about analyzing the value chain, Able will see that the customer is making logical choices about re-sharpening versus buying new blades so that behavior will not change unless Able drops the price of its blades close to $200 which may destroy its economic model.

The answer is to look at the value chain and see how Able can harvest some of the value Baker is providing. If Able is in the business of making machinery, it might design, build and sell a machine the mill can use to sharpen its own blades which will save time and transportation costs. If Able's machine costs $10,000 and can sharpen 200 blades, the customer will no longer be interested in using Baker's service since the customer can now sharpen its own blades for about $50 each. Able's machine is creating $150 of value on each blade it sharpens which is the difference between the cost of sharpening using its machine and using Baker's service. If Able were sophisticated, it might harvest for itself a greater fraction of the value it has created. Suppose it decides to split the $150 of value created evenly with its customer. To do that, the cost of each sharpening would have to rise to about $125, which is the base cost per sharpening of $50 plus half the additional value created which is $75. At a cost of $125 per sharpening and a life of 200 sharpenings, Able could charge $25,000 per sharpening machine and still create substantial value for the mill.

By examining the value chain, Able discovered that it can harvest $25,000 that would have gone to another vendor and in the process of providing this new service it can cement its relationship with its mill customer. Another alternative would be for Able to lease the machine to the mill under terms that would average about $125 per sharpened blade.

A somewhat different view of how to create and harvest value is illustrated in the case of Metal Fab, Inc. an Iowa company that makes parts for metal corn cribs, grain silos and other metal farm storage structures. The business is fairly competitive and margins are thin.

Farmers typically pay $30,000–$100,000 per structure. Metal Feb supplies metal parts (kits) to erectors that is, companies which act as general contractors, to assemble the structures. A $100,000 structure might have the following cost break down as shown in Table 7.1 Metal Fab Cost Analysis.

Table 7.1 Metal Fab Cost Analysis

Metal Fab, Inc. kit	$25,000	25%
Erector's direct labor	$60,000	60%
Misc. Erector's cost	$5,000	5%
Erector's Profit	$10,000	10%
	$100,000	100%

Erector's labor, is about $30/hours so for the above building about 2,000 hours was required. Erection is a labor intensive process because metal panels are bolted together about every 8" along their joints to give structures strength.

Suppose Metal Fab redesigns their kits so that panels could be clipped or clamped together rather than bolted. If Metal Fab reduced the erector's assembly time by 1,000 hours, the erector's cost would be reduced by $30,000. If Metal Fab split the difference with the erector, it could raise the price of its kits from $25,000 to $40,000, and the erector's total cost would still drop by $15,000. In effect, Metal Fab is increasing its customer's profitability. What do you think will happen to Metal Fab sales?

Now consider the impact of this strategy on Metal Fab. Suppose its original COGS% was 70% and COGS per kit was $17,500 (70% × $25,000) and assume the new fastener technology cost an additional $5,000 per kit. Metal Fab's old gross profit would be $7,500 ($25,000 − $17,500 Old COGS) or a gross margin of 30% ($7,500/$25,000). After redesigning its product and harvesting a share of the value created its gross profit on a kit would rise to $17,500 ($40,000 price − $17,500 Old COGS − $5,000 fasteners). And, its gross margin would rise from 30 to 44% ($17,500/$40,000.)

Another example of harvesting value comes from Seigle's Inc. In the early 1990's they were mid-sized, a home center chain in the Midwest deriving about 60% of their revenue from retail customers and about 40% from builders. They decided they couldn't compete against Home Depot and Lowes superstores and refocused on builders. They looked forward in the value chain and found that what builders really wanted was someone who would supply, install and guarantee windows, doors and roof trusses and not just dump them at the curb. They harvested the value builders would otherwise pay to their carpenters and improved their margins. They also looked back down the value chain and decided they could increase their margins if they also manufactured most of what they sold. By harvesting the value in manufacturing they again increased their margins (Bailey 2003).

Think deeply about how the customer will use the product and what it will cost him or her to prepare and use the product. Ask whether there is any way to reduce that "cost of use." If there is, that represents unharvested value to both you and the customer.

Marginal Utility

If all the economists in the world were laid end to end, no one would care. That's how dry economic theory is. However, there are a lot of useful ideas in economics if one can find them. One of these useful ideas is the concept of marginal utility.

Marginal utility is the amount of satisfaction one gets by purchasing one more unit of a good or service. This theory holds that when faced with many choices customers will try to maximize their satisfaction, more specifically maximize their satisfaction on a per dollar basis (Mankiw 2007). So a Ferrari might provide more overall satisfaction than a Mustang, but when one considers the amount of satisfaction a consumer gets per dollar, the Mustang wins almost every time. This can be verified by comparing the number of registered Ferraris to the number of registered Mustangs.

So one way to increase sales is to lower price until the utility of a certain product divided by its price is higher than the competitors. But price cutting is a losing game because there is always someone with a loose screw willing to cut price until no one can make a profit.

A better approach is to find ways to increase customer satisfaction. For example, people are busy but they have to eat. So, prepackaged and semi-prepared foods have grown in popularity and generally have higher margins than unprepared foods. Examples include canned soup as compared to making soup from raw ingredients, soup ready to heat and eat as compared to canned soup which requires adding water and mixing, and soup in a microwaveable container as compared to soup which must be removed from a can to a pot or microwavable container and then cooked. Minute rice has replaced rice which used to take a quarter of an hour to cook. Reducing the time it takes to prepare a good for use is one way to increase satisfaction. Simplifying the use of a product also increases its utility. Increased marginal utility per dollar, will drive sales by driving the selection process.

Quick Second Strategy

A quick second strategy is one in which a company identifies a product made by another company and aggressively develops and markets its own version of that product. Often companies develop a new product and don't understand what they have; don't position it correctly in the market; price it too high; or don't aggressively market the product.

The computer industry is rife with examples of a quick second strategy. Thirty years ago, home computers were considered little more than interesting toys. But, IBM saw the potential in these devices for desk top business computing and used its manufacturing and marketing muscle to dominate the personal computer business (Pollack 1983).

When personal computers first came out, a person had to be a techno-geek to navigate DOS and get the computer to do anything. Xerox pioneered point and click technology and the graphical user interface that make computers simpler to use. But, Xerox didn't quite know what to do with this new innovation. Microsoft executed a quick second strategy by rolling out point and click and graphical user interface in its Windows Operating System (Mary 2007).

Another example of a quick second strategy in computing is the development of spreadsheets. In the beginning, personal computers were not that useful for solving business problems. Software Arts developed a program called VisiCalc, the first spreadsheet program. This software enable accountants and others to record, store, analyze and print financial data without being a programmer. Successors to VisiCalc extended the idea making the software even easier to use. Lotus aggressively marketed its spreadsheet which contained more features and was somewhat easier to use (Buell 1985). That was superceded by Excel which was even more aggressively marketed by Microsoft. It is not enough to simply copy someone else's product or service. To succeed with a quick second strategy, one must improve the product or service and find or create a marketing advantage.

The lesson is that the company that invents a technology is not necessarily the one that benefits from it. This suggests two strategies. First, keep any new technology under wraps until the company is ready, willing, and able to aggressively exploit it. Second, a company should constantly scan its market space for innovative new products and services. If one is found, the company should figure out how to roll out a better version of the product to a larger market.

Time to Market

Closely related to the concept of fast second strategy is the issue of "time to market." Companies that can get to market first and dominate the market can gain a first mover advantage. First movers tend to set standards and often acquire greater name recognition than later arrivals. Sure a company could start an on-line bookstore today, but when people search for books on-line most think of Amazon.com. What about starting an on-line auction? Can you say EBay? How about writing a new PC operating system? Can you say Microsoft? So for many products and markets, getting there first and establishing a large footprint confers substantial advantages. The point is that new product development cycles must be compressed so that products, goods and services reach the market as soon as possible.

Radical Product Innovation

Should a company struggling for survival be concerned with radical product innovation? A major cause of corporate distress is a competitor that introduces a radically new product. If you don't believe that, talk to a typewriter manufacturer. The question is what factors create a fertile ground for radical product innovation.

Things that make radical innovation more likely include (i) a corporate focus on emerging technology, (ii) a willingness to cannibalize existing core competencies and markets for the new, (iii) a failure-tolerant management, (iv) a focus on customer needs that have not yet been articulated and for which there are no existing products, and (v) a long term focus (Herrmann et al. 1989).

Culture of Technology and Innovation

Radically new products or services do not arise from rocky soil. They must be nurtured. Things that nurture new product development include an on-going research and development program, rewards and incentives for innovators which includes giving credit where it is due, constantly talking about products, product quality, new innovations, and new scientific developments, a systematic program to monitor competitor innovation and real candor about that fact that competitor's products may have superior features. A routine, perhaps weekly briefing on developing technology, scientific breakthroughs, and competitor's products helps build awareness of needs and opportunities. Executive, research and development, sales and marketing and production management should be included in these briefings.

A culture of innovation also implies fault-tolerance. Not every new project is going to succeed, so management must expect a certain percent of failures. Of course, fault tolerance should be tied to prudence. No project should be so large that its failure jeopardizes the well being of the company.

Toyota, for example, has a development system based on chief engineers with real development responsibility and the authority to make decisions on their product. This should be coupled with a knowledge capture system so that everyone can learn from the experience of others throughout the company. This knowledge base reduces errors and accelerates development because the amount of "reinvention" is minimized. The result is a system that tries many approaches to a problem, then gets the best product to the customer quickly. This minimizes both engineering and production cost. This system stands in marked contract to Ford and General Motors which seem to rely on hitting home runs with every project (Womack 2006).

Customer Focus, Technology Focus, Future Customer Focus

Sometimes a company must be flexible enough to hold two conflicting thoughts in its collective mind at once. While much of marketing orthodoxy, concentrates on known needs and wants, such action is not likely to produce a radically new product.

A focus on emerging technologies may translate into products customers have never dreamed about. This can lead to problems, if, for example, engineers develop gee whiz products they like, but for which the customers see no need. RCA, for example, developed and marketed a device that could read movies off a record the size of a diner plate and display them on an ordinary television. At the time, it was a technological marvel, and RCA sold the movies to go with the movie players at about $50 or $60 each. The problem was it was introduced about the time Sony introduced the Betamax video cassette recorders which enabled people to tape movies off the air for free. The real idea behind a technology focus is not just to build what engineers want to build, but to generate a broad and robust view of emerging technologies and the products that could spring from them. Think ahead to unarticulated customer needs and wants. Ben Franklin might never demanded a phone because he never have saw one, just as Abraham Lincoln might never demanded an airplane because he never saw one. But once telephones and airplanes were introduced, customers found them indispensable.

Core Competencies and Creative Destruction

Companies should focus on and develop their core competencies. But radically new products can destroy those core competencies. RCA was a leader in producing vacuum tubes, the mainstay of electronics until the mid 1950s. However, their promotion of transistors cannibalized the vacuum tube market. This is an example of creative destruction where new technologies shove aside old technologies (McConnell and Stanley 2002). But, if RCA had continued refining their old core competency in vacuum tubes rather than embracing the transistor, they would have been pushed out of the electronic supply business altogether. Likewise, companies must be willing to sacrifice products in its old market space to radically new products. When IBM introduced its PC, it sacrificed a large portion of its mini-computer market, including the System 23, but in the end, PC sales turned out to be much greater than the System 23 could ever be (Pollack 1983). The legacy phone companies like Verizon were so intent on protecting their land line phone business they lost a significant share of the business they could have had in the cell phone market (Dillon 2003).

Independent Organization

When radically new products reach the stage where they can be commercialized, commercialization should be given to an independent organization. For if radical new products have to compete for the time and attention of management with legacy products, the organization will tend to pull punches in favor of its comfortable, core competency. In effect, core competencies can be come core rigidities (Leonard-Barton 1992).

When IBM decided to enter the personal computer market, it give its group in Boca Raton, Florida an unusual amount of freedom from its bureaucracy. One year later, the IBM PC was introduced. The cycle time from conception to market could not have been as short had IBM insisted on using its normal management organization or practices (Pollack 1983).

Innovation Limits

Developing new and innovative products for new market niches is a proven strategy for growing sales. However, there are limits to this strategy. If too many products are forced through the development pipe-line, through-put may drop to zero.

Avery, for example, had so many new products in their development pipeline that there was no slack for critical tasks. That meant that if one product took longer than anticipated to develop, every product behind it in line was delayed. Scheduling slack is especially important for creative processes such as development because break-thoroughs don't occur on a fixed schedule. New products also introduce new variables in manufacturing and distribution creating bottlenecks where none existed before. Designing slack into the development process means a company will have to critically evaluate the products in development in terms of potential sales, contribution, and product life (Anders 2007).

Sales Person and Sales Territory Management

Sales force rationalization is a polite way of talking about eliminating poor performers. All sales people, even those compensated solely on commission represent some cost to a company. There are fixed costs, such as employee benefits, but opportunity costs can be much more important. In this context, the opportunity cost is the "lost sale," that is a sale another salesperson would probably have made.

Ranking salespeople by sales is one measure of performance, but total sales doesn't provide context. Ranking can be improved if some measure is used to adjust for the size of a person's territory. For example, suppose Murray and Slim sell bar supplies. Murray's territory is Manhattan where there are 4,000 bars and Slim's territory is Phoenix/Tucson where there are 600 bars as shown in Table 7.2.

Table 7.2 Analysis of Bar Sales

Sales person	Territory	Sales	Number of Bars	Sales per Bar
Murray	Manhattan	$300,000	4,000	$75
Slim	Phoenix/Tucon	$200,000	600	$333

By ranking sales persons by sales per bar you may find that Murray is dramatically under performing his peers. If Murray were eliminated, and Slim got even 2/3 the sales per bar in Manhattan that he did in Phoenix/Tucson, sales from Manhattan territory would almost triple to $888,000 (4,000 bars × 2/3 × $333 average sales per bar.)

Most sales people are assigned territories to work. The true measure of effectiveness is not just sales, but sales per opportunity. If a territory is large a sales person might achieve high sales simply by cherry picking a few large accounts. On the other hand, a territory with too few opportunities may yield a lower than average total sales for a superior salesperson. Equation (7.1) is a measure of the effectiveness of a sales person considering the opportunities in his or her territory.

$$\text{Sales per opportunity} \quad = \text{Sales}_i / \text{Opportunities}_i \qquad (7.1)$$

Where Sales_i are the sales generated by salesperson$_i$, and Opportunities_i is the number of sales opportunities in a territory. If sales per opportunity is low, that may mean that either this is a low producing sales person who should be replaced by a better performer or that the sales territory is too large for one salesperson to exploit. If a sales territory is too large for a salesperson to properly exploit, it should be split. But if a sales person is underperforming in a normal sized territory, he or she should be replaced with an average or better sales person which will increase sales.

Consider the example of MM Software which sells physician practice management software. Sales and opportunity data by territory and sales person are given in Table 7.3. What is the potential increase in revenue if the low performer is replaced by an "average" performer and oversized territories were split? Include all sales people when computing the average.

Analyzing the data in Table 7.3 we notice a couple of things. First, three sales people Ethyl, Lucy and Curley are below average in terms of sales per opportunity. But Ethyl and Lucy have very large territories. If these territories were split, Ethyl and Lucy would still probably generate nearly the same sales, say 80% of their prior sales, but from fewer opportunities 2,000 and 2,500 respectively. That would create two territories of 2,000 and 2,500 opportunities each. If they were staffed by average sales people, they would generate about $7,137,000 of new sales (2,000 × $1,586 + 2,500 × $1,586). Offset against that would be a 20% loss by Ethyl and Lucy totaling $2,500,000 (20% × $6,000,000 + 20% × $6,500,000). This move would increase net sales by about $4,637,000 ($7,137,000 – $2,500,000).

Curley is clearly a low performer and should be replaced. If he were replaced by an average performer sales would increase by about $1,172,000 (($1,586 – $1,000) × 2,000). So by splitting oversized territories and replacing low performers with average performers, sales are potentially increased by about 20.4% in this example ($4,637,000 + $1,172,000)/$28,460,000.

Table 7.3 Sales and opportunity data

Sales person	Territory	Sales ($)	Physician practices in territory	Sales per opportunity ($)
Fred	Arkansas	4,760,000	2,800	1,700
Ethyl	Kansas	6,000,000	4,000	1,500
Lucy	East Texas	6,500,000	5,000	1,300
Ricky	West Texas	4,000,000	2,000	2,000
Moe	Missouri	3,200,000	2,000	1,600
Larry	Louisiana	2,000,000	1,000	2,000
Curley	Mississippi	2,000,000	2,000	1,000
		Average sale per opportunity $1,586		

Sales Training and Lessons from High Performers

The better trained a sales force is, the more likely it is to succeed. Analyzing sales performance is not just an exercise in eliminating low performers. It is also an exercise in identifying top performers. These individuals should be analyzed to determine why they are so successful and whether those characteristics, strategies or methods can be generalized to improve the performance of the broader sales force.

New Sales Territories

As old sales territories are exploited, attention should turn to new sales territories. But there is sometimes a temptation to add new sales territories willy-nilly before existing sales territories are fully exploited. Expansion into new territories includes considerable cost, for example finding and training sales people for the new territory, sustaining those individuals through draws or advances until sales volume reaches a level that provides adequate compensation, logistics in terms of delivering a company's product or service in the new territory and servicing the product after delivery. If the products are consumer oriented, advertising will have to be purchased in the new territory to establish brand awareness and to let people know where to find the products.

Some products must be licensed and even for those that require no licensing, each new state's tax code will have to be analyzed so the appropriate state income and sales taxes can be paid. So while expansion is good, it is less costly to fully exploit an existing territory than it is to expand into a new one.

Sales Production

Monthly sales reports are too granular to manage a company and more detailed sales reports are necessary. Some companies have daily sales reports which compare daily sales to the sales that same day one year prior. This is an excellent and sensitive way to track trends and take prompt corrective action.

While sales should be reported and tracked daily, weekly sales reports are often easier for management to use. For one thing they are more compact. For another weekly reports smooth out deviations caused when a sales person gets backed up and submits two days of sales on the same day.

Weekly sales reports are best when they report a rolling 52 weeks of sales. This also helps highlight seasonal trends. For companies with multiple products or services sales should be broken down by product or service. Current year's sales should be displayed next to prior year's sales to provide context. Deteriorating trends may indicate that competitors have improved products or changed their pricing structure and it is important to detect such changes as soon as possible.

Conclusion

A company must grow or die, and growth does not just happen. A company must find a way to drive customers to its door by offering the best products and services at a fair price. Advertising alone will not drive sales. At most it makes people aware of a product, it features and where to get its. Advertising dollars should only be spent where there is a clear way to measure whether they are effectively driving sales.

Companies should take a long hard look at customer needs. Companies ignore this analysis at their peril. Why is a customer buying a particular product? What problem is the customer trying to solve? How are they using the product? What are the features of the best products on the market? Until a company knows the answers to these questions it cannot expect to achieve superior performance.

New product development is essential for growing market share. Customers get bored with existing products and competitors always improve their products. Companies should be manic about finding a killer app. for their market, finding new market spaces to fill, improving a product's marginal utility and harvesting value created for customers by new products.

A company should aspire to generate a certain percentage of sales each year from new products. Getting products to market quickly can lead to market dominance. With a quick second strategy, a company constantly scans the market for new products and ideas and then commercializes their own version of those products with explosive force.

There are many opportunities to grow revenue through sales force management. An analysis of territories can identify those that should be split. Low sales performers should be replaced with better performers and high sales performers should be analyzed to determine whether there is something they are doing that can be replicated across the sales force. And all these activities should be closely monitored with at least weekly sales reports if not daily sales reports.

Notes

1. ___ MBNA Company Profile www.mbna.com/company_profile/first-html downloaded Aug. 31, 2005.
2. ___ Topix.net www.topix.net/com/krb downloaded Aug. 31, 2005.
3. ___ CNN Money http://money.cnn.com/2000/01/10/deals/aol_warner/ downloaded Aug. 31, 2005.

References

Adamy J (2007) How Jim Skinner flipped McDonald's. Wall St J B1 and B2, 5 Jan
Anders G (2007) How innovation can be too much of a good hing. Wall St J, B3, 11 June
Bailey J (2003) Shift in customer base transforms a company. Wall St J, B5, 6 May
Buell B (1985) The big daddy of software keep getting bigger. Bus Week Acquisitions Section. p 40, 22 Apr
Byron E (2007) Can a re-engineered Kleenex cure a brand's sniffles? Wall St J, A1 and A13, 22 Jan
Dillon N (2003) Verizon dials down 2003 profit estimates amid weak demand, Fierce Competition, Daily News. www.NYDailyNews.com. Accessed 24 Sept
Herrmann A, Oliver G, Ulrich E (1989) An empirical study of the antecedents for radical product innovations and capabilities for transformation. J Eng Technol Manag 24(1/2): 92–120
Holcomb HJ (2007) A system for succeeding. Phila Inq D1 and D3, 23 Apr

Leonard-Barton D (1992) Core capabilities and cored rigidities: a paradox in managing new product development. Strateg Manag J 13(Summer Special Issue): 111–125

Levinson J (1993) Guerrilla marketing. Houghton Mifflin, New York

Lowe P (2004) Community innovation survey. Innovation & Technology Transfer, European Commission, Enterprise DG. http://europe.eu.int/comm/dgs/enterprise/

Mankiw NG (2007) Principal of economics, 4th edn. Thompson-Southwest Publishing, Mason, OH, p 463

Mary B (2007) The history of the graphical user interface or GUI – The Apple Lisa. About, Inc., A part of The New York Times Company, http://inventors.about.com/library/weekly/aa043099.htm. Sarah Drury, 2003. " Survey of New Media," Temple University, http://isc.temple.edu/sdrury/survey/timeline.html

McConnell CR, Stanley LB (2002) Economics, 15th edn, McGraw-Hill Irwin, New York, p 45, 402

Pollack A (1983) Big IBM has done it again. New York Times. Sec.3 p 1, 27 Mar

Sapsford J (2006) As Nissan sales hit Pothole, CEO starts shifting gears. Wall St J, B1 and B5

Steinberg B (2005) Putting a value on marketing dollars. Wall St J B2, 27 July

White B (1980) Synthetic diamonds shake up the drill-bit market. Bus Week, Industrial Edition, McGraw-Hill, Energy Section, p.98, 1 Dec

White B (2007) Cisco's homegrown experiment. Wall St J, A14, 23 Jan

Womack JP (2006) Why Toyota won. Wall St J, A16, 13 Feb

Young S, Peter G (2001) Motorola is full of history, but its future looks troubled. Phila Inq, C3, 11 Mar. Motorola failed to embrace digital technology and lost market share to Nokia

Young S, Peter G (2003) How phone firms lost to cable in consumer broadband battle. Wall St J, A1 and A6, 13 Mar

Chapter 8
Markets and Pricing

Introduction

Successful restructuring means every aspect of a company's business should be re-evaluated, including pricing. Revenue is just price times volume so getting the right price is critical to growing revenue. If a company sets its price too low, it will leave profit on the table. If a company sets its price to high, it will not reach optimum sales. The relationship of price to cost drives gross margin and a company with too low a gross margin is destined to fail. Sony, which was enormously successful with its PlayStation 2, priced its PlayStation 3 about 25% higher than Microsoft's competing system the Xbox360. As a result, only half as many Playstation3s were sold as Xbox360. This difference has long term strategic impact. More system sales mean more game sales. More system sales mean a larger installed base to migrate to the next generation product and a larger installed base means greater economies of scale (Wingfield, 2007).

Pricing is a major source of profit improvement. Even companies that have optimized their manufacturing and distribution processes (Stasz, 2003) often fail to properly execute a pricing strategy (Wood, 2006). Pricing is as much art as science. But, there are a number of approaches that have proven useful. No one approach is right in every case, and at every time. But, the more one knows about pricing, the more sophisticated pricing strategy can be.

Pricing decisions are complicated by the fact that the optimum price for a product changes over its lifetime, with the level of competition, and with a product's target market. This chapter discusses major approaches to pricing as well as the strengths and weaknesses of each. Those approaches include cost centered pricing, market centered pricing, engineered cost, price elasticity, product life cycle, opportunistic pricing, micro economic pricing and touches on the theory of brands.

Cost Centered Pricing

Cost centered pricing uses full absorption cost to determine price. There are two ways to use cost centered pricing. The first is mark-up, the second is

D.E. Vance, *Corporate Restructuring*, DOI 10.1007/978-3-642-01786-5_8,
© Springer-Verlag Berlin Heidelberg 2009

gross margin. With mark-up pricing, price is set at cost plus some percent as shown in Eq. (8.1).

$$
\begin{aligned}
\text{Price} &= (\text{Cost} + \text{Mark-up} \times \text{Cost}) \\
&= (1 + \text{Mark-up}) \times \text{Cost}
\end{aligned} \tag{8.1}
$$

For example, suppose a product costs \$4.00 and the mark-up is 70%, the price is:

$$
\begin{aligned}
\text{Price} &= (1 + 70\%) \times \$4.00 \\
&= \$6.80
\end{aligned}
$$

With Gross Margin pricing, management sets a target gross margin and prices products accordingly. Starting with the equation for unit gross margin (8.2), one can use algebra to find price as a function of target gross margin and cost as shown in Eq. (8.3).

$$
\text{Gross Margin} = \frac{\text{Price} - \text{Cost}}{\text{Price}} \tag{8.2}
$$

$$
\text{Price} = \frac{\text{Cost}}{(1 - \text{Gross Margin})} \tag{8.3}
$$

For example, suppose management has a target gross margin of 40% and the product costs \$4.00 then the price is

$$
\begin{aligned}
\text{Price} &= \frac{\$4.00}{(1 - 40\%)} \\
&= \$6.67
\end{aligned}
$$

The virtue of the mark-up method is its simplicity. The virtue of the gross margin method is that it automatically incorporates the gross margin goal needed for restructuring. The chapter on reverse engineering discusses the importance of adequate gross margin.

The disadvantage of both of these methods is that customers do not care about a company's cost. They are interested in the best price they can get. If the cost centered price is less than what customers are willing to pay, the company is leaving profit on the table. But, if cost centered price is too high, customers will not buy.

Cost is a function of volume and volume is a function of price. So a more sophisticated analysis of cost centered pricing would consider how cost will change in response to volume and the price needed to maintain gross margin at each volume level (Stasz, 2003).

Market Centered Pricing

Market centered pricing holds that internal costs are largely irrelevant to price setting, assuming of course that there is some profit in a product. Market Centered Pricing usually focuses on two factors

(1) The price of similar products in the relevant market place. Relevant market place is defined as the geographic area or distribution system in which the customer is likely to shop.
(2) The measure of value. For many products, there are dimensions along which products are compared: horsepower, CPU speed, bandwidth, production capacity, etc. A machine which costs twice as much as another one might be a bargain if it produces three times the output of the lower priced machine.

Market centered pricing requires on-going intelligence about the prices charged by competitors as well as a measure of value among competing products.

Engineered Cost

Engineered cost is a strategy in which a product's probable, or target market price is established prior to a product's final design. Given the target price, product features, and the forecast sales volume, the engineering team attempts to design a product and related production methods which will deliver the product at a cost which maintains the company's target profit margin.

For example, suppose market research indicates that the price of a high definition 60" flat panel television when the product reaches the market will be $1,000. Suppose further that the company's strategic plan calls for a target gross margin of 40%. If Gross Margin is 40%, then the Cost of Goods must be 60% because Gross Margin and COGS% must equal 100%. That means the full absorption cost of the product can only be: $600 ($1,000 × 60%).

The research, engineering, and production departments will continue to re-design the television until it can meet cost projections. If it can not meet cost projections, the product will not be introduced.

Pricing decay is a reality for most consumer and many industrial products. Price decay occurs when competition drives prices down. The rate of price decay is often predictable. If one projects prices 6, 12 or 18 months into the future, one can use an engineered cost strategy to forecast how production costs must decline to preserve margins. This enables companies to be proactive rather than re-active.

Price Elasticity

Price elasticity of demand deals with the effect of price changes on total revenue. Economics tells us that when price rises, less is sold. On the other hand, when price is reduced, more is sold. The question addressed by Price Elasticity is: What happens to total revenue?

If price is elastic, reducing price a little, dramatically increases the number of units sold and total revenue increases. However, if price is inelastic, a few more units will be sold, but not enough to make up for the price reduction on the units that would have been sold anyway, so reducing price reduces total revenue.

If price is elastic, increasing price reduces the number of units sold so much that total revenue declines. However, if price is inelastic, increasing price reduces the number of units sold a little, but total revenue goes up.

What makes a product's price elastic or inelastic? Generally, if there are a many close substitutes for a product, its price is elastic. This is another way of saying that customers are very sensitive to price. However, if there are few close substitutes for a product, its price tends to be inelastic.

Examples of inelastic goods include Porsche and ground breaking prescription drugs because there are few close substitutes. Examples of items with elastic price demand include compact cars and aspirin because many companies make similar products.

One take away lesson is to know whether the price elasticity of demand is elastic or inelastic. If demand is elastic, consider cutting price and grabbing more market share. However, if price is inelastic, raise prices and increase total revenue.

Another take away lesson is that it is very important to shift the perception of a product from elastic to inelastic. The more unique one can make one's product, the fewer substitutes there will be and the more inelastic its pricing will become.

Optimizing Gross Profit Versus Optimizing Revenue

Maximizing sales is not the same as maximizing profits. As long as demand is elastic, cutting price will increase revenue. But, this must be balanced against the effect of price cutting on gross margin as shown in Eq. (8.4).

$$\text{Gross margin} = \frac{\text{Sales} - \text{Cost of Goods Sold}}{\text{Sales}} \qquad (8.4)$$

Substituting price (P) times units (U) for sales and unit cost (C) times units (U) for Cost of Goods Sold yield Eq. (8.5). And with a little algebra, U can be factored out to give Eq. (8.6).

$$\text{Gross margin} = \frac{P \times U - C \times U}{P \times U} \qquad (8.5)$$

$$\text{Gross margin} = \frac{P - C}{P} \qquad (8.6)$$

In the case of elastic demand, reducing price increases sales, but reducing price eventually drives gross margin to zero and then negative. So a company with elastic demand can only pursue the strategy of price cutting so far. How far is a function of sales and marketing costs, other overhead, and financing costs. See chapter on reverse engineering.

What if price is inelastic? If price is inelastic, raising price will reduce the units sold somewhat, but overall revenue will rise because of the higher price on the units that were sold. Raising price will also increase gross margin as shown in Eq. (8.6) because price is increasing while cost remains the same. In addition, raising price causes fewer units to be sold, and the cost associated with those units vanishes. More revenue and less cost sounds pretty good. Making a company's products desirable and unique will increase their inelasticity which will permit a price raising strategy.

Product Life Cycle

Most products have a life cycle which affects price. Generally, there are four phases to a product life cycle (Byrnes and Gerald, 1995).

Introduction

During the introduction phase, the product is new; price is usually high; there is a scarcity of suppliers; and not all uses for the product have been identified. It is purchased by early adopters. Price is relatively inelastic because of lack of competition and the indifference of early adopters to price (Rogers, 1983).

Growth

During the growth phase customers become aware of the product and its features; there is a general acceptance of the product category; there is often a fight to determine who will set industry standards; demand may exceed productive capacity; and the product can command a premium price. Price is still somewhat inelastic.

Maturity

In the maturity phase, many companies bring capacity on-line; products become standardized; consumers identify key value features; and competitive pricing begins in earnest. Price flexibility is limited. Price becomes elastic.

Decline

In decline, the product has become standardized; the industry consolidates and is dominated by a few large companies; high quality and many features are demanded; low price producers fight for market share; non-low cost producers are driven from the market. Customers become very price sensitive. Price becomes highly elastic.

Length of Product Life Cycle

Different products have different life cycles. Fashion items and some toys have a short life cycle. For example, "Tickle Me Elmo" which was a stuffed, fuzzy doll that laughed when prompted, had a life cycle of a few months. Other toys, such as Barbie Dolls or GI Joe, have very long life cycles. Personal computers went from the hobby-experimentalist phase in the 1970's when computers were often sold as electronic kits, to a mature, commodity product in 30 years. Analog cell phones gave way to digital cell phones in a quarter that time. The product life cycle of every product is different and the trend is toward shorter product life cycles. On the other hand, products are sometimes "reinvented," and reinvention pushes products toward the beginning of their life cycle. For example cars were reinvented as trucks, station wagons, luxury cars, sports cars, compact cars, sport utility vehicles and hybrids. Hybrid cars are near the beginning of their product life cycle, probably in the growth phase, and command premium prices over their non-hybrid equivalents.

Pricing Implications of the Product Life Cycle

Pricing strategy should change over the course of a product's life. Recognize when prices are inelastic and maximize price and gross margin during those times. Eventually price competition is going to squeeze prices and profit margins, so plan to engineer costs downward as the product matures (Balachander and Kannan, 1998). The life cycle of a product can be manipulated to a certain extent. If the product is "re-invented," that is, if the product or its features are changed enough so the market perceives it as a "new," it can be shifted toward the beginning of its product life cycle (Parker, 1992).

Opportunistic Pricing

Sometimes a company is tempted to cut price to close a particular deal. Boeing, for example has a published list price for its aircraft, but one would be hard pressed to find any airline in the world that actually pays the published price. On the other hand, it has a target price which it tries to get on every sale.

A problem with selling below one's target price is that it sets customers price expectations unrealistically low. Once customers have purchased at a low price they will expect that low price going forward. Information about a low price offered to one customer often leaks to other customers creating expectations that the low price is really the fair price. Once price expectations are set low, it is very hard to raise them.

Never sell for less than variable costs because each such sale creates negative cash flow to the extent of the difference between price and variable costs. There are three instances when opportunistic pricing, that is pricing below targets can be productive (i) when the product offered is so different from regular products that it will not change price expectations, (ii) when there is a drive for the dominant market share, and dominance brings with it some competitive advantage, for example the ability to set standards which can be leveraged into future price increases, and (iii) when the sale is made to someone who is not a regular customer and there is no chance they will re-sell to a regular customer. Equation (8.7) provides a way to set a target price.

$$\text{Contract price} = \text{Variable cost} \times \text{Units} + \text{Special engineering} + \text{Target profit} \quad (8.7)$$

Where contract price is the price to be charged for the contract, variable cost includes all variable costs from manufacturing and commissions to variable administrative costs, units is the number of units to be sold pursuant to the contract, and special engineering is any special engineering that is related to this particular contract. This equation assumes that there is adequate plant capacity so fixed costs will not be increased by accepting this order.

For example, suppose Sally Aircraft manufactures carbon fiber airplanes with a variable cost of $40,000, and fixed costs of $20,000. She sells them for $125,000 each. The Belarus Air Defense Command wishes to order 20 planes for surveillance. The plane's cargo door will have to be enlarged to accommodate equipment and the engineering modification will cost $15,000. Variable costs will not change. Sally needs a contribution on this contract of $1,000,000. What should the price be?

$$\text{Contract price} = \$40,000 \times 20 + \$15,000 + \$1,000,000$$
$$= \$1,815,000$$

While this is less than Sally's target price of $2,500,000 (20 × $125,000) it might be worthwhile to accept the order because it will increase plant utilization and is unlikely to undermine the price expectations of other customers.

Microeconomic Pricing

If all the economists in the world were laid end to end, no one would care. Anyone who has read an economics book knows why it is called the dismal science. Never the less, microeconomics provides some useful insights into pricing strategy.

Demand, Supply, and the Market Clearing Price

Demand is the quantity of a good or service customers are willing to buy at any given price. As a general rule, the higher the price, the less customers are willing to buy. Conversely, the lower the price the more customers are willing to buy. The principal reason is the substitution effect. As price rises, customers find more economical substitutes for the good being offered. As price drops, customers substitute the good in question for more expensive goods and buy more of it (McConnell and Stanley, 2005). The quantity of a good customers demand has nothing to do with

Fig. 8.1 Supply and demand curve

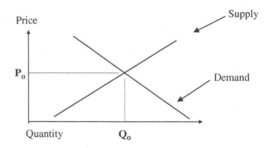

the company's cost of producing that good. Demand can be graphed as a line that slopes down and to the right as shown in Fig. 8.1.

Supply is the quantity of a good that producers are willing to supply at any given price. As a general rule the higher the price, the more suppliers are willing to produce. This makes sense intuitively because high prices provide a strong incentive for suppliers to bring more production on line. Conversely, the lower the price, the less suppliers are willing to produce. Supply can be plotted as a line that slopes up and to the right as shown in Fig. 8.1.

The point at which the Demand and Supply curves intersect is called the market clearing price. At that price point, the quantity people are willing to supply, exactly matches the amount people are willing to buy. Supply and demand are said to be in equilibrium. The quantity is Q_0 is the equilibrium quantity and the price P_0 is the equilibrium price as shown in Fig. 8.1. P_0 is called the market clearing price.

Supply and demand curves are not set in concrete. If, for example the Demand curve shifted to the right, it would intersect the supply curve higher up. That would mean a new market clearing price would be higher than the old market clearing price. One of the key strategies for shifting the demand curve to the right is to increase the perception of a product's value, utility, uniqueness or prestige. This can be done by improving the product, adding features, increasing reliability, improving the design and sometimes by creating an aura around the product through advertising.

Surpluses and Shortages

What happens if a price is set too high? See Fig. 8.2. If price is too high, say P_1, people will only purchase Q_1 units, because, by definition, the Demand Curve is the quantity people will buy at any given price. Of course at price P_1, a company will want to produce Q_2 units giving rise to a surplus (inventory overstock) equal to $Q_2 - Q_1$.

The opposite of a surplus is a shortage. See Fig. 8.3. if price is set below equilibrium, say, P_2, then buyers will demand Q_2 units, whereas suppliers will only want to

Fig. 8.2 Surplus

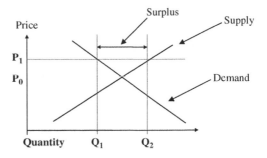

Fig. 8.3 Shortages

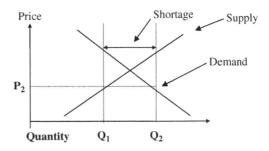

produce Q_1 units. This will create a shortage of $Q_2- Q_1$ Fig. 8.3. This is why price controls often result in shortages.

Price Implications of Surpluses, Shortages and Equilibrium Price

Chronic, inventory overstocks are a signal that price is too high. It is always less expensive to reduce production and sell all goods, than to keep production volume high and retain surplus inventory. The reasons are that (i) inventory ties up working capital, (ii) carrying charges such as warehousing, insurance, interest and inventory taxes erode profit margins, (iii) goods in storage frequently deteriorate from age, accident or inadvertence, and (iv) there is the risk of obsolescence. On the other hand, chronic shortages signal an opportunity to raise price.

Product Differentiation

An interesting feature of supply and demand is the unity of price. For most products, a market clearing price is set where supply equals demand, but look at the graph in Fig. 8.4, closely. Customers at C_4 are willing to pay more than the market clearing price P_0. There are customers at C_3 willing to pay more than customers at C_4, and

Fig. 8.4 Consumer surplus

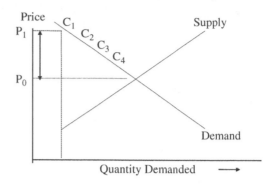

Fig. 8.5 Segregation of
customers along demand
curves

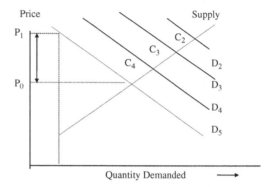

customers at C_2 are willing to pay more those at C_3. Since customers at C_1 are
willing to pay price P_1, but only have to pay price P_0, the product looks like a bargain
to them. The difference between P_1 and P_0 is called consumer surplus (Mankiw,
2007).

The difference between the market clearing price and the price particular customers are willing to pay is pure profit. Wouldn't it be great to harvest that profit by
charging every customer exactly what he, she or it was willing to pay?

If we sort customers into groups, and keep them from buying and selling across
groups, we can generate a set of demand curves which will cross the supply curve
at different points. This is a good approximation of charging each customer exactly
what he, she or it is willing to pay.

Figure 8.5 is illustrative. Those who shop at Neiman Marcus might be on demand
curve D_2, which intersects the supply curve close to the price they are willing to pay.
Those who shop at Macy's might be on the demand curve D_3 which will intersect
the supply curve near C_3. And Wal-Mart customers might be on demand curve D_5
which will intersects the supply curve near the market clearing price.

By positioning goods in different channels of distribution, packaging them differently, changing a few modest features, or giving them different brand names, a
company can segment its customers into different demand curves and charge each

near what they are willing to pay. For example, pharmaceutical companies sell the same medicine for premium prices in the US, lower prices in Canada, and sometimes very low prices in Africa and South America.

Brands

Brands and brand management are important and complex topics; far too broad to be treated comprehensively in this text. So the objective is not to make one an expert in brands, just to give one an appreciation of why brands work.

Supply and demand analysis assumes consumers have prefect information. But information is expensive, both in terms of the dollar cost of acquiring information and the time it takes to find information. As a result, few buyers get perfect information. Rational ignorance balances the cost of incremental information against its value in terms of a better purchasing decision (Byrnes and Gerald, 1995, p. 477).

One way for purchasers to reduce the amount of information they need is to purchase goods with a reputation for quality and value. The symbol of that quality/value combination is embodied in a brand name. Campbell Soup, IBM, Toyota, McDonald's are all brand names with which purchasers associate a tremendous amount of information.

Many marketing studies indicate that purchasers want a sense of safety more than anything. Brands provide that sense of safety. In doing so, they increase perceptions of product value, and therefore shift the demand curve to the right. That gives rise to a higher equilibrium prices for branded goods, assuming the brand has a favorable image.

Market

Companies sell into one of four basic types of markets and each has implications for growth, pricing and profitability. These markets are (i) pure competition, (ii) monopoly, (iii) oligopoly and (iv) monopolistic competition. Of course there are shades of gray between these markets.

Pure Competition

Pure competition is characterized by many buyers and sellers, selling products that are functional equivalents of each other. As a result, companies lose control over price. Customers have many choices among equivalent products; and a company that raises its price will find sales dropping rapidly because customers can get essentially the same goods elsewhere. Intense competition also puts downward pressure on price. Demand is highly elastic. So a key strategy for a company in pure competition is to relentlessly cut costs and cut them faster than competitive prices are falling.

Monopoly

At the other end of the spectrum is a pure monopoly. In a monopoly, there is usually only one supplier of a good, although the government defines a monopoly as anyone who so dominates a market that it can dictate price and quantity sold (Glass, 1999). Not all monopolies are prosecuted by the government. Many are endorsed by the government, for example water and sewer companies, and electric power distribution companies.

By definition there are no close substitutes when a company has a monopoly. Demand tends to be inelastic. A key strategy for monopolies is to look for technologies that threaten to undermine the monopoly. As threats emerge, a monopoly can enter that threat space, for example, after considerable hesitation, Verizon entered the cell phone market. Comcast fought back against the rise of satellite television by offering cable modems and voice over internet protocol services. Companies often get into trouble because they do not see a threat coming. No monopoly lasts forever.

Oligopoly

An oligopoly exists when a few large firms dominate a market. One characteristic of an oligopoly is that pricing and product decisions tend to move in near-lock step as each pricing or product decision is met with a counter move by other members of the oligopoly. Profits can be superior to those in pure competition because of barriers to entry like regulation, high start up costs, or a minimum size to reach economies of scale. However, in many oligopolistic industries price wars and overcapacity becomes ruinous.

To the extent that companies copy each others products, they tend to be close substitutes for one another. The only thing that keeps them from facing the ravages of pure competition is that each of the oligopolists has enough market power to influence supply. And since oligolopolists tend to monitor and mimic each others actions, they tend to raise and lower prices together. Improving the financial performance of an oligopoly depends on lowering costs; finding a way to differentiate ones product; and responding appropriately to the other companies in its market.

Monopolistic Competition

Monopolistic competition occurs where a company has many competitors, but the products are not all close substitutes for one another. Because products are not close substitutes each company will have a demand curve that is slightly different from its competitors. The strategy for a company in monopolistic competition is to differentiate its products in the market by continuously developing new products. To the extent they can make their products desirable and unique, they can create inelastic demand which gives price flexibility. The strategy for companies that are in pure competition as well as companies that are oligopolies is to reposition their products into the monopolistic competition market space.

Price Analysis

Every dollar a company can raise price without raising costs or losing customers is a dollar of pure profit. So, how can we apply pricing theory? Across the board price increases are difficult to get to stick unless all competitors adopt them. In addition, across the board price increases may result in loss of sales volume. A niche marketing strategy for pricing is more effective and will have minimal impact on volume.

Competitive Analysis

The best way to get started is to go through a candid and brutally honest evaluation of a company's products as compared to competitor's products. Table 8.1 provides a format for data collection. Starting with high volume, high profit products, a company's entire product line should be evaluated. Even if a company has thousands of products (SKUs) such an analysis should only take 3 or 4 weeks.

As a result of this analysis, one might find the market price of some products is so low that they are either losing money or the gross margin is so thin they should be discontinued to free up working capital. One might find products are under priced compared to the market and prices can be raised.

The competitive analysis might identify price points above which customer resistance increases dramatically. For example, if consumers resist paying more than $4 a box for breakfast cereal, one might price below that price point, but reduce the weight of the box to cut costs and maintain gross margin. Coffee and candy companies have been using this strategy for years.

A company might find it has products that are unique in formulation, design, capacity, or availability. Uniqueness means prices are probably inelastic so increasing price will increase overall revenue. The more unique the product, the greater the opportunity to increase price.

Slow moving inventory may mean a product is obsolete and should be discontinued. On the other hand, slow moving inventory may mean that there are few buyers but those buyers are willing to pay a premium for a product when needed. Marvin Davis, a legendry turnaround consultant, identified some items at an auto parts client where it was able to increase prices by 1,000%. Davis also contends that

Table 8.1 Pricing analysis

	Product/SKU	Cost	Advantages	Disadvantages	List price	Freight	Discounts	Other	Net price
Company									
Competitor A									
Competitor B									
Competitor C									
Company	Product/SKU	Cost	Advantages	Disadvantages	List price	Freight	Discounts	Other	Net price
Competitor A									
Competitor B									
Competitor C									
Company	Product/SKU	Cost	Advantages	Disadvantages	List price	Freight	Discounts	Other	Net price
Competitor A									
Competitor B									
Competitor C									

he has never had a client where he couldn't engineer some kind of price increase without losing sales volume (Davis, 2008).

Price Panels

Inevitably sales people will object to raising price. Price panels can be used to determine whether their objections are well founded. Lay out the company's products a few at a time, with no prices attached, and then have employees estimate the market value of each item. For example, six to eight employees might evaluate ten to twenty items at a time. Mean and median prices, computed after throwing out the high and low estimates should provide a good estimate of where prices ought to be (Davis, 2008).

Conclusion

Pricing strategy is an important element in restructuring a company. Every dollar that can be raised through price increases without losing sales volume is a dollar of profit.

Prices based solely on cost may be too high for the market which means lost sales or they maybe too low which means lost profits. Factors such as the price elasticity of demand help inform decisions as to whether prices should be raised or lowered to increase revenue and profits. The stage in a product's life cycle is a factor in selecting the appropriate price and cost strategy as is the type of market a company is in.

Microeconomics helps explain price effects and helps anticipate consequences of various price strategies. For example, surpluses tend to indicate produces are overpriced whereas shortages tend to indicate an opportunity to raise price. Micro economics also provides insight into the reason for segmenting the market and the appropriate pricing strategy for each segment.

A candid and brutally honest analysis of a company's products and prices can help identify products that should be discontinued as well as niches where products can be re-positioned, re-packaged or re-priced to increase revenue.

Since revenue is simply price times unit sales having the appropriate price strategy at the right time, for the right product, in the right market is an important key to success.

References

Balachander S, Kannan S (1998) Modifying customer expectations of price decreases for a durable product. Manage Sci 44(6) 776–786, June

Byrnes RT, Gerald WS (1995) Economics, 6th edn. Harper Collins College Publishers, New York, pp 448–487

Davis M (2008) Take no prisoners. American Management Association, New York, pp 35–45
Glass AJ (1999) Government demands microsoft be punished. Austin American-Statesman, 9 Dec
Mankiw GN (2007) Principals of economics, 4th edn. Thompson South Western, Mason, OH, pp 138–143
McConnell CR, Stanley LB (2005) Economics principals, problems and policies, 16th edn. McGraw-Hill Irwin, New York, pp 41, 373, 379
Parker PM (1992) Price elasticity dynamics over the adoption life cycle. J Mark Res 29, 358–367, Aug
Rogers EM (1983) Diffusion of innovations, 3rd edn. The Free Press, New York, p 248
Stasz JF (2003) Integration strategy: key to margin management. Financ Exec 44–48, July–Aug
Wingfield N (2007) Sony cuts playstation3 price to lift sales. Wall St J B4, 9 July
Wood A (2006) Achieving excellence. Chem Week p 5, 15 Nov

Chapter 9
Customer Service and Relationships

Introduction

Whether a company sells brilliant technological gadgets or is a simple retailer, customer service should be a key strategy focus. Without customers, a company has no sales, no profits and serves no purpose. Failure to focus on customer service is a hallmark of underperforming companies. It's not enough for a company to proclaim it is customer focused, it must be customer focused every day.

When a company gets a customer, it must do everything possible to close the sale, and provide enough value so the customer keeps coming back. Some companies fail because they focus on closing the current sale and not how the customer's experience will lead to the next sale.

In this chapter we will discuss the relationship between customer service, understanding customer needs at a deep level, and customer identification and tracking. We will also discuss firing customers.

Customer Service

Every contact with a customer should be a wow experience. Elements of a wow experience include prompt attention, a friendly demeanor, employees who know what they are doing and how to do it, advice and alternatives when asked, timely follow up calls, prompt delivery of goods and services, goods and services that meet customers needs, addressing customers by name and attention to details. There is nothing magic about good customer service, but it has a magical effect on a company's reputation and repeat sales. Unfortunately, few companies take the time to select, train and motivate employees to provide such wow service.

A nationally known pancake house opened in my area and my wife and I were anxious to try it. We waited 45 min to be seated although we could see half a dozen empty tables; it took another 25 min to get menus and another 20 min before we got up to leave. Only then did someone appear to take our order.

The management running this particular store didn't understand that customers wanted a relaxed place to have a good meal at a fair price. Instead, they provided an

D.E. Vance, *Corporate Restructuring*, DOI 10.1007/978-3-642-01786-5_9,
© Springer-Verlag Berlin Heidelberg 2009

experience that was frustrating and fatiguing. In the hour and a half we were there, we didn't see one employee over eighteen. While young workers can be excellent, they require a highly structured and supervised environment. Management fell down because it didn't put experienced workers in the store for the first few months to coach and train the young people it hired. Those who tried the restaurant were so disappointed by the service they never came back. The restaurant closed within a few months.

In contrast, Modell's, a sporting goods store, had thirty experienced sales people from other area stores deployed in a space of about ten thousand square feet when it opened. As a result, shopping was a wonderful experience. There were plenty of people to explain where to find things, how equipment worked and to provide other information. Modell's business boomed.

Business is about chasing customers, not chasing them away. To take the pressure off shoppers at Planet Honda in Union, New Jersey, the receptionist issues those who want it a "Just Looking" badge that tells sales people to back off. The owner of Planet says the magic happens when the customers take off the "Just Looking" badge. He claims sales have tripled since instituting this no pressure device (Kaihla et al. 2006).

So why don't companies focus on their customers? Leadership comes from the top and if executives don't value customer service no one else in the organization will. While it may be possible to reorient management to focus on customers, there might not be enough time to re-train everyone and selective personnel changes may be needed to jump start the process.

Responsiveness is an important aspect of customer service. Several years ago, there was a controversy about the roll-over hazard of Ford Explorers equipped with Firestone tires. Each company blamed the other, but in the final analysis, the public decided the fault lay primarily with Firestone and their sales plummeted. This of course created an opportunity for Goodyear to capture a significant share of Firestone's market. The owner of the Topline Tire and Auto Center in Brookville, Florida, sold Goodyear tires but said Goodyear never sent more than half the tires he ordered. It also took months for Goodyear to mount a sign on his store. "They just seemed to get caught up in their big-company bureaucracy."

Eventually, every window of opportunity closes and it closed for Topline when a Wal-Mart across the street started selling Goodyear tires at a deep discount. But the window of opportunity for Goodyear closed as well. In a year, the public had largely forgotten the problems with Firestone and Topline switched to selling Firestone tires. And Firestone was responsive; delivering tires as needed and providing the needed sign within a week.

Goodyear's lack of customer service cost it a high margin customer, Topline, which it replaced with a low margin customer, Wal-Mart. Apparently, customer service problems have been replicated nationally and Goodyear lost 2.4% of its market share when it should have been gaining 5 or 6% (Timothy 2003).

The way customer complaints are handled can have an impact on sales as well. For 10 years I was a loyal customer of a certain cottage cheese. But in the last 2 months, the top third of every container has had a milky white fluid in it instead of cottage cheese I was paying for. I called the customer service to let them know of the problem. The person answering the phone said, "It's supposed to be that way." as means of blowing me off. While I wanted to let them know about an operational problem, they wanted to tell me, the customer, that I didn't understand the Zen of cottage cheese. My response of course was that if that's the way it was supposed to be, then no customer should ever buy their product again.

Several lessons can be distilled from these situations (i) understand at a deep level, what customers are looking for, and give it to them. Customers rarely just buy a product; they are paying for an experience and service, (ii) when a customer asks for products to sell, move heaven and earth to get them product, (iii) when a customer offers to advertise your brand with posters or signs get them the advertising material they need, and (iv) make every contact with the customer a great experience; a Wow! experience.

What do customers hate? Inattentive clerks, sales people, waiters and waitresses that are hard to find or act as though they are avoiding customers, rude, indifferent and unknowledgeable employees, those who are condescending, those who hover or give unwanted attention, fail to return phone calls or are inflexible.

What do customers want? Courteous employees who act like they are glad to see you, who are polite and helpful, but not pushy, who know their products and where to find them, who can provide useful information to customers trying to decide among products, employees who empathize with customer problems, a no hassle return policy and warranties.

Expectations are so low that customers who get good service are bowled over by it. They become loyal customers and just as important, they tell their friends and family of their good experience. Of course the flip side is that when a customer gets bad service, the company not only loses that customer, but the company will get a bad reputation among the customer's friends and family (Smith 2006).

Holistic Approach to Customer Service

Customer service isn't just getting customer facing employees to be polite and return phone calls. A company must think of customer service in a holistic way, that is to say, the whole company, its operations, systems, website, phone system, order taking, delivery, set-up, and post sale service must all work together to create a great customer experience. If a company does 90% of everything right and 10% wrong, the customer will get the impression the company doesn't care about him or her.

So what is the action plan? Top management must make customer service a central theme and repeat that theme over and over again until it becomes ingrained in the company's culture. Employees must be trained to do their jobs efficiently as well as courteously. Customers should be involved in improving customer service. For example, customers should be involved in website design.

Many customers prefer to call companies rather than using websites or mail. Ask customers how phone queries can be made more efficient. Constantly collect customer feedback in the form of surveys and simply talking to customers. Finally, empower employees to solve customer problems. Empowering employees to fix problems builds employee morale as well as customer loyalty (Rosenberg 2005).

Building a business around customer service might seem like it runs counter to cost control and other strategies discussed in this book but it isn't. Good customer service drives sales and everything flows from sales.

Customer Relations

Customer relations is not about making a sale, it's about making the next sale and the one after that and the one after that. It is about building customer loyalty. Customer loyalty has to be a two way street. The company that treats customers as strangers and focuses solely on maximizing profits will have no customer loyalty. It will signal its customers that they better price shop to make sure they are getting a good deal. On the other hand, the company that makes its customers feel safe and comfortable and that is easy to do business with will build customer loyalty. There is no better example of this than Commerce Bank, a South Jersey Bank started by Vernon Hill.

Where most banks nickel and dime customers with fees for checking, ATMs and other services, Commerce provided free checking, free ATM, free pens and other free services like coin-counting machines for children of all ages. Commerce made it easy to do business with them by providing extended hours and being open 7 days a week. It also has highly trained employees who can quickly complete any transaction. Commerce also staffs its branches so that waits are minimal. Commerce Bank customers are extremely loyal because the bank has made its business developing relationships with people rather than focusing on selling products and charging fees. As a result Commerce has had one of the highest deposit growth rates in the nation (Brubaker 2007a, b).[1,2]

Responsiveness

One of the key elements in customer service is responsiveness. Few things frustrate customers like delay and delay often opens the window for competitors. For example, one major bank sent me a "pre-approved" credit card. I filled out the form and sent it back, but got neither the card nor acknowledgement for 3 weeks. When I made a follow-up call I spoke to six bank representatives all of whom asked the same questions and none of whom could provide any answers other than "we get 30 days to approve new credit cards." While on hold for representative number six I logged onto my credit union's website, applied for a credit card and received it in 48 hours. The bank's credit card arrived weeks later and I promptly canceled it.

There are number of things that can be done to improve customer response, for example, elimination and simplifications of tasks needed to service customers. Middle management by its very nature tends to elaborate processes which delays problem resolution. Flatter organizations, with less middle management, improve response time which improves customer service. Cross training employees to do several jobs can eliminate bottle necks that slow response time (Denton 1995). Responsiveness will also improve if employees know they are being measured on their performance.

Customer Service Training

Another key to good customer service is training. If everyone knows what they are supposed to do, and how they are to do it, the customer experience will be smooth. But if employees bumble through a customer encounter, enter the wrong order codes, fail to follow through on customer requests or generally do not understand the importance of customer service, the customer will have a bad experience.

At Commerce Bank every employee knows exactly what to do. This is no accident. Commerce Bank has invested heavily in training, running its own Commerce University.

Not so long ago, my wife decided to split her money between two banks. She bought a CD at Commerce Bank and it took less than 10 min. We went to another bank, the largest in the Philadelphia region and it took over an hour for her to get an equivalent CD even though she was the only customer. Who do you think customers will migrate to? (Wachovia Corporation, 2008).

Customer Tracking System

Making an initial sale to a customer is costly. A company must find the customer or customers must find it. This may involve advertising, sales calls, internet searches, direct mail or other means, all of which are expensive. Then the customer must determine whether the company has the goods or services, selection and quality which meet his, her or its needs. The customer must determine whether the company offers an appropriate price-value combination. Finally, the customer must have confidence that the company can perform.

Some believe that it takes five in-person sales calls on average to land a new customer for a commercial or industrial sale. Whether it is seven sales calls or three it is rare in any industry for every call to result in a sale. There is also an oft cited statistic that it is five times more expensive to find and sell to a new customer than it is to sell to an existing customer.

A repeat sale is easier to make than a first time sale because customers know where you are. If the customer had a good experience they are likely to go with a "proven winner" rather than to take the time and effort to find a new supplier. The bottom line is that existing customers are gold and should be treated that way.

Repeat sales are necessary to build any business and an important method for building business is to learn as much about your customers as possible without seeming intrusive. If a company can track its customers it can anticipate and fulfill their needs.

Another reason to track customers is to identify trends. If a company's customers are coming from a particular town, or area, it might want to focus intensive advertising on that town or area. If it knows most of its customers are female ages 21–29 it might want to advertise in a place or in a medium tailored to that target market.

A well designed customer tracking system will facilitate these objectives. So what does a customer tracking system do and how does it do it? If a company can capture a customer's name, address, telephone number and email address, it has the means reaching out to them individually as products or services come up that they might be interested in. Auto dealers, banks, and stock brokers capture this level of detail because of the nature of their transactions. Retailers with credit cards capture this information as well. Retailers without credit cards sometimes capture this information by asking people whether they want to sign up for catalogs or newsletters. Using a customer tracking system simply to send advertising is a fairly low level use of information. A better tracking system would catalog a customer's buying habits. When do they shop? What do they buy? Are they buying products which must be periodically replaced? How much do they buy? What styles and colors do they buy? What do they use the products for? Capturing and retaining this information helps anticipate customer needs so offers can be presented to them when their buying window is open.

What is a buying window? If one stopped drivers at random and asked whether they wanted to buy a new car, the vast majority would say no. Their buying window is closed. If you could ask them whether they were looking for a car every day, without annoying them, they might say no day after day until one day they say, "Yes. I am looking for a new car." At that point their buying window is open. They are receptive to information on cars, receptive to test drive invitations, and maybe even receptive to buying. However, as soon as they actually buy a car, their buying window closes again. And once the window is closed, even the most persuasive advertising, and the best deal, will be little more than sound and fury signifying nothing.

So what is the strategy? A customer tracking system should be designed to anticipate when the buying window is open and place the company's product or service in front of the customer at that time.

Consider a travel agency. Its customer tracking system could separate business and pleasure travelers. Then classify pleasure travelers as those who buy cruises, those who travel to theme parks, those who are international travelers, and those who want "adventure" vacations. Most people take vacations at about the same time of year because of work or school commitments so the agency should be able to determine when vacations are taken as well as how far in advance people plan their vacations. For example, a family of four, two adults and two children, might take their vacation in July, but plan for, decide on, and book their vacation in March. So the travel agency's strategy should be to package theme park and other family oriented brochures and send them to the specific family in question at the end of February or early March. They might offer a coupon of some kind to close the deal.

This same approach can be used to tailor advertising, sales calls and offers of other goods and services so it arrives when a customer's buying window is open.

Amazon.com has become a master of mining customer data. They track the books individuals buy and analyze purchasing patterns. People who buy a book on camping might also buy a book on rock climbing. So, if someone orders either the camping or rock climbing book, Amazon suggests the other title as an additional purchase.

Shopping recommendations are a form of up-selling. A person goes to a restaurant for bacon and eggs and the waiter asks, would you like juice with that? Shopping recommendations are taking on the characteristics of high art and involve web mining, user modeling and profiling as well as integrating reference information from other sources. Companies should explore such techniques because their competitors are probably already thinking about them (Aresti 2007).

Many companies ask for a buyer's zip codes at check out. Combined with census data, zip codes enable companies to estimate per capita income of their customer base. Location and income provides a two dimensional view of the customer. Zip code data can be used to more narrowly target advertising; determine the size of the geographic area served by a single store and can help qualify locations for future stores by income, proximity to other store and population.

Data that should be captured on business sales includes the industry the customer is in, and how a customer is using the product. The company can then target other companies in the customer's industry. The company can also find companies in other industries that use the product in a similar way and target them.

There are many other ways to analyze and use customer information. The point is that customer information should be collected and analyzed in a systematic way. A few ideas on using customer data are set forth in Table 9.1.

Lost Customers

Every business will lose customers from time to time. Lost customers provide a valuable source of information about the company's performance relative to the market in terms of price, service level, features, innovation, reliability and changes in customer behavior.

How do you know whether you have lost a customer? Many companies retain customer information in the form of order books and billing records. By knowing the frequency and volume of purchases one can predict sales level by customer and identify deviations from norms.

For example, suppose Shop Rite has a customer service card that shoppers present at check-out to qualify for discounts. Through this card, shopper identity is linked to the frequency and volume of purchases. Consider the shopping history for customer number 2323 given in Table 9.2. In the weeks when the customer purchased, he or she purchased an average of $142.22 (total purchases of $1,280/9 weeks). Seven weeks with no purchases is a strong signal that the store has lost this particular customer. The issue is what is the store going to do about it?

Table 9.1 Customer tracking system

Type of data	Uses
Name, address, phone number and email address	– Advertising, making offers tailored to an individual customer's buying pattern
Industry and product use for business customers	– Identify other businesses in the customer's industry
	– Identify businesses that can use the product the same way the original customer might
Purchase times, frequency of replacement purchases	– Determine when the buying window is open and make offers at appropriate times
Zip-code	– Target marketing to areas where customers live
	– Determine the per capita income of customers
	– Qualify areas for new store sites
	– Determine geographic market area of each store
Buying patterns	– Determine the types of items people purchase together and make recommendations as to products
Types of installed equipment	– Sell warranties and maintenance contracts
	– Forecast breakdowns and sell replacement parts and services.

Table 9.2 Customer purchase pattern customer No. 2323

Week	Purchases	Week	Purchases
Jan. 5	$150	March 9	$150
Jan. 12	$160	March 16	$30
Jan. 19	$130	March 23	$0
Jan. 26	$170	March 30	$0
Feb. 2	$0	April 6	$0
Feb. 9	$0	April 13	$0
Feb. 16	$190	April 20	$0
Feb. 23	$140	April 27	$0
March 2	$160	May 4	$0

One thing that can be done is to conduct a phone-based customer exit interview. Such an interview would ask why the customer no longer shops at the store and what the store would have to do to regain the customer's business.

The fix might be as simple as carrying a different brand of toothpaste, or cleaning the rest rooms more often. Or it might be that the price of a particular item like milk or pampers is too high. On the other hand, the reason for a customer leaving might be beyond the company's control. Table 9.3 provides the framework for a computer system to detect and report on lost customers.

Table 9.3 Algorithm for detecting loss of regular customers

This algorithm is only useful if sales can be tracked to a specific customer.

1. Maintain a summary history of customer purchasing activity. Purchases by week is probably granular enough in most instances. This history should contain customer identification information, the week of the sale, and the total amount of the sale.
2. Sort the sales history of all customers by customer id, then by date within customer id. A rolling 12 months of history is sufficient for most businesses. If a customer makes fewer than four purchases, they are probably not regular customers and should be eliminated from this analysis.
3. Average the days between purchases and you will have an estimate of how frequently a given customer purchases.
4. Compute the number of days between the customer's last purchase and the day the analysis is run. Divide days since the last purchase by the average number of days between purchases. If this number is greater than 3, the company has probably lost a customer.
5. Compute the average value of a purchase. Multiply the average weekly purchase times 52 weeks per year to estimate the amount of annualized lost sales.
6. Print the customer identification, average purchase, average number of days between purchases, date of last purchase and annualized lost sales.

The impact of Shop Rite losing a single customer might seem low, in the example above the customer was purchasing about $6,051 per year (($1,280 purchases/11 weeks of history) × 52 weeks). However, loss of individual customers may presage loss of many more customers. The impact grows rapidly.

In a perfect world, sales people would know when a reliable customer has moved on to another supplier. However, not all sales people are ideal, some are new, new to an account or to a territory, are focused on new customers, or are overwhelmed by paperwork.

A company must have a broader and more systematic method of tracking and predicting sales at a customer level and of knowing when it has lost a customer. At some level it needs pattern recognition software. The patterns in this case are buying patterns. Such reports can alert sales and marketing management to client loss in a timely manner so follow-up action can be taken to recapture the customer or learn why the customer was lost and take corrective action.

Customer Feedback

If you want to know how to improve products or services, ask your customers. In an industrial setting where each sale involves significant dollars, the new CEO or the turnaround consultant might actually visit current customers, potential customers, and lost customers and ask for suggestions. That is what Lou Gerstner did when he was hired to turnaround IBM after the company lost $16 billion in 3 years (Robert 1999). However, it's not always practical for a CEO or turnaround consultant to visit retail consumers. So a practical and low cost way to capture such consumer input is needed.

Customer Complaints

Customer complaints provide a gold mine of information. Employees rarely point out product flaws, shortcomings and bad service. Unlike employees, customers have nothing to lose and everything to gain by complaining and complaints can be the basis for substantial improvement.

Every place the company touches a customer, there should be a systematic means of capturing customer opinion. At retail outlets, on-line, attached to bills, everywhere, there should be a form that captures customer complaints. So as not to project a negative impression of this system, one might title the form "Complaints and Suggestions," with a little note at the bottom thanking the customer for taking time to provide input. Products and invoices for services should also contain a hot-line number and a website where complaints and suggestions can be filed.

At many companies, the complaint process is simply used to diffuse customer dissatisfaction. But at companies whose goal is to push the envelop of performance and customer service, complaints are carefully analyzed. Complaints can detect defects in manufacturing or service delivery that escape traditional quality controls. Timely complaint analysis can identify when things go off track by counting the complaints per day by product or service. When there is a spike in complaints, that spike should be promptly communicated to top management.

Complaints can also lead to new and better products. For example, complaints that a product is too thick or too thin, or too heavy or too light or that the product wears out too quickly or that it cannot perform the same functions as competitors products can drive changes in design and manufacturing. Complaints that a product is too difficult to use can lead to a more intuitive design or clearer instructions. Complaints about the difficulty in opening packaging can lead to simpler packaging. Many companies go through the motions of having a customer hotline, but fail to harvest the value such information provides.

Customer Hotline

The rule 80–20 applies to a customer hotline which means a small number of customers will provide the vast majority of input. It is more likely than not that the type of people who have the time, energy and drive to call the hotline once, will probably call many times if he or she it treated with courtesy and respect. Callers represent an invaluable window into what customers are thinking and each caller might reflect the feelings of hundreds or thousands of customers who don't have the drive or ambition to call.

There are a several actions a company can take to maximize return on the investment in a customer hotline

(1) Treat callers with sympathy and respect, the operator's job is not to defend the company, but to understand the customer.

(2) Keep detailed records of calls, caller contact information, the product involved, the nature of the issue involved and any suggestions the customer made.

(3) Summarize findings weekly. This applies to written and website complaints as well.

(4) Present findings to product line managers on an on-going basis.

(5) Make complaint logs available on an internal on-line website so that managers across products and departments can benefit from such customer feedback.

Customer Satisfaction Surveys

Customer satisfaction surveys are a more proactive way to collect customer information and should be utilized to the extent practical. Nissan dealerships make customer satisfaction calls and surveys after every service appointment. Pep Boys make customer satisfaction survey calls on a sample basis as does Cannon Leasing Services. Each of these organizations has excellent customer service because they take time to find out whether service has been good or bad and if service falls below standard, the organization takes corrective action.

ABB a leading power and automation technology company pushes the edge of customer satisfaction surveys with what it calls customer radar. Rather than simply trying to find out after the fact whether customers were satisfied, it actively probes customers for their performance expectations. And rather than asking generic questions about expectations, it has a specific set of inquiries designed for spare parts, another set of inquiries for repairs, one for emergency response, and yet another for planned maintenance (Denton 1995). By digging deeper into customer expectations they can focus more precisely on customer concerns.

Customer Research

Companies that are interested in understanding their customers should take the time to understand what their customers are buying when they buy. Customers rarely buy a product. They buy a solution to a problem or they buy something that is going to make them feel special.

Watch how customers use the product and talk to them about their experience during or after use. This should be an on-going process visiting a sample of customers every few months. Home Depot, for examples requires board members to visit twelve stores per year, usually unannounced, where they talk to customers, interact with employees and see whether stores are clean and well stocked. Medtronic requires engineers and designers to observe at least one surgical procedure a year in which a Metronic device is used in surgery (Kaihla et al. 2006). Such visits provide immediate feedback from customers, some good, some bad, but always valuable. This must be an ongoing process because customers change, their needs change, their understanding of their needs change and the competition changes.

Customer Selection

Many companies define a customer as anyone who buys its products. That is the wrong approach. Just as companies should be in the behavior selection business with regard to employees, they should be in the selection business with regard to customers.

Some customer volumes are so small that sales and marketing costs, order processing, fulfillment and customer service extinguish any hope of profits is too high. On the other hand, some customers are just too big.

The lure of a multi-million dollar contract with a large customer can induce a company to under-bid to the point where contracts become unprofitable. Contracts with large companies can be disruptive if their orders require a dramatic increase in output. In this context dramatic is an increase of 50–100%. Such dramatic increases can put a strain on existing personnel, reduce quality or require a company to make significant capital investments. Large companies often have large bureaucracies which delay payments or worse, deny them if any invoicing detail is imperfect. Some just have a slow pay policy to conserve cash.

There are three strategies for dealing with this situation. The first is to just say no to contracts with customers that are only marginally profitable or which strain resources. Second companies with an unprofitable contract should acknowledge the problem and ask the customer to renegotiate the contract. There is no guarantee the customer will allow such renegotiation, but if the company has provided excellent value and service the customer might be willing to renegotiate. Third, a company might seek a partner with more technical experience, more resources or more experience dealing with large customers. This might thin profits, but it should also help guard against losses (Leung 2003).

Firing Customers

While companies only exist to fulfill customer needs, sometimes particular customers must be fired for the good of the company. Customers that are abusive to staff, customers who won't or can't pay, customers who demand goods or services that are outside the company's area of expertise and customers who are disruptive should all be fired. Such customers drain time, energy and resources from the vast majority of customers who want excellent goods and services at a fair price and are willing to pay in a timely manner.

Firing a customer should be done without malice or acrimony. Customers being fired should not be mistreated, insulted or given inferior goods or services. Rather, a customer being fired should be treated with the utmost courtesy. One might say something like, "You have made it clear that you are unhappy with our products or services. We would like to refund your money and will give you a list of other firms where you can shop." Thereafter, if they come back, one might say, "I'm sorry, I cannot accept your order."

When firing a customer one should document the specific reasons why the customer is being fired. With dates and facts regarding their disruptive acts. There is no need to discuss these acts with the customer, such discussions will only serve to annoy prickly customers and encourage them to disparage your company. Never the less, the reasons for terminating a customer relationship should be on file.

Conclusion

Exceptional customer service can build repeat sales and customer loyalty. Customer service is involved in fielding inquiries; order taking; and fulfillment. Management commitment to customer service and on-going training are critical to good customer service.

A customer tracking system can be used to focus marketing efforts, send advertising, and anticipate customer needs. If a company can place targeted sales material in front of customers when their buying window is open, the likelihood of closing a sale is dramatically increased.

Customer complaints, customer hotlines, and customer satisfaction surveys represent an invaluable source of information for improving a company's performance, but only if information is summarized and analyzed by management. A better, but more time consuming way to find how customers feel about a good or service is to visit them while they are using the product or service and talk to them about their experience.

A hallmark of most underperforming companies is that they short change customer service. A hallmark of a companies that have superior performance is that customer service is among the top ranks of their concerns.

Notes

1. In October of 2007 Commerce Bank was acquired by TD Bank Financial Group of Toronto. As of this writing, there is considerable concern that the acquiring bank will destroy the culture that make Commerce great.
2. Prior to printing, Commerce Bank was acquired by TD Banknorth. Commerce customers are anxiously waiting to see whether service is maintained or whether TD Banknorth will reduce service as a cost cutting measure. http://philadelphia.bizjournals.com/philadelphia/stories/2007/10/15/story15.html

References

Aresti, A, Markellou P , Mousouroul L , Sirmakessis S , Tsakalidis A (2007) A movie e-shop recommendation model based on web usage and ontological data. JECO 5(3):17–34 July–Sept

Brubaker H (2007a) Canadian Bank agrees to purchase commerce. Phila Inq, A01, City D-Edition, 3 Oct

Brubaker H (2007b) Commerce Bancorp will be acquired by TD Banknorth. Phila Bus J, 15 Oct

Denton KD (1995) Process mapping trims cycle time. HRMagazine 40(2) Feb

Kaihla P, Baltatzis P, Collingwood H, Copeland M, Finn B, Hamner S, Jacobson D, Nachtigal J, Schonfeld E, Sloan P, Thomas O (2006). Best kept secrets of the world's best companies. Business 2.0 7(3):82–96, Apr

Leung S (2003) The lure and danger of big company jobs. Wall St J, B9 Sept 2

Robert S (1999) Valuable business lessons form IBM's turnaround CEO Lou Gerstner. *Bottom Line/Personnel*, www.bottomlinesecrets.com/article.html?article_id=153372. Accessed 15 Nov

Rosenberg JM (2005) Fixing customer woes with holistic approach. Phila Inq D11, 22 Aug

Smith J (2006) Businesses missing a key ingredient: customer service. Phila Inq D7, 13 Nov

Timothy A (2003) Deflated: how Goodyear blew its chance to capitalize on a rival's woes. Wall St J A1 and A10, 19 Feb

Wachovia Corporation (2008). Wachovia statement: Wachovia's board approves Wells Fargo Merger proposal. Wachovia Corporation, Press Release. Charlotte, North Carolina, 3 Oct

Chapter 10
Re-engineering, Process Mapping, Continuous Process Improvement and Outsourcing

Introduction

Most companies are inefficient, but don't realize it. All businesses can be improved. Factors that affect competitiveness include cost, quality, delivery, dependability, flexibility and innovation (Skully and Fawcett, 1993). Improvement can be driven in manufacturing, services and administrative processes.

To drive a company to peak performance, sometimes it's a question of making many small improvements and sometimes a quantum leap in productivity is needed. Performance goals, time available and resources determine the best mix of techniques.

There are many reasons for underperformance. Systems and procedures are rarely overhauled, yet products, services, technology, circumstances, and competitors change all the time. There may be a disconnect between management's goals and what is actually happening in the office or on the factory floor because goals are interpreted and reinterpreted many times as they filter down. Problems also arise when those at "corporate" specify methods that are ineffective and workers must improvise solutions. Turnover of managers and employees means an understanding of why things are done as they are done, is lost, and without understanding, procedures are misapplied. As a result, needless work is built into processes, and opportunities to improve are lost.

Previous chapters discussed increasing revenue and cutting costs. In this chapter we discuss techniques for improving operational efficiency. These techniques include (i) process mapping, (ii) re-engineering, (iii) continuous process improvement and (iv) outsourcing. No one method is best in all circumstances and several methods may be needed in the same company.

Process Mapping

Process mapping is about thoroughly understanding the tasks which make up a process so that value added tasks can be enhanced and non-value added tasks eliminated (Soliman, 1998, p. 811). Rather than trying to improve every task, process mapping

D.E. Vance, *Corporate Restructuring*, DOI 10.1007/978-3-642-01786-5_10,
© Springer-Verlag Berlin Heidelberg 2009

first asks, are these tasks necessary? In trying to understand the processes being mapped, one might consider the words of Rudyard Kipling, "I had six humble serving men; they taught me all I knew. Their names were what and where and when and why and how and who." Answering those questions will go a long way toward understanding the processes being mapped.

A process map can be represented as a table, or a flowchart or some other visual means. One advantage to flow charts is that people are used to seeing decision trees built into them (Linton, 2007, pp. 28, 30).

Each task is classified as an (i) operation, (ii) transportation, (iii) inspection, (iv) delay or (v) storage. The time it takes to complete each task is estimated as well as the distance goods or documents travel. Reducing travel reduces time, labor and equipment costs. The idealized map is then compared to real world operations and corrections are made (Linton, 2007, p. 26).

Public Service Company of New Mexico found it was reacting to service calls rather than being proactive. It applied a seven step process which consisted of (i) work identification, (ii) work prioritization, (iii) planning and scheduling processes, (iv) developing a workload management algorithm, (v) clear responsibility for execution, (vi) variance analysis and (vii) key performance measures. In their case, they documented processes "As is" and then looked for ways to streamline their methodology. A flowchart of how the system should work, a "To Be" version of the world was then developed along with supporting procedures, and made available to everyone so all would understand what needed to be done. The process of flowcharting the existing system for all to see turned up a number of obvious process improvements. Public Service was able to cut maintenance costs 10–15% (Cordova, 2005).

A value added task is something that enhances the value of a product or service to the customer. A non-value added task is something that does not. Focus on customer value is also a principal of lean manufacturing. Lean manufacturing adds a few additional criteria for evaluating tasks, for example, (i) verifying what the customer wants rather than assuming what the customer wants, (ii) using the least costly methods to achieve results which is a way of saying, "don't over engineer the process, (iii) following the shortest route through the plant, (iv) maintaining quality and (v) continuously re-evaluating processes to make sure they are as lean as possible (Hall, 2006).

What do we mean by non-value added processes? Delay does not add value, nor does transportation around the plant or storage. So the question is whether workflow can be redesigned so non-value added tasks can be eliminated or at least reduced. For example, can the factory be re-arranged so the output of one process flows directly into the next. This saves transportation. Processes should be timed so there is no delay between tasks. Delay increases lead time and wastes labor hours. Perhaps a just in time inventory management and tracking system be designed so that raw material and intermediate work in process storage is eliminated (Linton, 2007, pp. 26, 28).

Inspections add value to the customer in that they reduce the likelihood of failure, but could the risk of failure be reduced in another way? For example, if better suppliers are found, raw material inspections can be reduced or eliminated. If workers are trained to look for common defects as they work on a product, then intermediate inspections can be reduced or eliminated.

Process mapping also reduces processing time, defects and rework by better matching people and their skills with the needs of every process (Linton, 2007, p. 28). Process mapping can highlight bottlenecks and redundancies, reduce travel distance which reduces flow time and the cost of material handling. Reducing flow time reveals costly mistakes that would otherwise be hidden in intermediate storage so mistakes can be corrected (Adams, 2000). Another significant benefit of process mapping is that it clarifies responsibilities across departmental boundaries and identifies ways departments can coordinate work to improve efficiency (LaFerla, 2005, p. 17).

Eliminating steps can have a significant impact on performance. Some studies suggest that up to 70% of total process time can be eliminated using process mapping. Absecon Mills, for example, found the time to fill an order could be reduced from 28 days to 14 days by eliminating needless tasks and simplifying the remaining ones. This provides them with a significant competitive advantage over Chinese competitors who require 10–12 weeks to fill a similar order. But the quest for improvement never stops. Absecon's process mapping analysis revealed that actual manufacturing time was only three hours, so they continue to eliminate and simplify tasks (Holcomb, 2007). Reducing processing time will make a company more responsive to changes in customer demand and eliminating non-value added steps will save labor dollars as well as costs associated with equipment and space (Linton, 2007, p. 28).

Compared to re-engineering, process mapping is relatively low cost because it primarily involves eliminating steps rather than creating new ones. The principal cost is an engineer or skilled analyst who can study processes, gather input from workers, determine how to reorganize tasks and oversee implementation.

Lean manufacturing adds the additional principal that a processes should not be distributed across organizational boundaries where turf wars or other interdepartmental friction might interfere with efficient design. Lean holds that one process should take place in one organization. For example, order entry, picking and shipping should be in one department, not three departments. The idea is that unified command and unified responsibility drive efficiency (Hall, 2006). Table 10.1 provides Examples of Process Mapping Driven Improvements.

Continuous Process Improvement

Process mapping focuses on whether processes add value. Continuous process improvement, focuses on making each process as efficient as possible. Continuous process improvement has made Toyota one of the world's leading car companies. The theory, also called Kaizen, is focused on the cumulative effect of many small improvements. Some published reports indicate this incremental approach can result in a 100% increase in efficiency over the period of 12–18 months (Bond, 1999, p. 1327). However, improvement will vary from company to company in part dictated by how inefficient a company was at the time restructuring began. Investments

Table 10.1 Examples of process driven improvements

Description	Improvement
Component manufacturing (McKellen, 2005, p. 16)	
a. Increase frequency of supplier delivery to reduce inventory.	Reduce inventory
b. Have supplier provide bar stock in pre-cut lengths.	Reduce processing
c. Rearrange work flow so the output of one operation is positioned as input to the next operation.	Reduce storage and movement
d. Replace the lathe turning and grinding steps with a numerical controlled machine that is so precise grinding is not needed.	Eliminate process
e. Reduce set-up time.	Reduce time
f. Simplify design to reduce assembly steps.	Reduce processing
g. Eliminate inventory prior to shipping by using demand pull system.	Reduce inventory
h. Monitor production hourly and adjust schedules in real time to smooth work flow.	Increased throughput Reduced wait time
i. Work to a weekly customer schedule.	Reduce inventory
Aerospace company (Bevan and Waters, 2005)	
a. Co-locate design, development and production staff.	Eliminate movement
b. Relieve software design engineers of routine work like code testing	Appropriate processing
c. Standardize engineering design drawing format so they could be easily converted to maintenance manual illustrations.	Eliminate process
d. Eliminate requirement to send a complete set of engineering drawings to receiving for component selection and only provide minimal drawings necessary for inspection.	Reduce processing
e. Implement supplier procedures to improve materials quality.	Reduce inspections
f. Replace frequent and time consuming design review meetings with a requirement that all parties review designs prior to meetings and only meet to discuss problems.	Reduced time Increased throughput Reduced wait time
g. Independent tests by mechanical, software and systems integration engineers duplicated effort. Replace with comprehensive test strategy.	Reduce processing Reduce time
h. Streamline engineering changes by funneling work through a single change board and replace change specialists in specific disciplines with a cross-functional change implementation team to reduce bottlenecks.	Reduced processing Reduced wait time
Consumer products manufacturing (Adams, 2000; Denton, 1995)	
a. Reduce travel distance of parts through 1.2 million square foot plant from 20 miles to hundreds of feet.	Reduce time Reduce transportation
b. Reduce flow time through plant	Identify hidden errors Improve response
c. Reduce time it takes to transmit orders from sales to production from 5 days to 1 day by using automated drawing and cutting software	Improve delivery time
d. Install an 800 line for fax machine to increase faxed orders and improve order accuracy.	Reduce order errors
Textiles (Holcomb, 2007)	
a. Move tools closer to where used	Reduce movement
b. Paint shape of tool on storage rack	Reduce tool storage and retrieval time
c. Cut order processing paperwork	Improve customer response

in continuous process improvement are usually small due to the incremental nature of changes. Kaizen is driven by spontaneous, bottom up change (Bond, 1999, p. 1320). No one knows a production, administrative, or operating department like those working in it every day.

Targets of Opportunity

At Toyota, there are seven commonly accepted wastes that are targets of continuous process improvement (Hines and Rich, 1997, p. 47).

1. Overproduction – can occur both within work-in-process and in finished goods. Excess inventory, masks defects, because customers and workers can bypass defective goods and draw upon other production. Overproduction also interrupts the smooth flow of work and goods through the operation.
2. Waiting – Ideally there should be a smooth flow of goods from one end of a plant to the other. Increased time in the plant increases work in process inventory.
3. Transport – moving work-in-process inventory is considered a waste because it increases cost, but does not add to the value of the finished good.
4. Inappropriate Processing – Appropriate processing uses the simplest method and smallest machine necessary to produce the quality and quantity of goods required at the lowest possible cost. Inappropriate processing uses more complex processes and more expensive machinery than necessary.
5. Unnecessary Inventory – Unnecessary inventory masks problems which may be ignored since production workers and customers can draw upon an abundance of good inventory. It increases lead time and storage costs, increases risk of spoilage and obsolescence, and increases costs for insurance and taxes.
6. Unnecessary Motion – Workers that have to stretch, bend, lift, carry, or switch hands when using a tool can represent unnecessary motion. Unnecessary motion increases fatigue, workers compensation claims and slows production because time and effort spent on unnecessary motion is not spent on production. The goal is to create an ergonomically efficient workplace in which new work and parts are delivered to workers as they need them and finished work is removed from workstations as completed.
7. Defects – Defects create direct costs in a number of ways. For example, a hole drilled in the wrong place may require scraping an item with the loss of all work-in-process value that the item represents. An incorrectly assembled machine which must be sent to rework for disassembly and reassembly before it can be shipped increases costs. Defects not caught before shipment increase warranty costs, customer complaints, and can result in lost sales.

An organization that makes it the responsibility of every employee to identify and report on these seven wastes is much more likely to harvest the benefits of improved productivity than one that relies on management or consultants to identify such opportunities.

Organizational Factors

A key element in continuous process improvement is worker buy-in. Workers must be treated as valued contributors to the enterprise (Hall, 2006). Constantly training the workforce will help workers help the company by giving them a bigger picture of how isolated tasks fit into the whole production cycle. This also gives them the perspective they need to help with continuous process improvement. Training should include information on quality control techniques such as Root Cause Analysis (RCA), Pareto analysis and other techniques as well as an understanding of the key metrics that drive operational performance (Dadmum, 2007). Changing workforce culture to actively participate in continuous process improvement and providing training are long lead time activities. Therefore continuous process improvement should be focused on divisions the company plans to nurture rather than those it expects to close or sell.

Listen to worker suggestions without judging them. Ask an employee to explain his or her idea to coworkers. Care should be taken to make sure that improvements don't have negative consequences for workers. If an operation's efficiency improves ten percent, ten percent of the operations workforce should not be laid off. Give credit where credit is due. Make sure the individual(s) making the improvement are recognized. Share the benefit of the improvement with the workforce. Whole Foods, for example, shares a percentage of the money it saves by doing more work with less labor (Kaihla et al., 2006). This will create positive feedback and more ideas for improvement. For example, if a company's policy is to reward employees with 20% of first year savings, half might be allocated to the idea's originator and the other half might be distributed to the workers in his or her immediate work-group.

Units, operations and teams must be empowered to make improvements without seeking permission from six layers of management. Nothing kills initiative like a hierarchical management structure and budgets imposed from a central bureaucracy, indecisiveness, delay and paternalistic oversight (Bond, 1999, p. 1322).

Re-engineering

The term re-engineering, sometimes called business process re-engineering (BPR) implies radical change resulting in a quantum leap in performance (Williams et al., 2003). Re-engineering involves a total re-think of what is being done as well as how it is being done. Often re-engineering involves introduction of new technologies, and just as often investment of significant amounts of capital. As such, re-engineering is usually a top-down process.

Re-engineering Goals

There is no formula for re-engineering, but there are broad guidelines as to how to proceed. First, a company must understand, at a deep level, what business it is in, what its customers want, when they want it, how they want it, where they want it, how they use the company's products and services and how much customers are willing to pay.

Second, a company must understand the processes it uses to deliver goods and services to the customer. This should be a macro view of processes, rather than an analysis of the specific tasks that make up the processes. The description of the company should be "As-is" without any embroidery or wishful thinking.

Third, the company should establish a set of benchmarks for delivering goods and services. How much lead time should it take to deliver a new order? How much lead time to develop a new product? How can the customer measure the value added by the company's product or service? How reliable is the company's product or service? What features or competitive advantages does the company's product or service have compared to competitors? What is the price value relationship in the company's products or services? What is the cost to deliver goods and services, and are margins adequate? The company should develop a broad set of industry specific benchmarks, for example the number of labor hours to build a car, or the lapsed time to complete a product.

Fourth, a company should scrutinize both its competitors and companies in other industries to see how they are performing against these benchmarks. If competitors are doing much better, that should be a wake-up call that swift, decisive change is needed (Dadnum, 2007, p. 13). But even if a company's performance is in line with its peers, is that really good enough? Shouldn't the goal be superior performance?

The reason for looking at benchmark data from other industries is that other industries may face problems similar to the ones faced by the company under review. If a company can learn something from another industry that its competitors have not yet learned, that knowledge may provide the company with an opportunity for break-out performance.

Fifth, once a brutally honest analysis of performance is complete, a company can set new standards of performance. If a company wants to make a quantum leap forward, new standards cannot simply be small increments over old performance. Radical change is the essence of re-engineering and a radical improvement in goals will be needed to drive radical change.

Re-engineering Process

Once, the existing processes are outlined at a macro level and new target benchmarks are set, the company's engineers, operations managers, executives, and outside consultants should be briefed on the company's findings. Participants should prepare themselves for this conference by scouring the literature in the field for break-out ideas, methods and technologies. Most industries have journals that speculate on new innovations. Scientific and engineering journals often discuss break-out technologies long before widespread adoption. A university library is an invaluable source of scientific and technical journals and reference librarians can help zero in on relevant material. Where an incipient technology seems promising, the turnaround team should make an effort to contact the author of an article or articles on that topic.

As new technologies are identified a company should find engineering firms skilled in that technology. Such firms can give practical advice and provide estimates of the cost of implementing the new technology. The lead time in implementing a new technology is also important. If a technology takes to long to install, a company may face competitors who have installed the next generation of the technology before they have installed the base technology. Further, in a restructuring situation, a company might run out of time or money before re-engineering can show results.

Because significant investments of capital are often at stake in re-engineering, it should be subject to a capital budgeting analysis. Is the rate of return sufficient to justify the investment over the life of the technology? If not, then a company should consider alternative, less complex technologies, or seek other means to achieve a competitive advantage. The objective isn't to have the best "gee-whiz" technology, it is to win the performance race. Sometimes that can be done with simpler tools, used more effectively.

Targets of Opportunity

The targets of opportunity for re-engineering will be different in every company and industry. However, a few examples indicate what re-engineering can do.

Just as technology is a driver of competition and innovation, it is often a driver of re-engineering. One of the most widely used technologies for re-engineering is information technology. It can eliminate many routine tasks, speed communication and can be designed with built-in quality controls. Information technology built into machines that inspect raw materials, make processing decisions and control tools at machine speeds can radically improve performance (Koski, 2000). But to limit re-engineering analyses to information technology is to miss other significant opportunities for improvement.

Every place where a piece of paper is created may be an opportunity to streamline a process. Company's run on information, but often useless information is collected simply because it has historically been collected. Double checking and approving data also adds cost. The people most likely to get data right are the people who collect it initially, not supervisors or clerks downstream from the data source. Of course this means those collecting data must be properly trained and supervised. Reasonableness and validity checks on data are more efficiently done in computer systems than by legions of clerks.

Supply chains have been a significant target of opportunity for re-engineering. The automobile industry and its suppliers have harvested significant improvements in efficiency through better supply chain management and have built on techno-logical developments such as EDI (electronic data interchange) which effectively lets one company communicate with another company's databases (Kudyba, 2005). Motorola was able to improve the way in which it negotiated with its suppliers by re-engineering its whole procurement decision model (Metty et al., 2005). Hewlett-Packard optimized its supply chain through a total re-engineering of its processes, in part, by disseminating supply chain information more widely to decision makers (Laval et al., 2005).

Adtran, a telecommunications equipment manufacturer re-engineered its supply chain including (i) demand planning, (ii) sales order entry, (iii) delivery promises, (iv) procurement and receiving, (v) outsourcing, (vi) inventory management, (vii) manufacturing management, and (viii) order fulfillment and distribution. The re-engineered system was built around several software packages that it integrated in house. One of the key features of the re-engineered supply chain was a web based system that enabled buyers and suppliers to act on forecasts for raw materials, production and delivery schedules. Suppliers were invited to participate during the implementation so that they could see how Adtran's procurement and production schedule would impact their own production. The results of this re-engineering project were to improve delivery to request time from 70 to 92% and to reduce inventory by 60% (Dadnum, 2007, p. 15).

The nature of some large facilities means they are either producing or not producing. Examples include nuclear power plants, refineries and electric transmission grids. Every day, and every hour such facilities are off-line costs significant amounts of money. Re-engineering preventive maintenance at the API refinery in Falconara Marittima, Italy was used to reduce both unplanned outages and scheduled down time for preventive maintenance. Maintenance that had only been performed during total plant shut down will now be performed while the plant is producing. This reduces preventative maintenance down time while increasing reliability. Overall, preventive maintenance hours were reduced by 16.5% and maintenance costs were reduced by 12.6% (Bevilacqua et al., 2005, p. 731).

The plastics industry is characterized by intense competition, high raw materials costs and narrow margins. So, this industry is always searching for the kind of quantum leap in productivity that re-engineering can provide (Williams et al., 2003). Furniture manufacturers are re-engineering their plants to radically increase automation which reduces labor and material costs, lowers inventories, and reduces set-up time which shortens order to delivery time. This change was driven by a tripling of wood prices over the last 10 years, a demand for customized furniture, reduced lead time, and the competitive threat of Chinese imports (Koski, 2000).

Human Dynamic

Re-engineering, by definition involves significant investment of capital and wrenching organizational change. Therefore, it is important to get top management's commitment to the process. Comparative benchmarks help drive home the need for change and the capital budgeting process should emphasize the financial payoff, but often that is not enough. Keep executives informed of progress through meetings and presentations at which they have an opportunity to ask questions and offer input (Dadnum, 2007, p. 15). Throughout the process, there will be those who seek to derail or devalue the process or cut its allocated resources or in some other way obfuscate or delay. Employees have seen efforts to improve efficiency over and over again and many probably think all they have to do is keep their head down until this blows over and then they can go back to doing what they have been doing (Wood, 2006).

Logically, one might want those most familiar with the old processes to lead or participate in the restructuring team. However, this could have adverse consequences such as impeding a search for radical improvement (Bevilacqua et al., 2005).

Those in affected departments should be kept informed of progress, but more important they should be educated as to why change is needed and trained in whatever new technology is being implemented. Training and education will go a long way toward gaining enthusiastic cooperation rather than grudging acceptance. Remember, an unwilling workforce can kill the most promising innovation.

Criticisms of Re-engineering

There are some legitimate criticisms of re-engineering as it has been practiced. But knowing the pitfalls of a process is the first step in avoiding them. Among the pitfalls are

(1) Loss of knowledge of company processes, customers, suppliers and regulations as headcount is reduced.
(2) Declining morale. Those remaining may feel overwhelmed by the work they have to do. Most processes within a company require the trust of the employees, but layoffs erode that trust.
(3) Loss of communication as layers of middle management are stripped out of a company.
(4) Excessive headcount reductions, only to find out that those laid off must be rehired to keep the company running.

Each of these criticisms is valid if re-engineering just means hacking people off an organization. For example, lost of knowledge is a real short term problem, but procedures, manuals, and training can help a company quickly regain most lost knowledge. The role of middle management in communication is a more doubtful matter. The more layers that a company's goals are filtered through, the less likely the workforce will receive them in tact. Laying off too many employees only to rehire them seems like bad judgment pure and simple.

Nothing increases job security like profits. Job security will increase morale. Morale will further be boosted if the company demonstrates its willingness to respect and take care of its remaining employees.

Setting Goals

The first step toward identifying improvement, is to articulate the goals of a function, department or subsidiary. Unfortunately, goals are often stated in vague, self-aggrandizing terms. Restructuring requires in-depth interviews and re-interviews with senior and middle managers to get beyond rhetoric and generalities to specific, implementable and measurable goals. By implementable, we mean goals that can be reduced to executable policies and procedures.

For example, management might state the goal of the production department is to produce the best possible products for the least cost. Admirable, but how do people implement such vague goals? A more precise statement of goals might be to reduce costs of goods sold by 10% per year this year and 5% per year for the next 4 years; reduce warranty claims by 20% this year and ten percent for the next 5 years. Notice that goals are framed in a way that requires continuous improvement. If a company improves one time and stops, while its competitors improve every year, it will eventually lose the race.

Finally, as with everything else, increased efficiency must be balanced against its impact on other corporate goals such as customer service and quality control. Everything in life is a balance. Genius is knowing where that balance lies.

Setting Priorities

Two constraints on any restructuring are time and money. So focus where the payoff is quickest and greatest. There is no point in improving divisions identified for closure or product lines identified for elimination. Process improvement in divisions identified for sale should be limited to those that are quick and low cost. Federal government contracts limit the amount of profit a company can make so improving efficiency in divisions that sell primarily to the government should have a lower priority. Areas which require a high level of staffing or high expenses or which require a large investment of capital or working capital should be prioritized.

The restructuring team should spend a couple of weeks constructing a map of all the divisions, departments and functions needed to run the company. This map need not be pretty, but it should be accurate and readable. This map should help the turnaround team visualize company operations and how it should deploy its resources.

How does one begin to map the functions in a company? First obtain an organization chart, if one exists. If one does not exist, one should be developed. Every person need not be on this chart, but it should reach down to the level of managers responsible for sales, production and administration at every facility and should indicate the number of people he or she manages.

Second, interview high level executives starting with the CEO, and Turnaround Committee and the CEOs direct reports to document their understanding of business operations. Get them to describe their markets and customers, the products and services offered, and the flow of information, products and services through the unit. Ask similar questions, as appropriate to each of his or her direct reports. The important things to glean from these discussions are the objectives and functions of each department. Most companies have functions and processes that made sense at one time, but no longer make sense because of changes in organization, products and markets, bureaucratic inertia and lack of perceived authority to change processes. This often results in unnecessary and duplicative work. However, to know whether work is unnecessary or duplicative one must flow out the work being performed from order taking, to manufacturing, delivery, billing and collection, and measuring customer satisfaction

At each point, and in each process, the two questions which should asked are (i) does this contribute to management's articulated goals and (ii) is there a simpler way to perform a function?

Technique Selection

In restructuring a company, it is important to use the right technique under the right circumstances. Re-engineering can result in a quantum leap in productivity, but it requires a significant investment of capital and learning a new technology. Process mapping is lower cost and can be implemented more quickly because current processes are being adapted. Continuous process improvement is relatively low cost, but it requires workforce training and a significant cultural shift before the workforce will feel empowered and safe making recommendations. This makes continuous process improvement a long lead time technique. Sometimes several techniques can be used together (Williams et al., 2003).

For example, Ford UK re-engineered its computer systems so that hundreds of machine tools on its automated engine production line could be monitored simultaneously. This provided an immediate increase in productivity. After installation, management continued to look for, and discover, new ways to use the data generated by this system to improve scheduling and solve problems. Ford has increased output by 50% and reduced headcount by 75% (Antony, 2003). The differences in these techniques should be exploited when prioritizing restructuring tasks as shown in Fig. 10.1.

Outsourcing

Outsourcing is subcontracting out some aspect of company operations. Outsourcing need not mean sending work out of the country. There are many domestic companies that provide outsourced goods and services.

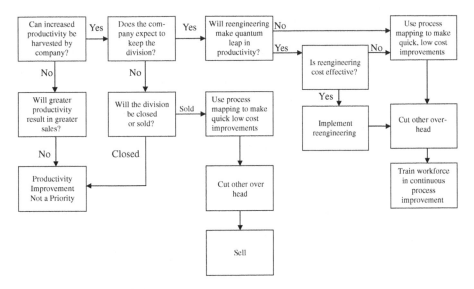

Fig. 10.1 Technique analysis

Most companies want to control their core business functions, but outsource peripheral ones; or maintain control over production and design and outsource components. Some companies aspire to become virtual companies in which almost every business activity is outsourced and management becomes the puppet master pulling the strings on a series of outsourcing companies. There are many advantages to outsourcing.

(1) It might be easier to outsource a function than to develop expertise in an area.
(2) Recruiting, training, and motivating staff becomes someone else's problem.
(3) Facilities costs: rent, heat, light, insurance and maintenance can be saved.
(4) Capital expenditures for: equipment can be eliminated.
(5) Employee related overhead such as vacations, holidays, overtime, health and pension benefits can be eliminated, as can costs associated with employee litigation for sexual harassment, discrimination, ADA, etc.
(6) Seasonal ramp up and build down problems can be eliminated.
(7) An outside contractor may be much more sensitive to management's needs than an internal organization because outside contractors know they can lose the work.

On the other hand, when a company's value added functions are outsourced, the company becomes less and less relevant to its customers (Blaxill and Hout 1991, p. 94). Broadly speaking, the decision rule is that companies should do internally those tasks that are the most value added and consider outsourcing routine tasks (Rosenberg, 2006).

Outsourcing is a classic make or buy decision. To determine whether outsourcing is useful, one must be able to identify the real cost of making a good or service in house rather than buying it from outside.

When considering outsourcing, be careful to consider only costs that can actually be eliminated. For example, full absorption cost includes allocation of fixed costs that may not be eliminated when a good or process is outsourced. Variable costs provide a rough estimate of costs that can be avoided through outsourcing. However, in the long run all costs are variable.

Time is a critical restructuring issue and while a company might be able to reduce internal costs over the long haul, an outsourcing contractor might be able to provide those savings in a short period of time.

There are several elements to successful outsourcing. First, specify exactly what is needed. It's easy to write a specification for spark plugs, it's much more difficult to write a specification for something as complex as information technology where requirements change over time. Second, there must an objective standard of quality. Third, the company doing the outsourcing must implement appropriate supply chain protocols to timely communicate orders, order status and inventory. Fourth, the company must commit to an on-going program of inspection and quality control. Relying on the subcontractor for quality control is a recipe for disaster. Fifth, the contract for outsourcing must be contingent on the outsourced goods or services meeting specifications, quality and delivery schedules. Often a client must put staff in the outsourcing company for an extended period of time to make sure it has the proper people, procedures, training and quality control in place.

While outsourcing is a useful cost control tool, it is not a magic lantern that solves all of a company's problems. Cost savings don't always materialize, and customer service and repeat sales can be negatively impacted if product or service quality deteriorates.

Quality and Reputation

Poor quality can destroy a company and customers don't really care whether the poor quality was because of errors by an outsource contractor or by a company's own personnel.

For example, Foreign Tire Sales, Inc. of Union, New Jersey had to recall 255,000 tires made in China because they lacked a safety feature called a "gum strip," that fits between the steel belts in tires to make them more durable (Rosenberg, 2007a). Fisher-Price, a division of Mattel, Inc. had to recall 1.5 million Chinese made toys because of lead paint (Rosenberg, 2007b). Nokia, a Finnish cell phone company outsourced battery production to Matsushita, a Japanese company. Nokia announced that 46 million of its phones had defective batteries that could overheat and be potentially dangerous (O'Brien, 2007). In March of 2007, the US Food and Drug Administration linked contaminated wheat gluten used in pet food to Chinese manufacturers. Other contaminated and defective products have been linked to China including toys, seafood and toothpaste (Zamiska and Miller, 2007).

Recalls and the adverse publicity they generate can have a devastating impact on sales. Protecting the company's reputation is an issue whether the subcontractor is foreign or domestic.

Hidden Costs

There are a number of hidden costs in outsourcing. One of the difficulties is coordination across ten or twelve time zones. Suppliers are working when employees of the company are asleep, and suppliers are asleep when their client's are awake. Even with email, many outsourcing issues must be resolved in real time which means phone or video conferences across time zones. This gives rise to perpetual jet-lag in the individuals coordinating operations on both ends of the relationship.

Cultural differences and limited language skills can cause problems as well. For example, a hardware wholesaler in New Jersey ordered two million dollars worth of brass mail slots and when they were received, the word "Mail" was upside down. A company that outsources to a foreign supplier must also consider the impact of consumer reaction to foreign working conditions and the environmental impact of production methods.

Savings Erosion

Labor costs are lower in underdeveloped countries, but rise as a country's economy develops, increasing the prevailing wage, which in turn reduces the cost advantage of outsourcing. Early outsource production was sent to Japan, and as Japanese wages rose through the 1960s and 1970s, companies began outsourcing to Taiwan. As Taiwanese wages rose, companies outsourced to China, Viet Nam, and India.

Labor savings can erode rapidly. Munjal Shah, a Silicon Valley entrepreneur with a company called Riya Inc. opened a software development office in Bangalore, India in 2005. At the time he was paying engineers a quarter of the market rate in the Silicon Valley. In 2006 he had to pay 50% of the Silicon Valley rate to stay competitive and by 2007 he was paying 75% of Silicon Valley rates. Considering the added cost of coordinating development across time zones, he concluded there was no longer an advantage outsourcing and closed his Bangalore office (Tam and Range, 2007).

Periodic fuel price spikes can raise transportation costs to the point where foreign outsourcing becomes too expensive. Other hidden costs of outsourcing include: costs to identify and coordinate with an outsourcing company, which must be amortized over the life of the outsourcing contract, and difficulty withdrawing from an outsourcing relationship if cost savings or quality erode.

Nevertheless outsourcing can be a valuable strategy if it is focused on goods services which are generic, highly standardized, low value added, and which have low margins (Blaxill and Hout, 1991, p. 100)

Conclusion

There are a variety of approaches for improving efficiency, none of which are appropriate all the time, but each of which are useful under the right circumstances.

Process mapping involves breaking a process into tasks and eliminating non-value added tasks. For example, transportation and storage add no value for the customer and should be eliminated. Process mapping requires minimal capital investments and can be implemented relatively quickly.

Continuous process improvement is based on the cumulative effect of many small improvements in productivity. This is a bottom up process in which the workers, those who know processes best, make suggestions for improvement. This is a relatively low cost means of improvement. However, it requires worker training in principals of operations and quality control and a cultural shift in which workers are empowered to make suggestions and benefit from improvements. A cultural shift might be a long lead time item.

Process re-engineering usually involves completely rethinking what a company wants to do and how it wants to do it. Goals are stated in terms of a quantum leap in productivity. New technology and processes are usually required and this translates into a relatively long lead time and a significant capital investment.

At some level, the concepts underlying continuous process improvement, process mapping, and reengineering overlap and feed into one another. This is not a problem as long as one focuses on meeting performance goals and not the minutia of each specific technique.

Outsourcing can be used to improve productivity, but it is not the solution to every problem. Companies generally perform high value added processes internally and outsource generic and low value processes. Successful outsourcing involves clear specifications as to what the subcontractor is to do; integration of procedures for ordering, problem solving and inventory management; quality controls and sensitivity to cultural differences.

Through an appropriate combination of process improvement strategies and outsourcing a company can significantly improve its cost structure and efficiency.

References

Adams L (2000) Mapping yields manufacturing insights. Quality 39(5):62–66, May
Antony A (2003) Ford uses data analysis to boost productivity by 50% at Dagenham. Computer Weekly, 17 June. Article 00104787
Bevan J, Waters M (2005) Journey to lean. Eng Manag 15(4):10–13, Aug/Sept
Bevilacqua M, Ciarapica FE, Giacchetta G, Bertolini, M et al (2005) A application of BPR and RCM methods to an oil refinery turnaround process. Prod Plann Control 16(7):716–732, Oct
Blaxill MF, Hout TM (1991) The fallacy of the overhead quick fix. Harv Bus Rev pp 93–101, July–Aug
Bond TC (1999) The role of performance measurement in continuous improvement. Int J Oper Prod Manag 19(12):1312–1334
Cordova AV (2005) Just the facts: implementation of a fact based work management system within a utility. AACE Int Trans. PS.10.AACE International. PS.10.1–PS.10.12

Dadmum TL (2007) Re-engineering the supply chain to meet the changing demand: Adtran's experience. J Bus Forecast, vol. 26, Iss. 1, 12–17, Spring

Denton KD (1995) Process mapping improves cycle time. HR Magazine 40(2) Feb

Hall J (2006) Making business processes lean. Manag Serv. Winter. pp 18–20

Hines P, Rich N (1997) The seven value stream mapping tools. Int J Oper Prod Manag 17(01): 46–64

Holcomb HJ (2007) A system for succeeding. Phila Inq, D1 and D3, 23 Apr

Kaihla P, Baltatzis P, Collingwood H, Copeland M, Finn B, Hamner S, Jacobson D, Nachtigal J, Schonfeld E, Sloan P, Thomas O (2006) Best kept secrets of the world's best companies. Business 2.0 7(3):82–96, Apr

Koski J (2000) Throughput improvements shorten delivery times. Wood & Wood Products. pp 71–78, Dec

Kudyba S (2006) Enhancing organizational information flow and knowledge creation in re-engineering supply chain systems: an analysis of the U.S. Automotive Parts and Supplies Model. Int J Innovation Management. vol. 10, Iss. 2, 163–173, Aug

LaFerla B (2005) Mapping the way to process. Engineering Management. vol. 13, Iss. 6, 16–17, Dec 04/Jan 05

Laval C, Feyhl M, Kakouros S (2005) Hewlett-Packard combined OR and expert knowledge to design its supply chains. Interfaces 35(3):238–247

Linton J (2007) Process mapping and design. Circ Assem, 26–30 Feb

McKellen C (2005) Mapping techniques. Metalworking Prod, 15–16 Feb

Metty T, Harlin R, Samuelson Q (2005) Reinventing the supplier negotiation process at Motorola. Interfaces 35(1):7–23

O'Brien K (2007) Nokia warns of defects in handset batteries. Phila Inq. 15 Aug, C2

Tam P-W, Range J (2007) Some in silicon valley begin to sour on India. Wall St J, A1 and A15, 3 July

Rosenberg JM (2006) More small firms use outsourcing. Phila Inq, C2, 30 Jan

Rosenberg JM (2007a) Distributor recalls 255,000 tires made in China. Phila Inq citing the Washington Post, C3, 10 Aug

Rosenberg JM (2007b) Business news in brief: fisher-price probed over lead paint in toys. Phila Inq, C3, 7 Aug

Skully J, Fawcett SE (1993) Comparative logistics and production costs for global manufacturing strategy. Int J Oper Prod Manag 13(12):62–78

Soliman F (1998) Optimum level of process mapping and least cost business process re-engineering. Int J Oper Prod Manag 18(9/10):810–816

Williams A, Davidson J, Waterworth S, Partington R. (2003) Total quality management versus business process re-engineering: a question of degree. Proceedings of the Institution of Mechanical Engineers, Part B, Engineering Manufacture, vol. 217, pp 1–10

Wood A (2006) Achieving excellence. Chem Week 5, 15 Nov

Zamiska N, Miller J (2007) Chinese goods draw scrutiny from EU, Asia. Wall St J, A2, 3 July

Chapter 11
Cost Analysis and Finding Waste

Introduction

The best advice a client ever gave me was, "You got to hunt where the deer are," by which he meant you have to focus effort where the payoff is greatest. There is no magic bullet that can cure the ills of a distressed company. The more views one has of a company's cost structure, the more likely one is to identify and trim waste. While controlling labor costs will improve a company's performance, control of non-labor costs can be decisive.

The first section of this chapter discusses cost targets. The second section discusses techniques for analyzing costs and the third section of this chapter discusses targets of opportunity for cost reduction.

Establishing cost targets for overhead and cost of goods sold provide the turnaround team with clear goals and provides the turnaround committee with a tool for measuring progress. Goals also help staff and management come to grips with the painful change necessary to improve performance.

Three cost analysis techniques are (i) payment analysis, (ii) functional analysis and (iii) audit programs. Payment analysis begins by ranking expenditures by vendor which automatically prioritizes high payoff vendors. Functional analysis examines the cost components of each function for high payoff targets. Audit programs systematically step through income statement and balance sheet accounts looking for savings. Targets of opportunity are areas in which substantial savings have been found in many companies. Among the most fertile areas for cost reduction are facilities, vehicles, insurance and telecommunications.

Cost Goals

Overhead

Overhead is a great killer of companies and should be a prime target for cost reduction. For purposes of this discussion overhead is defined as expenses other than cost of goods sold, financing costs and taxes. Overhead is not used to make a product or deliver a service. Overhead tends to accumulate at a company the way barnacles

D.E. Vance, *Corporate Restructuring*, DOI 10.1007/978-3-642-01786-5_11,
© Springer-Verlag Berlin Heidelberg 2009

accumulate on the hull of a ship and from time to time overhead must be scrapped off, just as barnacles must.

A good way to begin analyzing overhead is to compute overhead as a percentage of sales (Overhead%) for the company for the last 3 years. If sales are increasing Overhead% should be decreasing. Overhead% should also be compared to the company's best competitors. A company's goal should be an Overhead% at least 10% lower than its peer group. Why 10%? A company that strives only to be good as its peers is doomed to lose the race. A company should aspire to beat its competitors by a significant amount. The formula for Overhead% is given in Eq. (11.1). The formula for new target overhead is given in Eq. (11.2) which can be derived from Eq. (11.1).

$$Overhead\% = Overhead/Sales \tag{11.1}$$

$$Target\ Overhead = Industry\ Average\ Overhead\% \times 90\% \times Sales \tag{11.2}$$

Suppose a company has sales of $20 million, overhead of $5 million.

$$Overhead\% = \$5\ million/\$20\ million$$

Assume industry average Overhead% is 22%. What should be the target overhead in dollars?

$$= 22\% \times 90\% \times \$20\ million$$
$$= \$3.96\ million$$

One goal of this company's turnaround team should be to find and eliminate about $1.04 million of overhead ($5 million in current overhead less $3.96 million in target overhead.)

The more specific the recommendation, the more likely it can be implemented, so let's look inside overhead. Overhead breaks down into two major components (i) selling and marketing costs and (ii) other overhead. Selling and marketing costs tend to rise and fall as sales rise and fall, among the reasons for this are that commissions and sales related travel and entertainment follow the rise or fall of sales.

Dollars spent on other overhead should not rise when sales increase. Other Overhead as a percent of sales (OO%) should decline as sales rise. Other overhead percent (OO%) is given in Eq. (11.3).

$$OO\% = (Overhead - (Selling\ Costs + Marketing\ Costs))/Sales \tag{11.3}$$

This ratio should be compared to the company's historical ratio and to competitors' ratios. Not every company reports selling and marketing costs in their financial statements. So, it might not be possible to compare OO% to industry norms. In that case, the general overhead targets given in Eq. (11.2) will have to suffice as a turnaround team goal. However, where selling and marketing costs can be isolated from overhead, other overhead targets can be estimated using Eq. (11.4). Again, the objective isn't to reach industry average OO%, but to best it by some amount, for example 10%.

$$\text{Target Other Overhead} = \text{Industry Average OO\%} \times 90\% \times \text{Sales} \qquad (11.4)$$

One of the most common reasons OO% goes out of control is the proliferation of staff functions as discussed in the chapter on controlling labor cost. But there are other reasons as well. Knowing that overall costs are excessive and setting OO% targets establishes a framework for action and a way to measure the effectiveness of overhead reduction efforts.

Cost of Goods Sold

Non-labor costs are often a significant factor in cost of goods sold. Cost of goods sold (COGS%) should be compared to historical trends as well as those of competitors. The equation for COGS% is given in (11.5).

$$\text{COGS\%} = \text{Cost of Goods Sold/Sales} \qquad (11.5)$$

Suppose a company has COGS of $15 million, sales of $20 million what is its COGS%?

$$= \$15 \text{ million}/\$20 \text{ million}$$
$$= 75\%$$

Where companies or competitors report segment information segment COGS% should be computed and used to assure measures are comparable. Target COGS including the goal of outperforming (OP) the competition by 10% is given in Eq. (11.6).

$$\text{Target COGS} = \text{Industry average COGS\%} \times (1 - \text{OP}) \times \text{Sales} \qquad (11.6)$$

Suppose a company has COGS of $15 million, sales of $20 million, the Industry Average COGS is 72% and its goal is to beat the industry average by 10% what should its COGS in dollars be?

$$= 72\% \times (1{-}10\%) \times \$20 \text{ million}$$
$$= \$12.96 \text{ million}$$

This means the company's goal should be to cut COGS by a little over $2 million ($15 million–$12.96 million).

Appropriate Goals

Setting cost targets 10% better than a company's competitors may seem aggressive, but experience shows there are inefficiencies in even the best run companies. There are many examples of companies setting and achieving high performance standards, there are few examples of companies reaching high levels of performance when they set low standards.

In this chapter we talk about setting goals for overhead, other overhead and cost of goods sold. We also talked about setting goals for these measures in the chapter on reverse engineering. How do the two fit together?

In reverse engineering the task is to find a combination of cost reductions that will enable a company to reach its goals. One issue is how to allocate cost cuts in a reasonable manner. In this chapter we talk about goal setting based on industry norms. Both methods provide a means for estimating what goals should be. The actual goals approved by the turnaround committee may be those from reverse engineering or those based on industry norms, but in all likelihood approved goals will be somewhere between the two.

Payment Analysis

Vendor Payment Analysis

One way to pin point excess costs is to determine where and to whom a company makes most of its payments. Vendors that a company pays large sums to should become targets of opportunity for cost reduction. This is an example of "hunting where the deer are."

Most accounts payable systems contain vendor history information that provides cumulative, Year to Date (YTD) payments by vendor. Often prior year payment totals are maintained for comparative purposes. Sort vendors from highest to lowest YTD payments and look at high dollar vendors. Are these expenses required to make the product; sell it; or ship it? Or are they overhead items? If overhead, can they be dramatically reduced? An analysis of high dollar vendors is a quick way to identify cash diverted to consultants, temp worker agencies and others that should be targets for reduction or elimination. It can also point out whether excessive payments are being made to lawyers or accountants. If a company's trusted advisors are billing excessive amounts, perhaps it is time to get more trustworthy trusted advisors.

As a general rule 80% of dollars are paid to 20% of the vendors. The bills of vendors representing 80% of dollars paid should be audited for excessive price, quantities billed and not shipped, and hours billed with no verification or no detailed justification. Invoices for mission critical vendors should also be scrutinized because there is always the temptation to purchase non-mission critical goods from these vendors to avoid scrutiny.

It is probably not worth while to scrutinize every vendor in detail. For example, vendors whose total payments constitute less than one half of one percent of accounts payable should be bypassed at this point to concentrate on higher value targets. For vendors whose total payments are greater than one half of one percent, management should know exactly why such payments are being made and how these purchases adds value.

This method has been used successfully to identify a significant amount of excess cost and waste. It would not be surprising to cut the cost of goods sold by two or three percent and operating expenditures three to five percent using this technique alone.

Category Payment Analysis

Category analysis is very similar to vendor analysis except that it stretches its net a little wider. Often managers spread purchases across several companies or several divisions of a company to stay below the radar. For example, rather than hiring fifty consulting programmers from one company and having to justify a million dollar invoice each month, some managers spread the work across a half dozen smaller consulting companies.

A cost object is a general description of the purpose of a cost; it is a way to categorize expenditures. If a company's accounting system tracks payments by cost object it should be relatively simple to extract cost object detail from accounts payable; summarize by cost object; and then sort the objects from high to low. In most companies, this process will identify a number of areas where expenditures exceed expectations. These areas should become targets of additional scrutiny.

The 80–20 rule should apply here too. Eighty percent of cost dollars will probably be in about 20% of cost objects. Concentrate on high dollar objects during the initial phase of restructuring and leave analysis of low dollar objects until the company achieves its larger financial goals.

Functional Analysis

Functional analysis looks at cost in terms of major income statement divisions. The four major sections or functions that should be uppermost in this analysis are (i) cost of goods sold, (ii) overhead, (iii) financing costs and (iv) taxes. Functional analysis addresses improvements both big and small. But, in the end it's minding the details that makes the difference between a company that just limps along and one that is spectacularly successful.

Cost of Goods Sold

Cost of goods sold is a highly productive area for cost reductions because savings have a multiplier effect. Targets of opportunity within Cost of goods sold include (i) production costs, (ii) facility utilization (iii) suppliers and (iv) product design.

Production Costs

Prepare, or have someone prepare a cost summary that identifies the percent of costs in every expense category contributing to the cost of goods sold. Suppose cost of goods sold broke down as shown in Table 11.1. We can see that small changes in assembler labor and the cost of circuit boards will have a much greater impact on COGS than cutting some cost categories like Connectors in half.

Study high payoff areas in detail. Are assemblers waiting for parts? Do they have the right tools and equipment? Is the assembly line shut down because of equipment failure? These questions bear on the productivity of the assemblers, and product cost.

Is the productivity of assemblers being measured? If not, one might find that some assemblers complete 20 units per hour and others only 6. The next question should be what techniques do the most efficient assemblers use? Is it the way they set up a job? Have they fashioned a special jig or do they use a special tool, or have they developed a more efficient assembly method? If they have, then their methods should be studied and replicated. For assemblers who are abnormally slow, do they require more training? Or are they simply not diligent? Either way, once underperforming workers are identified a solution to low productivity will present itself.

Table 11.1 Analysis of production costs

Cost element	Amount	Sub-total	Percent(%)
Direct labor			
Warehousemen	300,000		6
Assemblers	1,800,000		34
Testers	300,000		6
Packagers	400,000		8
Direct labor		2,800,000	
Direct materials			
Circuit boards	900,000		17
Wiring harnesses	300,000		6
Connectors	90,000		2
Packaging	300,000		6
Direct materials		1,590,000	
Variable factory overhead		140,000	3
Fixed factory overhead			
Management	300,000		6
Depreciation	350,000		7
Other	50,000		0
Fixed factory overhead		700,000	
		5,230,000	100

Can a more cost effective supplier of circuit boards be found? Are costs excessively high because 1 out of 10 circuit boards fails, or 1 out of 100, or 1 out of 100,000?

Look at the relationship between cost categories. Is packaging excessive for the type of good produced? What is the purpose of packaging? Is it another point-of-sale advertisement? Is its purpose to protect the product? If packaging can be simplified, perhaps savings can found in both packaging material and packaging labor.

Facility Utilization

Under-utilization of facilities is a common problem in troubled companies. Facility under-utilization can cause a number of problems including,

(1) Opportunity costs in the form of lost sales
(2) Increased costs if work has to be subcontracted out
(3) Excessive cost of goods sold if fixed manufacturing costs are spread over an inadequate number of units.

Physical plant is expensive and most physical plant costs are incurred whether or not used. McDonalds recognized this fact about 30 years ago. Prior to that, they were only open from about 11:00 A.M. to 10:00 P.M. and sold mostly hamburgers, French fries, cokes and milk shakes. That only gave franchisees 11 hours per day to amortize facility costs. Now, most McDonalds are open from 7:00 A.M to 11:00 P.M which gives their franchisees 16 hours per day to amortize facility costs and generate additional profits.

Suppose Fitz Corporation makes wooden desks that wholesale for about $275 each and they can build about one desk per hour. Demand is 384 desks per month, but they only build about 264 desks per month because of limited plant capacity. They outsource 120 desks per month which costs them about $200 per desk.

After examining records it was determined that they were effectively running a one shift operation which was masked by staggered start times. Going to two shifts they were able to bring the subcontract work back in house. Table 11.2 is an analysis of production as it is currently and what it could be if they added a second shift.

Through better plant utilization, Fitz can produce all their desks in-house, avoiding subcontractor costs. Spreading fixed factory overhead across 384 units vs. 264 units further lowers the Cost of Goods Sold. By bringing all production in-house, their gross margin rises to 51% (($275 − $134.38) / $275) from the current 40% (($275 − $165.63) / $275).

Suppliers and Purchasing

One philosophy says that suppliers should be played against each other and forced into price concessions without limit. Many large companies play this game

Table 11.2 Facility Utilization

	Hours per Months						
Theoretical plant capacity	662	24 hours/day	×	7 days/week	×	4 weeks/month
Reasonable efficient utilization	480	24 hours/day	×	5 days/week	×	4 weeks/month
Actual plant utilization	264	11 hours/day	×	6 days/week	×	4 weeks/month

	Units	Current cost	Units	Revised cost
Demand per month in units	384		384	
Less internally produced units	264		384	
Raw materials $55/unit		14,520		21,120
Direct labor $40/unit		10,560		15,360
Variable factory overhead $5/unit		1,320		1,920
Fixed factory overhead $13,200		13,200		13,200
Subcontract units $200/unit	120	24,000	0	0
	384	63,600	384	51,600
Average cost per unit		$165.63		$134.38

especially when they command so much of a supplier's output that it would be catastrophic for the supplier to lose the company's business.

A competing philosophy says a company can improve performance by integrating suppliers into its strategy. At this point you are probably thinking – "Ah, yes. Supply chain." Supply chain analysis is useful because it minimizes inventory by sharing scheduling and order information among all the parties in the supply chain from raw materials to the final consumer.

Really successful companies move beyond sharing logistic and demand information to sharing product design and production know how. Suppliers brought into product development can share technology that may improve or simplify the product's ultimate design. Early supplier involvement with designers can reduce new product lead time.

Successful companies understand that suppliers must be profitable otherwise logistics and quality will suffer and suppliers may cease to exist. On the other hand, companies need suppliers to supply material at the lowest possible cost. One strategy for achieving both goals is to analyze supplier production and encourage them to support efficient manufacturing and management practices. This may mean helping them identify and eliminate unneeded tasks, reduce inventory, and apply more effective manufacturing methods. This is only possible if the supplier trusts the company to do what is in its best interests and only if the company trusts the supplier not to share information with competitors. Toyota invests heavily in this supplier relationships and that maintains the supply of high quality, low cost components on an "as needed" basis. They do it by continuously analyzing every step in their shared design and production process to eliminate waste and improve quality (Womack, 2006).

Product Design

Product design has an enormous impact on cost. Product design dictates materials, fabrication and assembly methods, packaging and shipping costs, and reliability which translates into price and warranty costs.

While competition and customer needs play important roles in shaping product design, that doesn't mean a company should abdicate all responsibility for good design. Good industrial design refers to aesthetic qualities and ease of use. However, good design from a cost and efficiency perspective includes goals like minimizing weight, minimizing the number of parts, and simplifying the assembly process.

Make or Buy

Assembly simplification shades into the make or buy decision. Should a company make sub-assemblies or buy them? In part this turns on incremental cost. The total cost of making a sub-assembly in a company is irrelevant if a portion of those costs would be incurred anyway. An example of a cost that would be paid by the company whether a part was made or bought would be allocated overhead.

The simplest way to think of a make or buy decision is to compare the variable cost of manufacturing an item (direct labor, direct material and variable factory overhead) to the cost of purchasing the item plus transportation in and import taxes if any.

Functional analysis can be used to analyze services, administrative functions or almost any element of a company.

Targets of Opportunity

There are some pockets of waste that are so common across troubled and underperforming companies that they deserve special and prompt attention.

Consultants

Consultants are enormously expensive, but used in moderation, they can be an effective source of new ideas or temporarily provide a skill the company lacks. Once hired by a company, consultants tend to find new work for themselves and costs expand far beyond original missions. Some missions are open ended and executives resort to use of consultants to avoid increasing headcount.

Every consultant should be identified and listed on a report that indicates what the consultant was hired to do, how long they have been working on the project and when they will be done. The report should also list how much has been paid to that consultant year to date this year and last year.

Unless a consultant's skill is unique and needed only temporarily, the consultant's contract should be terminated and the work brought in house. The skill of a architect designing a building is unique and temporary. Computer programming consultants hired to supplement the programming pool are not.

Office Space

Corporate headquarters and other office space represent a cost that should be heavily scrutinized. While there are a few occasions when a headquarters must be close to key customers or suppliers, such situations are rare. Often better space can be leased or bought by moving a few miles outside major metropolitan areas. The quantity of office space should also be analyzed and not excessive. Staff reductions should translate into less space.

Facility Consolidation

Consolidating production is another way to address unutilized capacity. A company can sell excess facilities. Real estate is expensive in terms of taxes, insurance and maintenance. Selling a facility will generate cash for the turnaround. All or a portion of a facility can be sublet. Subletting provides an income stream and will preserve the facility if production requirements expand later. If the facility is leased rather than owned, one might negotiate with the landlord to release a certain amount of space back to him, her or it. I used this approach to save a client about $100,000 per year.

If administrative organizations are being consolidated with a subsequent reduction in headcount, the square footage of space needed to support the consolidated staff should also be reduced. If each worker utilizes 120 ft^2 of space and a company eliminates 300 employees, it should expect to harvest for sale, sublet, or release about 36,000 ft^2 (120 × 300). The space per worker doesn't just include the space occupied by the worker but some share of common space such as aisles, rest rooms, break rooms, copy rooms and so forth. If space costs $40 per ft^2 for rent, heat, light, water, sewer, insurance, taxes and security, the cost saved by eliminating 36,000 ft^2 in this example is $1,440,000 per year.

Of course when reducing space, one should look ahead 6 months to a year and if the space will be needed in a relatively short period of time it may not be practical to sell, sublet or release it. On the other hand, most companies tend to overestimate the amount of space they need.

Airplanes

Unless the company is an airline it probably doesn't need airplanes. While there is an argument that a corporate jet is needed to get to places, on schedules not served by commercial airlines, there is also the argument that commercial air service is frequent, reliable and goes practically everywhere. Chartering jets for specific flights is almost always cheaper than owning or leasing an airplane, having pilots on salary, and paying for maintenance, insurance, fuel and landing fees. Shareholders are more impressed by profits than how executives get to meetings.

Cars

Companies spend a tremendous amount of money to acquire and maintain cars. Lease payments, insurance, gas, oil, and maintenance adds up quickly. Liability for accidents involving company cars can be huge and even if the company's insurance company pays the immediate claim, most commercial insurance policies are experienced rated which means claims show up in higher, future premiums.

Strict guidelines should be developed as to who is entitled to a company car and those guidelines should be enforced. For example, the CEO or CFO might be entitled to a company car and even a limo if he or she does considerable work going to or from the office or to or from functions for the company's benefit. Outside salespeople may need company cars to transport clients or samples. However, few middle managers or other employees need cars.

An inventory of company cars should be developed and matched against the company's guidelines. This usually flushes out a considerable number of cars which can be eliminated. For those who claim they need to drive for company purposes, let them use their own cars and bill the miles back to the company on an as needed basis.

Trucks

Trucks are another expensive asset requiring insurance, fuel, road taxes and routine maintenance. A truck fleet should be scrutinized for utilization and underutilized trucks should be sold. Whether a truck is heavily used or not, it will still generate costs in the form of insurance, depreciation and road taxes.

A major expense of truck fleets is unscheduled maintenance. If a truck breaks down on the road, the cost of tow service, local maintenance where ever it is, and load spoilage or delay can be costly. However, there are several excellent services and software packages that track utilization, estimate component wear and schedule preventive maintenance which dramatically reduces the cost of unscheduled maintenance.

Phones and Phone Lines

Phones tend to get overlooked as a opportunity to save cost. However, reduction of phone lines, trunk lines, and specialized high speed lines can be an excellent target of opportunity when a company has significantly downsized. Phone lines, once ordered, stay on a company's phone bill forever unless the company makes a conscious decision to eliminate them.

The individual(s) responsible for a company's telecommunications should have a list of all the company's phone numbers, how those lines are being used; and who is using them. When employees leave or are terminated their phone lines should be pruned.

Cell phones present the same problem. As employees are hired, especially out-side sales people, consultants and managers, they are often issued cell phones. A log of people issued cell phones should be kept and matched to cell phone bills. Such a match can be quite revealing. Cell phones being billed to the company at a monthly rate which have no activity should be identified and that service can-celed. Occasionally, this type of analysis will identify former employees still using company cell phones. Former employees should be billed back for cell phone usage.

Insurance

Companies are often either under insured, which puts them at risk, or over insured, which costs them money. Over insurance is the more likely problem when a com-pany is down sizing. As headcount is reduced and facilities sold or closed, insurance policies should be reviewed and premiums adjusted downward.

The value of assets insured as well as their replacement value should be moni-tored. For example, the replacement value of computers is dropping continuously, yet premiums on computers will not drop until the company takes the initiative to request less coverage.

Travel and Entertainment

Travel and entertainment is often abused. Reasonable guidelines should be estab-lished and monitored. Business class air travel should be sufficient for most employees instead of first class travel, just as mainstream hotels should suffice versus luxury hotels. Entertainment should be reasonable and necessary, but not excessive.

The real payoff in cutting travel and entertainment is to send a message from the top down that the company is in trouble and everyone has to give up something, not just the day laborers. It's difficult to convince labor that it has to sacrifice when corporate executives are partying.

Executive Perks

Country club and gym memberships, chauffeurs, health plans not offered to other employees, and other executive perks should be eliminated. First and foremost this is leadership by example. It helps signal that the company is serious about restruc-turing. The symbolism of eliminating executive perks should not be underestimated. Reducing the cash drain on a troubled company is a secondary, but important effect.

Financing

Companies in trouble often slide into using high cost means of financing. For exam-ple, while factors do a good job of credit and collections, they are expensive. A company using factors might consider re-establishing or strengthening its own credit and collections capability.

A company might find it is referring a significant percentage of credit sales to collection agencies. If a company were able to strengthen its own credit department and credit criteria it might be able to avoid referring receivables to collections. Likewise, a company might find it is hiring lawyers to sue customers for money due and owing. Collection agencies might be a more cost effective way to chase delinquent customers.

Long term financing with bonds costs less than bank financing and is less risky because bondholders demand fewer covenants and less eager to find a company in default. Banks, on the other hand, view technical covenant defaults as an opportunity to squeeze a company for fees, expenses, higher interest and more collateral. Private bond issues, placed through investment banks, are simpler, cheaper and can be made for smaller amounts than public bond issues. The point is there are many options for financing a company, even a troubled ones. A company should consider its financing options broadly (Vance, 2005).

Taxes

Taxes are a significant cost factor for every company. Property taxes, for example, must be paid whether or not a company is profitable. Property values go up and down as do tax appraisals. Make sure county and municipal appraisals are consistent with current fair market values and appeal if they are not.

Most states impose sales taxes on goods sold to consumers. However, most states allow companies to avoid sales tax on the materials they purchase. Check the situation in the state where the company is located and analyze invoices for sales tax charges.

Federal tax law allows a company to carry back losses for 2 years which means that income tax paid in prior years may be refunded to a tax payer with a loss in the current year. Tax losses in the prior 15 years may be used to offset profits in a current year if they have not been previously used or disallowed.

Another tax minimization strategy is to make use of the General Business Tax Credit which covers a large number of items such as investment credits for energy and rehabilitation, research, welfare to work, alcohol fuels and employer social security credit. A comprehensive discussion of tax strategy is beyond the scope of this book. However, the turnaround team should discuss these issues with the company's tax counsel.

Audit Program

An audit program is a systematic plan for evaluating a company's performance. Pioneered by public accounting firms, audit programs have been adopted by internal auditors, investment bankers conducting due diligence, and others. Typically, an audit program is designed to analyze company performance by examining income statement and balance sheet accounts one at a time. The virtue of this method is that it is systematic. A drawback is that audit programs initially give high value and low value items equal weights. However, after working through an audit program one time, high value items will become apparent. A sample audit program is provided in Table 11.3.

Table 11.3 Sample audit program

Revenue

Has a correct price been set?

  See Markets and Pricing

Are prices being correctly applied to invoices?

  This is a particular problem where prices are derived from application of discounts, experience, or contract terms. In a large company, it wouldn't be surprising to find several millions of dollars in pricing errors.

Are there excess returns?

  This might signal quality control or other service problems.

Are excessive credits given for returns?

  If customers order inventory for a "seasonal" selling period and return inventory later at full price, the company risks damage and obsolescence while incurring material handling costs. A solution might include a 10% "Restocking Fee."

Are sales or other taxes that can be passed along to the customer properly calculated, billed and recorded?

  This is a particular problem for companies that sell to consumers in interstate commerce. Internet and mail order companies must generally collect and remit sales tax in their home state, but do not have to collect sales tax on out of state sales. Mistakes in tax collection can be costly.

Cost of goods sold

Is there a professional purchasing staff that actively seeks low cost, high quality sources of supply?

  Purchasing has become a highly sophisticated function involving source identification, price negotiation, quality control, and delivery scheduling for just in time manufacturing. Without a professional purchasing staff, raw material and equipment costs could be excessive.

Are there appropriate controls over payment processing?

  Are there controls to match purchase orders, receiving reports and invoices? Vendors often bill for more than they ship or incorrectly extend price and quantity on invoices. Are there controls to prevent, and or detect duplicate payments? Almost every company has made duplicate payments.

Are the correct expenses charged to products?

  If inappropriate expenses are charged to a product its cost will be inaccurate and that could cause prices to be inappropriately high or low. High prices reduce sales volume. Low prices thin margins.

Are allocated expenses appropriate?

  Errors allocating expenses among products distort cost.

Are labor and material variances tracked and investigated?

  Over time, all processes go off track unless there are standards to measure against and discrepancies are investigated.

Table 11.3 (continued)

Are scrap, re-work and rejects being tracked?
> Improving the yield on a production process from 90 to 91% can decrease the cost of goods sold about 1%. Are errors tracked and resolved?

Is overtime being tracked, managed and minimized?
> The premium pay in overtime can destroy a businesses' economic model.

Is facility and equipment utilization appropriate?
> Under utilized facilities increase the cost of good sold, and may result in other costs such as sub-contracting. Under utilized equipment is not productive. Can facilities be sold, sublet or returned to the landlord?

Are there any functions that can be economically out-sourced or subcontracted?
> Companies are often good at their core function, but bad at ancillary functions. Subcontracting or outsourcing can often reduce costs and improved quality.

Sales and marketing costs

Do sales commissions support the businesses' economic model?
> Are sales commissions' based on contribution or some other measure of profits or on gross dollars sold? Do sales commissions consume a disproportionate share of gross profit? If so, they can destroy the viability of a business.

Is the commission structure simple enough so that a sales people know exactly what is at stake on every sales call?
> Commission structures that are too complex do not serve as a motivator.

Are commissions only paid on "collected" sales?
> If not, there is the risk that sales people will sell to un-creditworthy customers to make a commission.

Is there an excessive number of people in Marketing as opposed to Sales?
> Sales people often perceive marketing is a higher status, lower pressure job and lobby for marketing jobs. This can cause over staffing in marketing. But sales are everything (Watson, 1954).

Are there controls in place to measure the benefits of advertising and promotional campaigns?
> Without measurement controls, it is hard to determine what is working and what is not. Without measurement, unproductive behaviors are often repeated, and successful campaigns go unrecognized.

Are other sales costs, such as point of sale displays, and point of sale dispensers, properly captured and integrated into Sales Cost%?
> Without properly analyzing these costs turnaround cash can be wasted and the financial model can be undermined.

Other overhead

Is all of the company's real estate: land, buildings, leaseholds, absolutely necessary?
> Bricks and mortar are expensive. Costs include: rent or financing cost, taxes, insurance, utilities and housekeeping. Physical plant should be kept to a minimum. Offices only need to be clean and functional, not spectacular.

Are personnel costs appropriate?
> See labor costs

Are there excessive staff functions?
> Over time, companies often develop specialized staff units that are not directly related to generating revenue or controlling costs.

Are there expenses for the "comfort of officers" vs. the service of clients?
> Examples of expenses for the comfort of officers include: airplanes, limousines, cabins or condos, golf courses, health club memberships, expense account lunches, junkets, or corporate retreats to vacation destinations. All these should be eliminated in a turnaround.

Table 11.3   (continued)

Are there excessive support staff?
> Support staff include: secretaries, print shop employees, and drivers, to name a few. Few middle managers need individual secretaries vs. departmental secretaries. Print shops can often be outsourced, and most executives should drive themselves.

Is an excessive amount of work delegated to consultants?
> Consultants are expensive, usually don't have a long term interest in the company, and often take their learning about a company's best practices to other companies.

Are outside accountant and lawyers' fees appropriate and audited?
> There is a temptation, even among a company's most trusted advisors, to go to the well too often if not watched.

Financing costs

Are financing costs being properly analyzed to determine the true cost of money?
> The true cost of money includes: interest, fees, penalties, discounts, underwriting costs, and imputed interest on leases. If financing costs are not being analyzed and alternative funding sources aggressively cultivated, a company will overpay. Many non-bank financing alternatives are available and discussed in Raising Capital (Vance, 2005) and similar books.

Conclusion

Two promising targets for cost reduction are overhead, specifically overhead not used for selling and marketing and cost of goods sold. Goals for cost reduction can be estimated based on Overhead% and COGS% for a companies best competitors plus some improvement against those benchmarks.

There are a variety of techniques for cost reduction including (i) high dollar vendor analysis, (ii) analyzing functions to identify the highest cost elements, and (iii) use of audit programs that analyze costs on an account by account basis. There are also specific targets of opportunity for cost reduction based on experience such as facilities, vehicles, communications and insurance.

The more techniques one uses, the more likely one is to identify excess costs. And that may be necessary to drive a company to peak performance.

References

Vance D (2005) Raising capital. Springer Science + Business Media, New York
Watson T Sr (1954), Nothing happens until a sale is made. President & CEO of IBM c
Womack JP (2006) Why Toyota won. Wall St J, A16, 13 Feb

Chapter 12
Information Technology

Introduction

Information technology (IT) can be a tremendous tool for driving productivity or it can bleed a company dry. It is not just the cost of computers, software and program-mers that can drag a company down; computers can make and replicate mistakes far faster than an army of clerks. Such mistakes can be ruinous.

On the bright side, computers can replace an army of clerks, reduce workload, enable people to communicate quickly and accurately, help identify, sell to, and ser-vice customers, and improve supply chain management. Well thought-out systems provide management with the means to keep its finger on the pulse of a company in near real time; identify problems; and change course to meet new threats and challenges. Companies also tend to collect vast databases which can be mined to improve operations. But few companies take full advantage of the opportunities information technology presents.

Alignment of Strategy and Information Technology

Historically, strategy has been developed in the executive suite, handed off to line managers and eventually somebody working for a line manager calls the IT depart-ment to develop or modify a system to perform a particular task. There two problems with this approach. First the person requesting the work, the user, is likely to focus on what he or she needs to accomplish in his or her job versus focusing on whether that application meets the broader strategic goals of the company. Second, even the best computer professionals can only design within the knowledge of their users. If the user lacks strategic focus, the IT department cannot possibly have a strategic focus.

To solve these problems, IT leadership must be involved in development of the company's strategic goals. This will give them the perspective they need to rec-ommend global solutions rather than responding to a patchwork of requests from lower level managers. When strategy is stated in terms of goals rather than spe-cific systems, IT can suggest options that executive management might not even know exist.

D.E. Vance, *Corporate Restructuring*, DOI 10.1007/978-3-642-01786-5_12,
© Springer-Verlag Berlin Heidelberg 2009

At one point Frito Lay found it took 12 weeks to get sales reports. In the fast moving world of retail, tastes can change overnight, competitors can launch new products and steal share, and customer needs change. In other words, Frito Lay was barely able to keep up with operational demands let alone gain insight for real time brand management. No department head, no regional vice president, and no product line manager had the strategic outlook to recognize the problem or the resources to fix it.

Mike Jordan, who took over as CEO of Frito Lay didn't call the IT department and ask for a system. Instead he asked, "What is our strategy? What do we have to do to become world class competitors?" In order to provide top flight service to customers, minimize inventory, make sure that all inventory was fresh, and to hold people accountable, he realized he needed a real-time sales, inventory and accounting system. He worked with top executives across the company including IT executives to come up with an overarching architecture that met the company's strategic goals. Among other things, Frito Lay equipped sales people with hand-held computers which allowed them to capture and record information as it was generated. As a result, the company got the tools it needed to dramatically improve execution; it increased sales from $3.0 billion to $4.2 billion in 3 years; and it saved between 30,000 and 50,000 hours of paper work per week (Feld and Stoddard, 2004, p. 74).

Cost and Needless Complexity

At the end of the day, computers can only do a half a dozen things (i) store information, (ii) retrieve information, (iii) sort data, (iv) make calculations, (v) apply simple logic tests, and (vi) communicate over distances. Everything IT tells you about how great a system is going to be is built on these six capabilities.

There is an unfortunate tendency among professionals to make things more complicated than necessary. Engineers do it. Lawyers do it. Accountants do it. Not surprisingly, IT people do it. The risks in complexity are that (i) productivity enhancing projects are delayed, (ii) programming costs increase, and (iii) systems are more error prone. Complexity also makes management timid about asking hard questions.

Examples of complexity include a variety of hardware platforms, programming languages, and telecommunication systems. Complexity is compounded by the fact that each application system was independently designed, uses different database software, has different rules for classifying, analyzing and computing transactions, and different data element definitions. In addition, most companies still rely on legacy systems that were designed before point of origination data capture.

Lack of a unified systems platform costs money (Feld and Stoddard, 2004, p. 76). When database software from multiple vendors is used, each must be paid license fees, interfaces for each will be different, updating a data element in one database does not automatically update it in other databases, computer staff must be trained and retrained in different software, and transition of staff among applications using different software is more difficult. In markets where customers expect information to be updated and coordinated in near real time, navigating and coordinating multiple applications using different software can try customer patience and reduce repeat sales. Every company should have a long term initiative to bring all systems into a common architecture with common databases, telecommunications, application design and programming languages (Feld and Stoddard, 2004, p. 76).

Management should ask exactly how each system is going to work. Accepting an answer like "its complicated," or "I can't explain it to you unless you know more about programming," or "you wouldn't understand," or "everybody does it this way," or "trust me," is abdicating responsibility. Do not accept an answer full of technical jargon or gobbledygook. Make the IT department explain every system in plain English (Feld and Stoddard, 2004, p. 74). If the IT department cannot explain how a system works, that means they don't understand it either.

Integration of Computer Professionals

A chronic problem is that computer professionals are culturally isolated from the rest of the company. Whereas engineers, lawyers, sales people and accountants have learned to communicate in the common language of business, computer professionals have continued to speak, think and act from a techno-centric point of view. This is not entirely their fault.

Management must take the initiative to educate computer professionals in business concepts, the company's business model (how it makes money), the key determinants of success, and how computer systems support strategic goals. Everyone must understand the company's business.

As a first step, one might send IT professionals to courses like "finance for non-financial managers." Then they should routinely be exposed to presentations on company operations. At the same time they should also be educated as to the company's plan for rebuilding the systems infrastructure to use common databases, languages, rules of operation and data element descriptions. The cost of this education is relatively little, but the payoff is great.

Treatment of IT professionals as professionals means they must embrace professional standards. These standards include more accountability and measurement. Computer department managers should be expected to execute their game plan with the same precision expected of sales, operations, engineering and accounting. Discipline and simplicity will lead to speed and efficiency (Feld and Stoddard, 2004, p. 77). As with other areas, those who don't, won't or can't embrace these new goals, should be eliminated.

Inventory Computer Systems and Projects

Computer systems are expensive to build, install and maintain. Couple this with the fact that management tends to defer to experts in the IT department and this creates the potential for out of control costs. By one estimate, IT departments waste 20%

Table 12.1 Systems inventory

System/purpose/user	Priority	How it furthers company goals	Adverse impact of elimination	Staffing required
ARDAMSII / Manufacturing management system/Paul Whittle, VP Manufacturing	1	ARDAMSII is used to schedule production, explode production into a parts list using a bill of materials database, mange raw materials, work in process and finished goods inventory and to track manufacturing labor	It would be difficult to translate the production schedule into a parts list and impossible to manage inventory efficiently	Jarmal, J. Mgr. $80,000 Murdock, R, Analyst $75,000 McName, J. Sr.Programmer $65,000 Bede, M. Sr. Programmer $60,000 Larson, L. Programmer $35,000 Jackson, P Programmer $35,000
...	...	...	...	...
...	...	...	...	...
...	...	...	...	...
Vantage/computer user tracking systems/Jay Simon, AVP systems	45	It tracks the number of users on-line minute by minute	Won't know system utilization until the end of the day	Arbogast, R. Syst. Pgmr. $65,000 Kinison, D. Syst. Pgmr. $60,000

of their budgets on purchases that don't contribute to corporate objectives (Feld and Stoddard, 2004).

To get a quick overview of computer systems, have the IT department compile a list of computer systems, their name, purpose, user department and contact, how the system furthers the goals of the company, the adverse impact of eliminating the system, if any, and the number of programmers, analysts and data entry clerks it takes to maintain the system. The survey should also list the names and salaries of people assigned to a system which will help quantify the cost of each system. Table 12.1.

Systems should also be ranked from most mission-critical to least mission critical. Ranking forces people to make the tough choices required for restructuring. Rankings should be based on user input and not just computer department input.

For systems under development, a similar list should be compiled along with the estimated cost to complete and a completion date. A copy of the design specifications of systems under development should be provided with this list. If there is no design specification, a question should be raised as to how one is to gauge its usefulness and how programming is going to know what to build. These systems should also be ranked as shown in Table 12.2.

A separate list should be compiled of operations and systems software staff. These people are often hard to allocate to a particular system or project. The total

Table 12.2 Systems in development

System/purpose/ user	Priority	How it furthers company goals	Estimated time and cost to complete	Staffing required
NOW/Internet order entry and tracking / Dan Dolan, VP Sales	1	Allows customers to enter orders online and allows sales people and customers to track orders from placement to delivery.	9 months from the date of this report (June 30, 2xxx). Est. cost to complete $625,000	Proj. Mgr. $80,000 Analyst $75,000 4 Programmers $60,000
...	...	...	...	...
...	...	...	...	...
...	...	...	...	...
EAASII/Expense Acct System / Bob Rob, Actg Mgr.	25	Helps analyze expense vouchers for excess travel expenses	12 months from the date of this report (March 31, 2xxx). Est. Cost to complete $90,000	$\frac{1}{2}$ Analyst $30,000 Programmer $60,000

number of people assigned to maintain and develop systems plus the operations and systems software staff should reconcile to the headcount of the IT department.

Consultants, contract programmers and temp workers are a perennial feature of computer departments. If they are used to develop or maintain systems, they should be reflected in the staffing associated with each system.

A traditional, but brutish method of cutting computer costs is to make a 10% cut across the board. A better approach is to fully fund high priority systems and eliminate low priority systems. High performing people assigned to low priority systems should be saved and low performing people in high priority systems should be targeted for elimination.

IT Outsourcing

Outsourcing information technology is a common way to cut short term costs, but it might not be the best thing for the company in the long run. When all IT functions are outsourced, it is usually done using a long term contract. Such contracts are often designed to show dramatic first and second year cost reductions, but costs generally escalate in future years.

As a general rule, core, value-added functions should be done internally and generic, low-value functions outsourced. In a very real sense, computer systems represent a company's nervous system. That makes it a core, value added function. However, that doesn't mean no IT function should ever be outsourced. The issue is whether and when it is appropriate. Key decision factors include (i) whether in-house staff have the expertise, (ii) whether the service is needed continuously, like desk top support, or intermittently, like installation of branch office equipment,

(iii) and the fixed cost incurred or avoided through outsourcing. For example, extracts and report writing may be within current IT staff's expertise, but development of an interactive website for commercial transactions may not be. The cost of new expertise includes recruiting and paying new staff, or retraining existing staff plus the ramp up time it takes them to mature in their expertise. It may not pay to hire or develop expertise which will become another fixed cost. The alternative is to outsource projects which require expertise not needed on a continuous basis.

Payroll System

An in-house payroll system might be a target of opportunity. When a company maintains its own payroll system, it must have payroll accountants who are experts on the ever changing rules, regulations and taxes that apply to payroll and the company must also constantly update the system to reflect new requirements.

The alternative is an outside payroll service. These services have become efficient and relatively low cost. They automatically remit taxes which saves accounting time and effort and they provide insulation against fines for untimely tax remittance.

Essentially the choice of in-house payroll processing versus service bureau processing is a break even analysis problem. For in-house processing, maintaining expertise and updating computer systems represents a high fixed cost, but the variable cost of processing payroll for each employee is less than a service bureau would charge. On the other hand, a service bureau might cost more to process payroll for each employee, but the fixed costs, from the point of view of the company are zero because the service bureau amortizes its fixed cost over many clients.

If a company has less than 1,000 employees it should probably use a service bureau. On the other hand, if a company has 10,000 employees it might be more cost effective to do payroll in-house. Between 1,000 and 10,000 employees the computer and accounting departments should have to justify the expense of an in-house payroll system.

Web Hosting

Web hosting is an example of a service that a company might consider outsourcing. Fixed costs include building an in-house facility and hosting expertise, the cost of equipment and software and operators to run the equipment 24/7 (Flandez, 2007). Web hosting contractors can often harness economies of scale not available to individuals companies to cut their costs and reduce charges to customers.

Equipment and Software Costs

There is a tendency for the IT department to constantly upgrade and expand computer equipment and software. Often companies aren't fully utilizing the resources at their disposal. Most computer operating systems keep detailed records of what they are doing, how they are doing it and where they are storing information. Often these details can be exploited to find significant cost savings.

At one company I found the computer department was spending about $10 million per year for new equipment when they weren't effectively utilizing the equipment they had. After a utilization analysis they were able to save about $3 million per year or about 30%.

Errors

Unlike people, computers can make errors at the speed of light, which means they can make lots of them. Errors can be caused by programming mistakes or omissions, errors in reference and edit tables, unexpected circumstances, using a computer system for an unintended purpose, data entry errors and the list goes on.

Computer errors can have a substantial drag on a company's financial performance. For example, I have found several million dollars of under billings and overpayments due to computer errors. Errors can also be costly when they result in failure to timely process customer orders or update customer accounts. In 1999, Hershey Foods found errors and other problems in newly implemented systems that

Table 12.3 Common types of computer system errors

System interface
> Interface errors arise when records are lost between systems. One cause of lost records is that record codes and formats acceptable to the first system are rejected or dropped by the second system.

Reference tables
> To be flexible, systems are often designed to use reference tables to look up supplemental data, to edit records, to price items or to classify transactions. Incomplete or obsolete reference table data can result in lost, miss-priced or misapplied transactions.

Repurposed systems
> Systems designed for one purpose, but used for another are error prone. Repurposing is so common there is a dictionary word to describe it. The word is kludge. The problem with repurposing systems is that old code treats transactions or calculates values in unexpected ways.

Edit and validation routines
> Edit and validation routines are useful to make sure a database does not become loaded with useless data. A problem can arise when systems reject transactions and do not give a clear reason for the rejection or the when system deletes a rejected transaction without giving a user a chance to correct it.

Inadequate testing
> Systems are often put into production with inadequate testing or systems are modified on the fly without adequate testing. Failure to adequately test can result in significant quantifiable errors for lost orders, lost customer history, over or under-billing, over payment, delayed service and general customer irritation. There is a rule of thumb that says every three changes to a system introduce one new error. Whether that ratio is 3:1, 5:1, or 20:1, changes bring with them a risk in increased errors. Testing reduces this risk.

put delivery of $100 million of Halloween candy at risk (Koch, 2002). Table 12.3 provides some idea of what to look for.

Simple controls such as accounting for the records and dollars input and passed from module to module and system to system can help identify lost or rejected records. Procedures to periodically validate reference tables can reduce errors. Computer systems should be designed so that diagnostic reports can be switched on at various points in a computer system so that intermediate results can be validated.

The two most severe constraints on any restructuring are time and money so while much can be gained by analyzing computer systems, it might not be practical to validate every system while a company is fighting for its life. Therefore, a company should focus on the most severe problems and address them. Such problems often surface in the form of customer complaints, or computer output that seems unreasonable on its face. Special attention should be placed on pricing, billing, collection, and payment systems. One should never assume an answer is correct just because it's produced by a computer.

Productivity

Computer systems can usually improve productivity anytime something is written. If a data entry device can be placed where the paper records are created, the paper record can be eliminated saving a down-stream data entry step. Point of source data capture also reduces errors because the person entering the data knows what needs to be input better than data entry clerks, poor handwriting is eliminated as an issue, data are available for further process more quickly and edit and validation criteria can be build in to make sure the data is clean and usable as it is input.

How does one identify targets of opportunity for point of source data capture? Look for any area in a company were there is a data entry pool, where there are large numbers of terminals or where telephone operators capture or provide data.

The next step in the evolution of point of source data capture is to have customers input data directly into a company's computer system. This shifts the burden outside the company which further improves productivity. Examples of shifting data capture to customers includes bank automatic teller machines (ATM), on-line job, loan and insurance applications and electronic tax filing.

There are many other areas in which systems can enhance productivity. Any place were people spend most of their time looking up data, making computations, pricing, or recording values such as time, temperature or amount should be targets for automation. Anything that is repetitive in nature is probably a candidate for automation. The issue during restructuring is to identify the high payoff targets and harvest productivity in those areas.

Mining Existing Data

Companies with computer systems tend to collect vast amounts of data, but only use it in the most straight forward manner. For example, an order entry system might capture data necessary to fulfill and bill a sale, but a company might not analyze that data to gain insights as to who is buying what, and when to improve the efficiency of sales campaigns. Mining data is making new uses of existing data (Anderson, 2007).

There are many levels of sophistication in data mining and some marketers have taken it to a high art complete with complex statistical analysis. Data mining can be used to identify costly exceptions. The 80–20 Rule says that 80% of profits come from 20% of customers or products. Turning this around, 80% of the losses on unprofitable business comes from 20% of transactions. Often a company underperforms not because of any inherent weakness in the company, but because some of its transactions, customers or products are unprofitable. If one can identify and shed things that are unprofitable, one can substantially improve performance.

Heartland Express, Inc., a trucking company, has a profit margin of 12% in an industry where 3% is the norm. Heartland's founder and CEO, Russell Gerdin, gets a computer report every Saturday morning that lists the details of every haul the company makes. This report lists: customers, destinations, routes, revenue and expenses. It also lists "dead heads," trips between points that don't generate revenue. Other trucking companies get similar reports. What makes the difference? The answer is that Mr. Gerdin, personally scours the statistics looking for unprofitable trips, substandard pricing, poor routing, or unexpected costs. Then he calls his mangers and asks them to justify each unprofitable, or low profit haul. In other words, one of the key strategies Heartland uses to improve profitability is to avoid unprofitable transactions (Bailey, 2001).

Ford UK uses operating statistics from its automated engine manufacturing plant to improve scheduling, resource management and trouble shooting (Antony, 2003). Credit card companies, mortgage companies, insurance companies, banks, airlines, retailers, construction companies, and others can use data mining to identify and avoid unprofitable transactions. Of course, identifying unprofitable transactions is one thing. Focusing management on avoiding unprofitable transactions in the future is another. Some management's are so fixated on growing revenue that they take on new customers with no regard for the profitability. This disregard of profitability is one of the reasons companies get into trouble.

The potential payoff in mining a company's data creates a new demand on the restructuring team. It must have one or more members who can access and manipulate large quantities of data. Simply having IT department support will not do because other priorities will come before the restructuring effort. Integrated databases often come with report writers which are simplified extract, sort and print programs. Such report writers can be exploited by a restructuring team. An alternative is for the IT department to provide extracts of databases that the restructuring team can manipulate with its own software. Some fairly sophisticated analyses can be performed with Microsoft Access. The key is for the restructuring team to have a dedicated and computer savvy person on its staff.

Conclusion

Information technology can dramatically enhance profitability or be an enormous drain on resources. IT professionals should be brought into high level strategy meetings so resources are deployed in a strategic manner and not piece meal. IT professionals should also be educated in business principals and the company's economic model.

Management should insist on knowing the systems the company is relying on, who the users are, and at what cost. Similar information should be demanded for systems in development. If the IT department cannot explain how a system works or how it is supports the company's mission, then it probably not as important as they think it is.

The inventory of systems should be prioritized. Priorities should be based on user input and not IT input. Rather than cutting IT budgets across the board, cut low priority, low payoff systems.

There is a natural tendency to for IT to want to run systems in house when they can be better run by a service bureau. The premier example of this is a payroll. If payroll is being run in house, it might be a target of opportunity for outsourcing. Another example of service that might be efficiently outsourced is web hosting.

IT departments tend to want to purchase new software and hardware on a regular basis. They should be challenged to show that they are fully utilizing the resources they already have before new resources are purchased.

Computer systems tend to get very complex very fast. Complexity increases the risk of errors. Common errors occur (i) at system interfaces, (ii) in reference and edit tables, (iii) in the logic of repurposed systems, and (iv) in edit and validation routines and (v) when systems are inadequately tested. Errors can be expensive in the through overpayments, under-billings, delay or errors which negatively impact customer service. Mission critical systems should be reviewed to make sure such errors are not occurring. Customer complaints can sometimes help identify computer errors. Audits and internal controls can minimize other errors.

Companies tend to accumulate vast amounts of data which are not fully exploited. Mining this data is a way to identify new marketing opportunities as well as to pin-point operational deficiencies.

References

Anderson LC (2007) Data mining: what is data mining? www.anderson.ucla.edu/faculty/jason.frand/teacher/technologies/palace/datamining.htm. Accessed 11 May 2007

Antony A (2003) Ford uses data analysis to boost productivity by 50% at Dagenham. Comput Wkly, 17 June. Article 00104787

Bailey J (2001) For one trucking entrepreneur, success is in the details: CEO makes heartland express envy of the industry with printouts and short-haul trips. Wall St J, B4, 27 Nov

Feld CS, Stoddard D (2004) Getting IT right. Harv Bus Rev 73–79, Feb

Flandez R (2007) Shopping out IT gets more complex. Wall St J, B8, 7 May

Koch C (2002) Supply chain: Hershey's Bittersweet Lesson. CIO published by the International Data Group. 15 Nov 2002. http://www.cio.com/article/31518/Supply_Chain_ Hershey_s_Bittersweet_Lesson Accessed 10 May 2007

Chapter 13
Financing the Turnaround

Introduction

A major challenge is finding the resources to keep a troubled company going while it is being restructured. When a company is doing well, everyone is willing to invest in, or lend to it. But when a company is in trouble, investors and lenders vanish. Yet there are a few who, under the right circumstances, will provide financing at a price.

In this chapter we discuss banks, commercial credit companies, asset based lenders, PIPES and debtor in possession bankruptcy financing. Each of these funding sources is only available under very specific conditions, for limited periods of time, and at considerable cost. However, when a company is in trouble, these sources may be the only ones available.

Balance Sheet and Cash Flow Goals

Just as a turnaround team should have goals for assets, headcount, new products, market share and so forth, it should have cash flow and balance sheet goals. Once these goals are met, a company will have little trouble financing growth. Those extending capital to a company in the form of loans or investments need to manage risk. Their perception of risk will be greatly reduced once the following goals are reached:

> Profit Margin in the top 25% of the industry
> Debt to Equity Ratio of 2:1 or better.
> Cash Flow at least three times debt service.
> Current and Quick Ratios at least 2:1.

Profit Margin measures the relationship between revenue and expenses. Interest net of taxes is added back to net income to adjust for the fact that companies use varying amounts of debt. Once debt is adjusted out, companies can be compared. Profit margin can be calculated using Eq. (13.1).

$$\text{Profit margin} = \frac{\text{Net income} + \text{Interest expense} \times (1 - \text{Tax rate})}{\text{Revenue}} \qquad (13.1)$$

D.E. Vance, *Corporate Restructuring*, DOI 10.1007/978-3-642-01786-5_13,
© Springer-Verlag Berlin Heidelberg 2009

If a company has net income of $10 million, interest expense of $4 million, it is in the 25% tax bracket and it has $100 million in sales its profit margin is:

$$\text{Profit margin} = \frac{\$10\,\text{million} + \$4\,\text{million} \times (1\text{--}25\%)}{\$100\,\text{million}}$$

$$= \$13\,\text{million}/\$100\,\text{million}$$

$$= 13.0\%$$

Several financial services provide industry averages. One might also want to compute profit margin for a company's best competitors.

The Debt to Equity Ratio is the ratio of all debt to all equity as shown in Eq. (13.2). The debt equity ratio, below is quoted as 2:1.

$$\text{Debt equity ratio} = \text{Liabilities/Equity} \qquad (13.2)$$

Suppose a company has assets of $90 million, liabilities of $60 million and equity of $30 million.

$$\text{Debt equity ratio} = \$60\,\text{million}/\$30\,\text{million}$$

$$= 2$$

The ratio of cash flow to debt service measures whether a company is generating enough cash to cover its debt obligations and prosper. There are several versions of this ratio; a common version is given in Eq. (13.3).

$$\text{Cash flow to debt service} = \frac{\text{Net income} + \text{Depreciation and amortization}}{\text{Interest} + \text{LoanPayments} + \text{LeasePayments}} \qquad (13.3)$$

Suppose a company has net income of $10 million, depreciation and amortization of $2 million, interest expense of $1 million, loan principal payments of $2 million and lease payments of $1 million.

$$\text{Cash flow to debt service} = \frac{\$10\,\text{million} + \$2\,\text{million}}{\$1\,\text{million} + \$2\,\text{million} + \$1\,\text{million}}$$

$$= \$12\,\text{million}/\$4\,\text{million}$$

$$= 3\,\text{times}$$

The current ratio measures the relationship between assets expected to be converted to cash in a year and debts that must be paid in a year. Current assets are things like cash, accounts receivables and inventory. Current liabilities are debts which must be paid in a year and include things like accounts payable, accrued payroll, and the principal portion of loan notes, lease payments and bank loans due within a year. The current ratio is given by Eq. (13.4).

$$\text{Current ratio} = \text{Current assets/Current liabilities} \qquad (13.4)$$

Suppose a company has cash of $2 million, accounts receivable of $10 million and inventory of $8 million, accounts payable of $3 million and the principal due within a year on lease, mortgage and loan payments of $5 million.

$$\text{Current ratio} = \frac{\$2 \text{ million} + \$10 \text{ million} + \$8 \text{ million}}{\$3 \text{ million} + \$5 \text{ million}}$$

$$= \$20 \text{ million}/\$8 \text{ million}$$

$$= 2.5$$

Banks don't understand inventory so they want to know whether a company would be able to pay its current bills with current assets if inventory were valued at zero. The formula for the Quick Ratio is given in Eq. (13.5).

$$\begin{aligned} \text{Quick ratio} \quad &= (\text{Current assets} - \text{Inventory}) /\text{Current liabilities} \\ &= (\$20 \text{ million} - \$8 \text{ million}) /\$8 \text{ million} \\ &= \$12 \text{ million}/\$8 \text{ million} \\ &= 1.5 \text{ times} \end{aligned} \qquad (13.5)$$

Industry averages may point to somewhat higher or lower goals. However, industry averages cannot provide an absolute standard because a whole industry might be in decline at the same time.

If the afore mentioned goals have been met, there is little need to seek alternative sources of financing. However, companies in restructuring are usually far from those goals. So alternatives must be discussed.

Banks

No matter how long the relationship between a company and its bank, no matter how amiable the relationship, a company in crisis should expect its bank to withdraw support as soon as the trouble becomes apparent.

The Philadelphia Chapter of the Turnaround Management Association (TMA) sponsored a panel discussion on troubled companies. The panelists were commercial bank lending officers. The sole question before the panel was: "How can you help a company in a turnaround situation?"

The first panelist said, "Our policy is to disengage from any company that is in a turnaround situation." The second panelist said, "If one of our clients has breached their covenants because they were in financial trouble, we would charge them additional fees "for the increased risk," and then we do everything we could to get out from under the loan."

The third panelist said, "First we increase their fees and interest. Then we demand additional collateral and endless meetings and reports as a condition of getting back in our good graces. Then, after we torture them for a while, we dump them."

The moderator from the TMA, stunned at the bankers' responses, asked. "But what do you do to HELP a company turnaround? The answer from all three bankers was: "NOTHING." It was a very short panel discussion.

Bank Lending Agreements

Bank lending agreements that run a hundred pages or more are not unusual. Of that, the first paragraph states what the bank is going to do for the borrower and the rest is what the borrower must do for the bank. Very little of this has to do with repayment of principal and interest. Most has to do with covenants and penalties the bank can assess. One of the most draconian penalties is loan acceleration which is a demand for immediate repayment.

Covenants are promises a borrower makes to the bank such as a promises to remain profitable, have a minimum equity, maintain a certain debt/equity ratio, generate a certain level of cash flow and maintain ratios such as current and quick ratios within certain limits. Covenants are difficult to keep when a company is in trouble.

Banks also require personal guarantees for all but very large companies. A personal guarantee means that if a company fails, the bank can seize the owner's assets including his or her home, retirement accounts and so forth.

When a borrower breaches a covenant, the loan is often transferred to a bank's Workout Department. The objectives of the Workout Department are to get the bank out from underneath the loan and charge the debtor as many fees as possible. A bank might argue its Workout Department is simply managing risk. True. It is manages risk in the same way a deer hunter manages risk by carrying extra ammunition. Once a company has been transferred to the Workout Department, no matter what it does after that point, it will never get back into the bank's good graces. Look for alternate financing.

Facility Renewals

Most companies rely on banks for mortgages, term loans, letters of credit, leases and lines of credit. Banks call each credit-related service a " facility." Most term loans must be paid off in 3–5 years. When a company is doing well, it is not difficult to get such loans renewed. However, when a company is in trouble, the bank may simply not renew these loans. A line of credit must be paid off within 1 year and that makes it a current liability. Again, if a company is in trouble, the bank may simply decline to renew the line.

Line of Credit and Borrowing Capacity

Bank lending agreements usually include a formula for borrowing capacity. Borrowing capacity is the maximum amount a bank will lend a company at any point in time. It is possible to negotiate a loan of $10 million dollars but only be able to get $2 million because of limited borrowing capacity.

Borrowing capacity is usually defined as tangible net worth excluding bank loans, times some borrowing factor. At no time may outstanding bank debt exceed the borrowing capacity. If loans exceed borrowing capacity, lending agreements require outstanding balances be paid down to the borrowing capacity on the day the over-capacity borrowing is discovered.

Tangible net worth is assets less non-bank liabilities, less intangible assets such as copyrights, patents, trademarks and goodwill. Also excluded from tangible net worth are loans to officers, directors, employees, and accounts receivable over a certain age, usually 90 days. Some banks exclude pre-paid assets from tangible net worth and some banks exclude accounts receivables over 60 days old. Once tangible net worth is calculated, it is multiplied by a factor, usually 80% to get borrowing capacity.

When the economy begins to turn down, as it does from time to time, or when the bank is illiquid, or when a company falls into disfavor with the bank even though it has not violated any covenants, the bank, at loan renewal, can change the accounts receivable criteria to exclude receivables over 60 days from tangible assets and it can reduce the factor to 70%. Both of these actions significantly reduce the amount that can be borrowed from a bank.

Bank Crisis and Surprise

A significant problem with banks is that they don't give customers adequate lead time if they decide not to renew a credit facility. Prior to the renewal date, most companies ask "will my loan be renewed?" Banks tend to answer obliquely using words like, "we're working on it," or "it's under review," or "it's in process." If banks gave advanced warning of non-renewal, a company could look for alternative financing. Bank delay in telling a company of non-renewal can push a troubled company closer to insolvency. So the lesson is that as soon as your bank twitches, look for other financing, even if it is more costly.

Even troubled companies can get financing if they know were to look. The balance of this chapter discusses alternatives to banks.

Factors

A factor enables a company to sell on credit, and get paid a substantial portion of the sale price immediately. Factored transactions are often structured as an interest bearing loan from the factor to the selling company until the accounts receivable is collected. If the customer pays promptly, the factor charges little interest, but if the customer is a slow payer, the factor will charge the seller more interest. A factor makes money by charging a fee structured as a discount and by charging interest.

The discounts and interest rate charged are based on the nature of the accounts receivable and the type of contract. Factoring with recourse means that if the factor cannot collect the account, it gets to sell the account back to the company for what it paid. Factoring without recourse means the factor bears the risk that the account is uncollectible. Discounts for factoring without recourse are much higher than factoring with recourse.

The amount advanced by the factor to the company is the amount of the account receivable, less the discount fee, less expected interest and less some reserve in case interest is greater than anticipated. When the sale is with recourse, the company might expect to get about 85% of the invoice price promptly and a little more after the invoice is collected.

For example, suppose a company has an invoice for $10,000 and the factor's discount is 5%. The factor advances the company 85% of the invoice price or about $8,500. Assume the factor collects in 50 days and charges 18% interest on uncollected invoices. The interest charge will be about $209.59 ($8,500 × (50 days/365 days per year) × 18%). Of the $10,000 invoice, the factor keeps the 5% fee, $500, plus interest of $209.59 for a total of $709.59. So, out of $10,000, the company is entitled to $9,290.41 ($10,000 less $709.59). Since the factor has already advanced $8,500 to the company, it will remit the final $790.41 after it collects the account.

The benefit of factoring for the company is that it receives cash immediately plus the excess reserve when the account is collected. Many factors for business to business companies also check the credit worthiness of customers before goods are shipped or services provided. Off loading credit checking to the factor reduces cost and improves the likelihood that customers will promptly pay.

Every factor has slightly different terms so it pays to shop around. For example, if a factor could be found that takes a 3% fee and charges only 12% interest, the cost of factoring in the above example would drop to $439.73 ($10,000 × 3% + $8,500 × (50 days/365 days per year) × 12%).

Asset Based Lenders

Banks want to know that a company made a profit last year, that it will make a profit this year and that it will make a profit next year. In contrast, asset based lenders are more concerned with the quality of a company's assets and how easily they can be converted to cash if the company fails to repay its loan. The fact that they calculate risk differently than banks make asset based lenders an option for troubled companies.

Asset based lenders will lend against accounts receivable, inventory, property plant and equipment and real estate. However, they usually value these assets at their exit value, which is the value the assets would have if the company ceased to operate. Exit value, sometimes called fire sale value, is less than fair market value and usually much less than book value. This limits the amount of money that can be raised.

Asset based lenders vary widely in the types of businesses they will lend to, the collateral they accept, the value they place on the collateral, and the size of the transaction (loan) they are interested in. Some place geographic limits on where the collateral must be located. Some asset based lenders only lend to fairly stable companies and others specifically target companies in a turnaround situation. When dealing with an asset based lender, it is important to get their lending criteria before any substantive discussions take place otherwise, talks are a waste of time.

Tranche B Lenders

A tranche B lender, also known as a junior capital lender, is a lender that will take a second lien on assets. Tranche B lenders step in when banks get nervous about potential down turns in the economy or when banks undervalue assets.

Banks tend to value assets conservatively. Tranche B lenders may value assets higher than banks. Table 13.1 is an example of the impact of the different valuations placed on assets by banks and Tranche B lenders.

Table 13.1 Tranche B lending analysis

	Book value	Bank's value	Tranche B value	Difference
Accounts receivable	1,000	700	800	100
Inventory	1,000	800	850	50
Equipment	1,000	800	800	0
Real estate	1,000	800	2,000	1,000
	5,000	3,100	4,450	1,150

Where a bank might value assets at $3,100 a Tranche B lender might value those same assets at $4,450. If a bank has a lean on $2,500 of assets, the Tranche B lender could take a subordinated lien of $1,150 based on the excess value it sees in the assets. Tranche B lenders charge more than banks because their risk is greater.

There are a significant number of Tranche B or junior capital lenders in the market place. As with other lenders it is important to obtain their lending characteristics at the outset to see whether the company qualifies for their services. The solicitation letter from ABC Capital Partners, (the company name changed to protect confidentiality) reproduced in Table 13.2, tells us the lender is interested in working with middle market companies and that assets need not be concentrated in particular states.

Table 13.2 LBC capital partners solicitation letter

I have recently co-founded ABC Credit Partners, a member of United Capital Partners, a family of private investment management firms. United Capital member firms have an aggregate of more than $4 billion in capital commitments under management.

ABC Credit Partners provides privately negotiated junior capital and other structured credit products to companies with annual revenues less than $500 million on a national basis.

I look forward to working with you in the near future.

Adam Bingham Cohen
ABC Credit Partners, Inc.

Junk Bonds

The idea behind junk bonds is that almost any company can raise money if the yield to investors is high enough. Junk bonds look and feel like other corporate bonds except that they are issued by companies that are either little known, and therefore considered risky, or companies that are in financial trouble.

These bonds are called junk because they are too risky to be investment grade. A bond can become a junk bond in two ways. It could be a bond that was investment grade when issued, but has been down graded to junk because the issuing company has fallen on hard times. Pre-bankrupt General Motors (GM) bonds are an example. This type of junk bond is called a " fallen angel." Other bonds are classified as junk bonds from the day of issue. This second category of junk bonds is relevant for financing a company in trouble.

Realistically, there are limits on companies issuing junk bonds. Junk bonds sold to the public must be registered with the SEC, and registration is expensive, so it only pays to issue junk bonds if a company plans to raise more than $200 million. Privately placed junk bonds can be issued in a cost effective manner if a company is raising at least $40 million.

It is easier to issue junk bonds if the company is publicly traded. Publicly traded companies already have audited financial statements and have a public track record that bond purchasers can evaluate. Junk bonds have an advantage over bank loans in that they have few restrictive covenants. As long as a company makes interest payments when due, and makes payments to a sinking fund (a fund to retire the bond principal) if the bond indenture requires such payments, then a company is fairly free to do as it pleases.

Securitization

Securitization is a way for a company to raise capital independent of its creditworthiness or future prospects. Securitization is an alternative to bank financing; there are no covenants; and it costs less than bank loans.

The concept behind securitization is to create a company with no liabilities and very little risk called a Special Purpose Vehicle (SPV) and use this company's pristine credit history to sell A rated bonds. Such bonds pay very low interest rates, usually much lower than the prime interest rate charged by banks.[1]

To raise money through securitization, a company must identify a pool of assets that can be sold to an SPV. Examples of assets pooled for sale include: mortgages, leases, credit card balances, auto loans, notes receivable, and accounts receivable. Theoretically, any separable assets with a predictable cash flow can be securitized (Kothari, 2003).

Bonds are a form of security. Bonds sold as interests in pooled assets are called Asset Backed Securities. The market for Asset Backed Securities is several trillion dollars. About 70% of this total is for mortgaged backed securities. The remaining

30% include securities backed by student loans, mobile homes, vehicle loans, home equity loans and credit card backed securities (Furletti, 2002). A Special Purpose Vehicle (SPV), also sometimes called a Special Purpose Entity (SPE).

The company raising cash will sell the cash generating assets to the SPV. The SPV will then sell bonds whose return will be based on the cash flow generated by the asset pool. The SPV purchases the company's assets at a discount from the expected value of the cash flow. The discount covers the cost of servicing cash inflows, paying bondholders, and provides an allowance for uncollectible accounts.

If a company sold bonds directly backed by assets, and the company went bankrupt, the assets underlying the bonds would be subject to attack by the company's creditors. So the main reason for selling assets to a SPV is to get the assets out of the troubled company and protected from attack. The assets will only be protected if there is a true sale of assets which means that the company originating the assets must give up control over those assets.

To make the separation of the assets from the company complete, a company will hire an investment bank to set up and manage an SPV. Investment banks get fees to set up SPVs, for asset management, and for selling SPV bonds. The investment bank should also engage an agency to rate the bonds the SPV plans to sell. Such ratings reduce the information asymmetry between bond buyers and the SPV and allow the SPV to issue bonds with lower coupon rates.

The cost of funds to the company originating the assets will be based on the cost of funds to the SPV. If the SPV issues bonds, and the bond yield is 6%, servicing costs are 0.6% and the risk inherent in the underlying cash flow from assets was valued at 0.8%; the SPV would purchase the assets at a discount of 7.4% (6% + 0.6% + 0.8%). The higher the bond rating, the lower the SPV bond yield will have to be. The lower the bond rating the higher the bond yield will have to be.

One strategy to increase a bond's rating is to issue both senior and junior bonds secured by the same pool of assets. Suppose $200 million of bonds were being sold, $185 million of senior bonds and $15 million in junior bonds. The fact that senior bonds will get paid first means that to the senior bond holders, the pool looks like it has an extra cushion of $15 million against default. This will raise the credit rating of the senior bonds and lower the overall cost of funds for the SPV.

It is only cost effective to sell SPV bonds to the public if it expects to raise more than $200 million. However, if the bonds are sold in a private placement, then the minimum drops to about $40 million. The cost to set up a securitization transaction can be as little as $200,000 for a private placement or as much as $1 million for a public issue (Stonehenge Financial Partners, LLC, 2003).

Asset securitization is not the answer for every company or every investor. In the last few years large numbers of sub-prime mortgage loans of have been securitized. Sub-prime mortgages are loans to homeowners with questionable credit histories. Because the recent (2007–2009) slippage in real estate values, and mortgages issued without traditional underwriting standards, the high default rate on sub-prime securitized loans is reducing investors' appetite for securitized bonds (Times Wire Services, 2007).

Private Investment in Public Entities (PIPES)

Sometimes a company has such poor performance that its bank has cut them off, it has few unencumbered assets to borrow against and no cash generating assets to securitize. Junk bonds work if a company has marginal performance, but if it is really in trouble, there will be little market for bonds. Are there any other alternatives? Yes.

If a company is publicly traded, and its stock price is at least $3 per share, it might consider a Private Investment in Public Equities (PIPE) which is an alternative of last resort. In a PIPE transaction, a private investor provides capital to a public company in a private placement following the requirements of Securities and Exchange Commission (SEC) Regulation D. After the placement, the securities involved are registered. Registration is much more complex and expensive than Registration D. However, registration allows stock to be sold to the public. Registration is the key to a PIPE because it converts what would have been an illiquid investment of private capital, into a liquid asset in the form of stock that can be sold to the public (Chaplinsky and Haushalter, 2002).

PIPES can be structured in a number of ways limited only by the imagination of the parties and their relative bargaining power. Suppose a company in trouble is publicly traded with shares selling for $5 each and it needs $10 million. It might find a private investor to purchase $10 million of preferred stock convertible to 4 million shares of common stock. This means that on converting the preferred stock to common stock, the private investor will have purchased its common at $2.50 per share ($10 million/4 million shares).

At the time the deal is closed, a Form 8-K is filed with the SEC providing a detailed description of the terms of the PIPE. After a short period of time, perhaps a month or two, the company will register the common shares held by the private investor. Once the registration is effective, usually 20 days after filing, the private investor can sell its shares in the market place.

If the price of the stock in the company maintains its $5 price, the investing company will have made 100% on its investment. However, if a company is in trouble, the share price might not hold. If the price slips to $4 per share the investor will get $16 million ($4/share × 4,000,000 shares) on an investment of $10 million, still not bad for capital at risk for less than 6 months.

How does an investor protect itself from dramatic stock decline? One way is to incorporate a "reset" term in the investment contract. In the above example, it was anticipated that the investor would be able to buy stock for $2.50 per share which was about half price. A reset option would allow the investor to "reset" the conversion price one time if the market price of the stock slipped below some predetermined value. For example, the investor might have the option to reset the conversion price to 60% of market value if the market value slipped below $4. After the reset condition is triggered, the timing of the reset is up to the investor. He, she or it might wait until the market price slips to $3 and then reset the conversion price to $1.80. If the stock rebounded before the investor liquidated his, her or its position, so much the better.

However, if the stock price slips below some threshold value, the stock may be delisted from its exchange and delisting makes a company's stock hard to sell. So, a private investor may find he or she is stuck with illiquid securities.

Bankruptcy and Super Priority Loans

Filing for Chapter 11 bankruptcy does not necessarily cut a company off from capital. The purpose of Chapter 11 is to hold creditors at bay for some period of time until the company reorganizes itself. The bankruptcy code recognizes that sometimes additional money is needed to maintain the value of assets, for example if an office building has a flooded basement or leaky plumbing, those problems must be fixed otherwise the value of the building will rapidly decline. Sometimes a company needs working capital to buy raw materials or meet payroll needs. Since a company is more valuable if it is operating than if it is closed, courts are sympathetic to the idea of a company taking on more debt, even though it is holding off paying its old debts.

However, no one would lend money to a company in bankruptcy if they were an unsecured creditor and had to stand in line with other unsecured creditors. Therefore, the code provides that a post-petition lender can get a super priority loan which gives it preference over all other unsecured creditors if certain procedures are followed. This loan must be for actual and necessary expenses in the ordinary course of business. The court must approve the loan after notice and a hearing at which other unsecured creditors can contest the necessity of the loan. If the court approves, it will issue an order giving the loan a priority over all other unsecured creditors except, for court fees, attorney costs, and administrative bankruptcy expenses.

There are many commercial credit companies, private investment firms and small business investment companies (SBIC) that specialize in lending to companies in Chapter 11. Such lending isn't risk free. A company may not be able to reorganize and there may not be enough assets to pay off the loan. So even though a post-petition lender gets a super priority, it still needs to evaluate the details of a particular bankruptcy situation before deciding to lend.

Commercial Credit Companies

Commercial Credit Companies covers a wide variety of companies that invest in leases, working capital loans, factoring, sale and lease back and other special financial situations. Many do not fit neatly into the categories discussed above. A company that needs non-bank financing and does not want to give up equity might want contact a commercial credit company.

Every commercial credit company has a slightly different risk/reward/transaction size/time to exit profile. Time to exit is the amount of time until a lender wants to get his, her or its money back.

Unlike a pure asset based lender, commercial credit companies sometimes extend credit on the basis of both assets and a company's ability to generate income.

Table 13.3   KBR capital corporation criteria

KRB Capital Corporation describes itself as an asset based lender headquartered in Forth
  Worth, Texas (KRB Capital Corporation, 2001). General Financing Criteria:

- Transaction Size $50,000–$5,000,000
- Chapter 11 Financing, Seasonal and Turnaround Financing
- Minimal Covenants, limited or no personal liability
- Does NOT finance construction, medical or personal accounts receivable

Working capital financing:

- Finances 90% of eligible accounts receivable
- Finances 65% of eligible inventory
- Facility terms generally up to 2 years

Term loans and leases:

- Finances 90% of appraised value of machinery, based on liquidation value
- Interest only terms while equipment being brought on-line
- Finances 85% of appraised fair market value of owner occupied real estate
- Facilities usually 2–5 years

Commercial credit companies always charge rates that are higher than bank rates.
However, they rarely demand personal guarantees as banks do.

Table 13.3 and Table 13.4 provide some examples of the criteria used by
commercial credit companies to screen credit risk.

Table 13.4   Transamerica business capital

Transamerica asset based loans range from $10 to $150 million (Transamerica, 2002).

Characteristics of companies that qualify for Transamerica financing include:

- Actively involved management, with a track record of good performance in the company's
  industry
- Adequate assets
- Historical profitability that is "spotted" to consistent
- Moderate to high financial leverage
- Realistic projections, consistent with historical data

Required loan to asset value(s):

- Accounts receivable, up to 85% based on the quality of accounts receivable (this usually
  implies accounts receivable are less than 90 days old, often less than 60 days old.)
- Inventory, up to 75% of eligible (lower of cost or market) inventory
- Machinery and Equipment – up to 80% of appraised, orderly liquidation value (this usually
  means, the business is closed, and assets are sold via regular markets. This might be a small
  fraction of fair market value.)
- Real Estate – up to 65% of appraised fair market value (if property is already subject to a
  mortgage, then only the net equity is available for collateral.)

Terms and repayment:

- Repayment consistent with liquidation of assets
- Loan terms up to 7 years
- Rate: Floating rate over prime or LIBOR with fixed rate pricing available. (LIBOR is the
  London Interbank Offer Rate).

Summary of Financing Alternatives

Troubled companies have many alternatives to banks. The key is to match as closely as possible, the company's circumstances to the requirements of each alternative (Table 13.5).

Table 13.5 Financing alternatives for troubled companies

Option	Advantages	Disadvantages	Requirements
Factoring	Quick and easy. Factors can under-write credit risk	More expensive than bank loans. Company may have to buy back bad accounts	Very few
Asset based lenders	Relatively quick and easy. Losses less important than the value and liquidity of assets	More expensive than bank loans	Assets must be in good condition and there must be a ready market for assets
Tranche B lenders and Junior capital	They often value assets more highly than banks	More expensive than bank loans	They lend based on the difference between their asset valuation and that of banks
Junk bonds	Rates may be comparable to bank loans and there are far fewer covenants	Bonds sold to the public must be registered which is expensive	Cost effective if $200 million or more is raised in a public bond sale. Cost effective if $40 million is raised in a private offering
Securitization	A way for companies to raise capital independent of their credit rating	Problems with sub-prime mortgage backed bonds have chilled the appetite for such bonds	Must have separable assets that generate an on-going cash stream
Private Investment in a Public Company (PIPE)	A company can raise substantial capital that it does not have to repay	Dilutes the equity of existing shareholders because common shares are issued far below market price	Publicly traded company with a share price of at least $3 per share
Super priority loans	Can get financing for a company in Chapter 11 bankruptcy	Company must be in bankruptcy. More costly than bank loans	Company must be in bankruptcy. Must get court approval for financing
Commercial credit companies	Very flexible and can see opportunities where others do not	Every commercial credit company is different. Much more costly than banks	A company must match the criteria of the commercial credit company exactly

Conclusion

When a company gets into trouble, it should expect its bank to withdraw support, increase fees and terminate outstanding loans. It makes no difference whether the company has a long history with the bank or even whether it pays principal and interest on time. Some bank facilities like a line of credit must be renewed every year. Banks are not always candid about whether they intend to renew a credit facility. Lack of warning can push a troubled company closer to bankruptcy. So the first time a company's bank twitches, it should seek alternative financing.

If a company needs receivables financing it can use a factor. If a company has a lot of unencumbered assets it might get financing through an asset based lender. If it needs to borrow more than the amount that bank will lend against its collateral it might consider a Tranche B lender, also called a junior capital lender. If a company is underperforming, but not loosing money and it needs to raise $200 million or more it might issue junk bonds. If a company has a pool of cash generating assets that are separable from the assets used to operate the company it might consider asset securitization. If a company is publicly traded, with a stock price above $3 per share it might consider a PIPE transaction. If a company is in Chapter 11 bankruptcy it might consider a super priority loan.

Commercial credit companies do not fit neatly in any particular category. They look for assets to secure loans, but also consider a company's operating performance. Every commercial credit company is different in terms of risk tolerance and situation analysis. So, it is important to find a commercial credit company whose criteria match the company's circumstances.

Most troubled companies can get financing, even while in restructuring. However, it will be significantly more expensive than bank financing.

Note

1. Steven L. Schwartz, Professor of Law, Duke University Law School, "Securitization Post-Enron," 25 Cardozo Law Review 2003 Symposium Issue on "Threats to Secured Lending and Asset Securitization" submission draft 23 Oct 2003, pp 4–6

References

Chaplinsky S, Haushalter D (2002) Financing under extreme uncertainty. University of Virginia, Darden Graduate School of Business Administration, chaplinskys@virginia.edu, 434-924-4810, unpublished paper draft Sept
Furletti M (2002) An overview of credit card asset-backed securities. Payment Card Center Discussion Paper, Federal Reserve Bank of Philadelphia, 1–2 Dec
Kothari V (2003) Securitization: the financial instruments of the New Millennium, Academy of Financial Services, Calcutta – 700 039 India, p 4
KRB Capital Corporation (2001) Fort Worth Texas, www.kbkcapital.com/commercialbusinesscredit.htm 5 Aug 2001

Transamerica (2002) Transamerica business capital, www.TransamericaFinance.com/tfc/Comm_Lending?TA_Biz_Credit. Accessed 3 June 2002

Stonehenge Financial Partners, LLC (2003) website www.stonehengefp.com/Securitization.htm. Accessed 12 Nov 2003

Times Wire Services (2007) Hedge funds warn SEC on bonds. Wall St J, C6, 14 June

Chapter 14
Internal Sources of Cash

Introduction

Raising capital for a corporate turnaround is difficult, time consuming and expensive. And at the end of the day, there is no guarantee a troubled company will find financing. So what are the alternatives?

Companies, especially underperforming companies, tend to have more assets than they need in the form of accounts receivable, inventory and plant property and equipment. Excess assets have to be funded through either debt or equity, and to the extent those assets are funded by debt, they represent a drag on earnings.

A company must grow or die and growth requires capital, not just for research and development, and not just for plant and equipment, but growth requires capital for accounts receivable and inventory. This chapter discusses methods for identifying excess assets so they can be converted to cash to fuel growth. It also discusses how to effectively use the assets a company has.

Sometimes, a troubled company just needs money to stay alive. Missing a payroll is fatal for most companies and failing to remit sales, excise or withholding taxes when due can be equally devastating. In this chapter we consider a number of techniques to keep a company alive while it restructures.

Appropriate Amount of Capital

One of the questions a new CEO or turnaround team should ask is whether the company has the right amount of assets. If the answer is yes, time and attention should be focused on other aspects of restructuring. However, most companies have excess assets.

Return on Assets

One method of determining whether a company has the appropriate amount of assets is to compare its Return on Assets (ROA) to the ROA of the company's best competitors. ROA can be computed using Eq. (14.1). This ratio compares income from operations to the assets that produced that income. If the ratio is high, management

D.E. Vance, *Corporate Restructuring*, DOI 10.1007/978-3-642-01786-5_14,
© Springer-Verlag Berlin Heidelberg 2009

is doing a good job of generating income from assets. If the ratio is low, it could indicate either the company has excess assets or management isn't efficiently using its assets.

$$ROA = \frac{\text{Net Income} + \text{Net Interest} \times (1 - \text{Tax Rate})}{\text{Average Assets}} \qquad (14.1)$$

Net Income is income after taxes, Net Interest is interest expense less interest income, Tax Rate is the company's effective tax rate which can be found by dividing Income Tax by Earnings Before Taxes and Average assets are the assets at the end of the current year plus the assets at the end of the prior year divided by two. This equation assumes assets were acquired evenly over the year, which is a good assumption unless there has been a major acquisition.

Some companies finance with as much debt as possible, some with moderate debt and some with no debt at all. To make companies comparable to one another, the effect of each company's financing strategy must be backed out. To do that, interest is added back to net income. However, total interest is not added back, just the net, after tax cost of that interest. For example, if a company pays its bank $100,000 in interest, that payment does not reduce net income by $100,000 because interest is tax deductible. If a company is in the 30% tax bracket, the $100,000 interest deduction will save it $30,000 in taxes ($100,000 deduction × 30% tax rate). So the net cost of interest is only $70,000.

Suppose Alpha company has Net Income of $300,000; Interest expense of $43,000; interest income of $3,000; it is in the 25% tax bracket; assets at the end of the most current year were $6.2 million and assets at the end of the prior year were $5.8 million. What is its ROA?

$$ROA = \frac{\$300,000 + (\$43,000 - \$3,000) \times (1 - 25\%)}{(\$6,200,000 + \$5,800,000) / 2}$$

$$= \frac{\$300,000 + \$40,000 \times 75\%}{\$12,000,000/2}$$

$$= \frac{\$330,000}{\$6,000,000}$$

$$= 5.5\%$$

Return on assets is always reported as a percent. The higher the return on assets the better. The best indication of whether a company's ROA is good or bad is to compare it to the ROA of other companies in its industry. Benchmarking is the process of computing ratios for the leading companies in an industry and using those ratios as the basis of comparison (Vance, 2003, pp. 20–23).

Industry average ROA can be used to estimate the amount of assets a company should have. Suppose the leading companies in an industry, Beta, Zeta, and Theta have return on assets of 10, 8 and 6%. The industry average ROA would then be 8%((10%+8%+6%) / 3). Equation (14.1) can be rewritten by multiplying both sides by average assets and dividing both sides by ROA to give Eq. (14.2). In rewriting the equation, we made several adjustments. Substitute Industry ROA for ROA. For Average Assets, substituted Target Assets which is the amount of assets a company should have for its income.

$$\text{Target Assets} = \frac{\text{Net Income} + \text{Net Interest} \times (1 - \text{Tax Rate})}{\text{Industry ROA}}$$

Filling in the information for Alpha company gives Target Assets.

$$= \frac{\$300,000 + \$30,000}{8\%} \tag{14.2}$$

$$= \$4,125,000$$

If a company has average assets of $6,000,000 and target assets of $4,125,000 then potentially, the company has $1,875,000 more assets than it is productively using. The restructuring team should identify excess assets and convert them to cash.

Limitation on Use of ROA

Return on Assets has no meaning if net income, adjusted for interest net of taxes is negative or close to zero. Companies with a negative ROA or an ROA close to zero cannot be used to compute the industry average ROA. Some companies so under perform that they cannot squeeze even a modest return out of their assets. In that case some alternative measure like Asset Turnover should be used to estimate target assets.

Asset Turnover

Asset turnover is a measure of the efficiency with which management is generating sales from assets. But, it can also be used to estimate the appropriate amount of assets. The formula for Asset Turnover (AT) is given by Eq. (14.3).

$$\text{Asset Turnover} = \frac{\text{Sales}}{\text{Average Assets}} \tag{14.3}$$

Average assets is the assets at the end of the current period plus assets at the end of the prior period divided by two. The higher the asset turnover, the more efficiently assets are being used to generate sales.

Suppose Alpha company has sales of $6 million, assets at the end of last year were $5.8 million and assets at the end of this year were $6.2 million. Using

Eq. (14.3) Alpha's asset turnover can be computed.

$$\text{Asset Turnover} = \frac{\$6,000,000}{(\$6,200,000 + \$5,800,000)/2}$$

$$= \frac{\$6,000,000}{\$6,000,000}$$

$$= 1.0$$

Asset turnover is a dimensionless number. Whether 1.0 is good or bad depends on the industry average asset turnover (Vance, 2003, pp. 23–24).

Equation (14.3) can be modified to estimate the amount of assets a company should have based on sales. Using algebra, asset turnover and average assets can be swapped. Target assets is substituted for average assets and industry average asset turnover is substituted for asset turnover giving Eq. (14.4).

$$\text{Target asset} = \frac{\text{Sales}}{\text{Industry Asset Turnover}} \tag{14.4}$$

Suppose industry average asset turnover were 1.4. Equation (14.4) can be used to estimate Alpha company's target assets.

$$\text{Target assets} = \frac{\$6,000,000}{1.4}$$

$$= \$4,285,714$$

Based on an analysis of asset turnover Alpha company may have $1,714,286 of excess assets ($6,000,000 average assets – $4,285,714 target assets). Excess assets should be identified and converted to cash.

There is no reason the estimate of target assets using the ROA method and the Asset Turnover method should be exactly the same. Both methods indicate there is almost $2 million of excess assets.

The Cash Cycle

The cash cycle begins when cash is used to purchase raw materials and pay for labor, and continues through manufacturing, sales and ends when accounts receivable are collected and converted back to cash. Compressing the cash cycle will generate cash in the form of a reduced investment in inventory and accounts receivable.

Accounts Receivable

What is a company really doing when it sells on credit? In a very real sense, it is making a loan to its customer. That loan uses cash that must be funded. On the Statement of Cash Flows, increases in accounts receivable are classified as a use of cash. Significant amounts of cash can be tied up in overdue accounts receivable (Whitney, 1996, p. 92).

What happens when a company collects an accounts receivable? Collections generate cash which reduces the need for capital. Companies that sell on credit are constantly making sales and collecting. The incremental capital needed to fund accounts receivable depends on whether it is selling on credit faster than it is collecting, or whether it is collecting accounts receivable faster than it is extending credit in the form of new sales.

Accounts Receivable Turnover

Credit and collections efficiency can be measured in terms of Accounts Receivable (AR) Turnover. Accounts Receivable Turnover is the ratio of net credit sales to average accounts receivable. AR Turnover has no meaning for cash sales. For a company with both cash and credit sales, some method must be used to distinguish between cash and credit sales.

Most companies either sell for credit or sell for cash. Retailers sell for cash. In this context cash includes cash, checks, credit cards and debit cards. Most business to business sales are on credit.

The formula for computing Accounts Receivable (AR) Turnover is given as Eq. (14.5).

$$\text{AR Turnover} = \frac{\text{Net Sales on Account}}{\text{Average Accounts Receivable}} \tag{14.5}$$

Where Net Sales on Account is credit sales less returns and allowances, and Average Accounts Receivable is the average of this year's and last year's accounts receivable balance.

Suppose a company has Credit Sales of $10 million. Accounts receivable at the end of the current year is $2.1 million and at the end of the prior year it was $1.9 million.

$$\text{AR Turnover} = \frac{\$10,000,000}{(\$2,100,000 + \$1,900,000)/2}$$

$$= \frac{\$10,000,000}{\$2,000,000}$$

$$= 5.0$$

Accounts receivable turnover is a dimensionless number. The higher the accounts receivable turnover the better. As with other ratios, a company's accounts receivable turnover should be compared to industry averages to determine how well it is doing.

Unless the company's billing and collection staff are trained accountants, a ratio like AR turnover is going to be pretty meaningless. And unless staff understands how they are being measured, they won't be able to improve. Days Sales Outstanding is a ratio that translates AR turnover into something more understandable. Days Sales Outstanding (DSO) is the average number of days it takes customers to pay their bills. The formula for DSO is given as Eq. (14.6).

$$DSO = \frac{365\,days/year}{AR\ Turnover} \qquad (14.6)$$

For example, suppose a company has an AR Turnover of 5.0. Substituting the Turnover into Eq. (14.6) gives:

$$DSO = \frac{365\,days/year}{5.0}$$

$$= 73\,days$$

The company in this example takes 73 days on average to collect. This is a long time for most industries. However, government contractors often have to wait this long or longer to get paid and physicians often have to wait this long to get paid by insurance companies.

AR Turnover and DSO provide two metrics that can be used to measure the efficiency of billing and collections. Trends in these ratios indicate whether these departments are getting more or less efficient. Improving efficiency is going to generate cash. Deteriorating efficiency is going to use cash.

Raising Cash from Accounts Receivable

Management must proactively manage accounts receivable as they would any other aspect of the business. They wouldn't just tell salespeople, operations or finance to do the best they can. Goals should be set for credit and collections.

Suppose management's goal is to squeeze a specified amount of cash out of its investment in accounts receivable. How can the goal be analyzed, quantified and communicated to the billing and collections department?

To raise cash from accounts receivable, average accounts receivable must shrink by the amount to be raised. Assuming credit sales are constant, a reduction in accounts receivable will drive up AR turnover. Equation (14.7) is a modification of Eq. (14.5) to account for the effect of raising cash from accounts receivable.

$$New\ AR\ Turnover = \frac{Credit\ Sales}{Average\ AR - Amount\ Raised} \qquad (14.7)$$

Suppose Credit Sales are $10,000,000; average accounts receivable is $2,000,000; and the amount the company wants to raise is $500,000.

$$New\ AR\ Turnover = \frac{\$10,000,000}{\$2,000,000 - \$500,000}$$

$$= \frac{\$10,000,000}{\$1,500,000}$$

$$= 6.7$$

While the goal of 6.7 turns might have meaning to a trained accountant, it may be hard to communicate this goal to billing and collections staff. Translating AR Turns into DSO using Eq. (14.6) makes it easier to understand.

$$DSO = \frac{365 \text{ days/year}}{6.7}$$

$$= 54 \text{ days}$$

The goal can now be stated like this. Currently customers pay in an average of 73 day. If that can be reduced to 54 days, the company can raise $500,000 of cash.

Another way to look at raising cash from accounts receivable is to determine how much cash can be raised if a company makes a given DSO the target. The target may be set arbitrarily or it may be set as the industry average or ten percent better than the industry average.

Suppose the company sets its collection goal at the industry average of 45 days. To find the AR Turnover necessary to reach that DSO modify (14.7) by using algebra to swap AR Turns and DSO; replace DSO with Target DSO; and replace AR Turns with New AR Turns to get Eq. (14.8).

$$\text{New AR Turns} = \frac{365 \text{ days/year}}{\text{Target DSO}} \qquad (14.8)$$

Substituting a Target DSO of 45 days into Eq. (14.8) gives:

$$\text{New AR Turns} = \frac{365 \text{ days/year}}{45 \text{ days}}$$

$$= 8.1$$

This can be substituted into a somewhat modified version of Eq. (14.5) in which AR Turns and Average AR are swapped using algebra; New AR Turns replaces AR Turns; and Average AR is replaced with Target AR to get Eq. (14.9).

$$\text{Target AR} = \frac{\text{Net Credit Sales}}{\text{New AR Turns}} \qquad (14.9)$$

Suppose Net Credit Sales is $10,000,000 and New AR Turns is 8.1. What will the New Average AR be? Substituting these values into Eq. (14.9) gives:

$$\text{New Average AR} = \frac{\$10,000,000}{8.1}$$

$$= \$1,234,568$$

If the old average accounts receivable was $2,000,000 and the new average accounts receivables drops to $1,234,568. The reduction in accounts receivable of $765,432 ($2,000,000 − $1,234,568) will generate an equivalent amount of cash.

Stated another way, this improvement in accounts receivable collections is equivalent to having someone give the company three quarters of a million dollars (Vance, 2005, pp. 308–313).

Accounts Receivable Management

Understanding that capital can be raised from better accounts receivable management and setting goals are both useful steps. The next question is how is it done?

Terms

What a appropriate terms for a credit sale? 30 days? 60 days? 90 days? 2/10 net 30? Should interest be charged on invoices over 30 days?

Unless the company is in the finance business, there is no reason to give 30, 60 or 90 day terms. Once a company has delivered a product or rendered a service, invoices should be due on receipt. That doesn't mean every customer is going to pay immediately. What it means is that the company should expect prompt payment once it has completed its part of the bargain.

Terms like 2/10 net 30 shouldn't be offered even though accounting texts recommend such terms. The terms 2/10 net 30 mean that a customer will get a 2% discount if they pay within 10 days and in any event the whole balance is due in 30 days. The argument is that giving a 2% discount and getting prompt payment is more cost effective than financing an invoice for the remaining 20 days. However, most companies have a policy of taking discounts when available, then paying whenever they please. Trying to collect improperly taken discounts is time consuming and annoys customers. The best approach is to not offer discounts.

Promptness

Prompt invoicing is a chronic problem in many companies. Invoices often languish for days or weeks after products are shipped or services provided before being prepared and sent out. Controls should be established to make sure invoices are sent the day merchandise is shipped or as soon as possible after a service is rendered.

Completeness

Another chronic problem is that invoices do not always provide enough information for a customer to fully understand what they are paying for. Lack of information can cause an invoice to be sidetracked from the normal processing routine. This is the first step in a customer "losing" the invoice. A company should put every bit of information it has in its invoices, and if necessary it should attach explanatory schedules. If the customer provides a purchase order (PO) number, make sure its PO number is on the invoice.

Follow-Up Calls

When is should to follow up calls be made? One highly successful billing manager used to call customers 3 days after sending an invoice to make sure customers got it, that it met their standards, and to ask when it might be paid. She would then diary a follow-up call 3 days after the date of the payment indicated by the customer. She was always firm, but polite and kept extensive collection notes on her computer as to what each customer promised. After a short period of time, it became evident that follow up calls weren't necessary for about 80% of her customer base. The remaining 20% got her full attention.

Follow-Up Letters

Traditionally, companies send follow-up letters or follow-up invoices, monthly. But that is just a custom. There is nothing sacred about a monthly cycle. If cash is low, try following up after 3 weeks. If payment or satisfactory answers aren't received, send another letter in 2 weeks. The point is to stay in the center of a customer's radar.

How Much Credit Should a Customer Be Allowed?

Should a company extend credit to everyone who wants to buy from it? If not, who should get credit? How much? And when should credit be cut off? Answering these questions are critical steps in managing accounts receivable. If a customer is a publicly traded, its financial statements will be available on the SEC's website www.sec.gov. Follow the links to Company Forms and find their form 10-K for the most recent year. From this data you can:

(a) Determine whether customers are profitable. If they are not profitable, a company may find itself an unsecured, low priority creditor.
(b) Estimate how long it takes customers to pay their bills. If a potential customer doesn't pay its other suppliers promptly, it is not likely to pay the company promptly. The time it takes a customer to pay its bills can be estimated as follows:

1. Compute Purchases. Purchase may be computed from information available in the customer's Form 10-K using Eq. (14.10).

$$\text{Purchases} = \text{Cost of Goods Sold} + \text{Ending Inventory} - \text{Beginning Inventory}$$
$$(14.10)$$

2. Compute Accounts Payable Turnover. Accounts Payable turnover may be computed using Eq. (14.11). Average Accounts Payable is the accounts

payable at the end of the current year, plus the accounts payable at the end of the prior year, divided by two.

$$\text{Accounts Payable Turnover} = \frac{\text{Purchases}}{\text{Average Accounts Payable}} \qquad (14.11)$$

3. Compute Average Days to Pay. Days to Pay represents the average time it takes for a company to pay its bills. Equation (14.12) can be used to compute Days To Pay (DTP).

$$\text{Days to Pay} = 365/\text{Accounts Payable Turnover} \qquad (14.12)$$

Suppose a company has accounts payable at the end of the current year of $11 million and accounts payable at the end of the prior year of $9 million; cost of goods sold of $100 million; ending inventory was $22 million and beginning inventory was $18 million. Using Eq. (14.10) purchases can be computed.

$$\text{Purchases} = \$100 \text{ million} + \$22 \text{ million} - \$18 \text{ million}$$
$$= \$104 \text{ million}$$

Then Eq. (14.11) can be used to compute accounts payable turnover.

$$\text{Accounts Payable Turnover} = \frac{\$104 \text{ million}}{(\$11 \text{ million} + \$9 \text{ million})/2}$$
$$= \frac{\$104 \text{ million}}{\$10 \text{ million}}$$
$$= 10.4$$

Finally, we can use Eq. (14.12) to estimate how long it takes a customer to pay its bills.

$$\text{Days to Pay} = 365/10.4$$
$$= 35 \text{ days}$$

If the company's goal is to reduce average collections to 40 days, this customer would fall within the guidelines. A customer paying in 60 days would not meet the goal. The company should either decline to give the slow paying customer credit or make other provisions. For example, the company might ask the customer to pay for the purchase on a credit card, ask it to pay cash, or the company might forego the sale altogether. Remember, the object isn' t to make the sale; the object is to get paid.

This computation may, on the surface seem burdensome. But, once the formulae are set up on a spreadsheet they can be used to evaluate any customer. All that is necessary is to capture five variables: Cost of Goods Sold, Beginning Inventory, Ending Inventory, Beginning Accounts Payable and Ending Accounts Payable.

If a company isn't publicly traded and the sale is for a significant amount, ask the customer to complete a credit application. The application should ask that financial statements be attached. If a customer says it hasn't been in business long enough to have financial statements they probably aren't a good credit risk. If a customer says that its financial statements are confidential, ask it to fill out a credit application that captures the data needed to compute days to pay: Cost of Goods Sold, current and prior year inventory and current and prior year accounts payable. If the customer refuses to provide this information, apologize and; say the company has strict rules about granting credit. Ask whether the customer can pay in cash, via credit card, through a letter of credit or in the alternative, decline the sale. It is always better to lose a sale than to make a sale and deliver goods that are never paid for.

How Much Credit Should a Customer Get?

The amount of credit that should be extended to any particular customer varies by time and circumstances. Even the best customer can run into cash flow problems; have staffing changes that affect payment regularity; have computer errors; or purchasing agents who suddenly question why they are paying so much; or staff that find your invoices not quite formatted to their liking. Whatever the excuse, even the best customers sometimes pay slowly.

So how much credit should a company extend? If a company knows for sure it will eventually get paid, for example if it is dealing with the federal government, relatively more. Can this customer be trusted with a month's worth profit? Should it be trusted with a week's worth of profit? A day's worth of profit? In part that answer should be informed by its payment history. Whatever the answer is, the credit and collections department should be provided with clear guidelines.

When Should Credit Be Cut Off?

One reference point is to ask the age at which the company's bank makes accounts receivable ineligible for the borrowing capacity calculations. If a company's bank considers accounts receivable over 60 days ineligible, then customers should be kept on a very short string. If the bank allows accounts receivable up to 90 days, a little more latitude might be granted, but not much. If a customer is unwilling to pay its bills in a timely manner, the company will have lost little in denying them further credit.

When Should a Customer Be Referred to a Collection Agency?

The general rule is to refer accounts to collections sooner rather than latter. There are several reasons for this (i) the fresher the account, the higher the probability of the collection, (ii) the sooner a collection company gets an account, the sooner it can convert it to cash, and (iii) collection agencies often discount their fees if accounts turned over are "fresh."

As a customer's receivables get close to the borrowing capacity ineligible date, send letters notifying customers that it is policy is to "release" accounts to collection agencies after a given number of days. If no payment is forthcoming, refer the account to a collection agency. Most are very professional and do an excellent job.

Inventory

A significant amount of capital can be locked up in inventory. Most companies have far more inventory than needed to support manufacturing and sales. When a company buys inventory, either in the form of raw material or finished goods, it is using cash. When a company sells inventory, it generates cash. If it buys faster than it sells, its net capital demand increases. If it sells inventory faster than it buys, it generates cash and reduces the demand for additional capital.

One of the traps companies fall into is maintaining slow moving inventory to satisfy the demands of small, occasional or non-strategic customers. Companies need to unlock this cash even if it means shedding customers so cash can be used to develop new products or find new strategic customers (Whitney, 1996, p. 93).

The inventory turnover ratio is a means of measuring the efficiency of inventory management. Inventory turnover is the ratio of Cost of Goods Sold to Average Inventory as shown in Eq. (14.13).

$$\text{Inventory Turnover} = \frac{\text{Cost of Goods Sold}}{\text{Average Inventory}} \tag{14.13}$$

Where Average Inventory is computed by averaging the ending inventory from the current and prior years.

Suppose Alpha Company has a Cost of Goods Sold of $6,000,000; the ending inventory of the current year and prior years were $2,200,000 and $1,800,000 respectively.

$$\text{Inventory Turover} = \frac{\$6,000,000}{(\$2,200,000 + \$1,800,000)/2}$$

$$= \frac{\$6,000,000}{\$2,000,000}$$

$$= 3.0$$

Inventory turnover is a dimensionless number. It indicates how many times a company sells its entire inventory over the course of a year. The higher the inventory turnover is the better. Whether a particular ratio is satisfactory is a function of industry norms. If a company generates substantially all of its revenue from services, this ratio has no real meaning.

Inventory turnover is another one of those ratios that it is difficult for staff to grasp and use. A better way to communicate inventory management performance is through the average number of days goods are in inventory. Days in Inventory (DII) can be computed using Eq. (14.14).

$$\text{Days in Inventory} = \frac{365 \text{ days/year}}{\text{Inventory Turnover}} \tag{14.14}$$

Suppose Alpha Company has an inventory turnover of 3.0. The average number of days a good is in inventory can be computed using Eq. (14.14).

$$\text{Day in Inventory} = \frac{365 \text{ days/year}}{3.0}$$

$$= 121.7 \text{ days}$$

DII is easier for most people to understand. It says, on average, 121.7 days elapse from the time a company acquires raw material until it sells its finished product. The more understandable a performance measure, the easier it is to drive improvement.

For manufacturing companies, inventory turnover is a measure of manufacturing efficiency. A company that can acquire new materials, convert it to finished goods and sell it quickly is more efficient than one that processes material more slowly. One key to improving inventory turnover is reducing the time it takes to manufacture goods. Two other keys are purchasing raw materials only as needed and producing only what can be rapidly sold.

Raising Cash from Inventory

Taking a proactive approach to inventory management, it is possible to reverse engineer a specific goal. Some of the capital tied up in inventory can be recovered if inventory turns are increased. The issue is what goal must the turnaround team set to raise a given amount of cash? Equation (14.13) can be modified by subtracting the target Amount Raised from the old average inventory to get the New Inventory Turnover giving Eq. (14.15).

$$\text{New Inventory Turnover} = \frac{\text{Cost of Goods Sold}}{\text{Average Inventory} - \text{Amount Raised}} \tag{14.15}$$

Suppose Alpha Company has a Cost of Goods Sold of \$6,000,000, old average inventory of \$2,000,000, and its goal is to raise \$400,000 in cash. What will New Inventory Turnover have to be?

$$\text{New Inventory Turnover} = \frac{\$6,000,000}{\$2,000,000 - \$400,000}$$

$$= \frac{\$6,000,000}{\$1,600,000}$$

$$= 3.75$$

Using Eq. (14.14) the new inventory turnover can be translated into target Days In Inventory.

$$\text{Days in Inventory} = \frac{365 \text{ days/year}}{3.75}$$

$$= 97.3 \text{ days}$$

If Alpha reduces its Days In Inventory from 121.7 days to 97.3 days it can squeeze $400,000 out of inventory (Vance, 2005, pp. 313–316).

Techniques for Reducing Inventory

It's easy for a consultant to tell a company to improve inventory turnover, but exactly how is it done? The 80–20 Rule is a useful way to think about this. In one incarnation, the 80–20 Rule says: 80% of a company's sales come from 20% of its customers. Adapting it to inventory, we might say that 80% of sales come from 20% of the items in stock. The problem is identifying the 80% that play a less significant role in sales and reducing the quantity of those items in stock.

Turnover Analysis by SKU

Most businesses have highly automated inventory systems in which items are tracked by part number or Stock Keeping Unit (SKU). It is possible to compute the turnover of every item in inventory using SKU information. Once slow moving items are identified, inventory of those items can be reduced to more realistically match demand.

Cost of goods sold at the SKU level is the number of items used times the cost of each item as shown in Eq. (14.16).

$$\text{Cost of Goods Sold}_{SKU} = \text{Sales in Units}_{SKU} \times \text{Unit Cost}_{SKU} \qquad (14.16)$$

Where Cost of Goods Sold$_{SKU}$ is the Cost of Goods Sold of a particular SKU, Sales In Units$_{SKU}$ is the number of units of a particular SKU that were sold, and Unit Cost$_{SKU}$ is the cost of each unit of a particular SKU.

As an alternative, if sales in units per SKU isn't tracked use Eq. (14.17) to estimate Cost of Goods Sold$_{SKU}$ using the gross margin approach.

$$\text{Cost of Goods Sold}_{SKU} = \text{Sales in Dollars}_{SKU} \times (1 - \text{Gross Margin}) \qquad (14.17)$$

Where Sales In Dollars$_{SKU}$ is the total sales of a particular SKU, Gross Margin is the difference between a product's price and its full absorption cost divided by the product price.

Once the Cost of Goods Sold for a particular SKU is computed, Inventory Turnover$_{SKU}$ can be estimated using Eq. (14.18).

$$\text{Inventory Turover}_{SKU} = \frac{\text{Cost of Goods Sold}_{SKU}}{\text{Average Units} - SKU \times \text{Unit Cost}_{SKU}} \qquad (14.18)$$

Inventory turnover at the SKU level is then converted to Days in Inventory for each SKU using Eq. (14.19).

$$\text{Days in Inventory}_{SKU} = \frac{365 \text{ days/year}}{\text{Inventory Turnover}_{SKU}} \quad (14.19)$$

Each of these computations will have to be performed for every item in inventory. For a company with a few dozen items in inventory, a spreadsheet can be constructed to make these computations. However, for a business of substantial size, computer programs will have to be written to extract the necessary data from inventory and sales records. The result will be a report that analyzes how many days supply the company has for each item in inventory.

Management judgment comes into play in deciding how many days supply is adequate. For custom built components, the number of days might be fairly high, considering the time and effort it takes for a supplier to build and ship that unique item. Most items a company needs are available in a few days or weeks. So management should set strict standards as to the number of days supply it needs to cover production and contingencies.

An interesting feature of this system is that it is self adjusting. Suppose, for example, sales of a particular item rise dramatically. As more is drawn down, the Cost of Goods Sold for that item will increase, which decreases Days In Inventory. If this slips below management's target days in inventory, this item can be flagged for reorder. If sales of an item slows, the amount of inventory can be flagged as excess so that it can be sold off to raise cash.

The average the Daily Usage of a particular SKU can be found by dividing the sales in units by 365 as shown in Eq. (14.20).

$$\text{Daily Usage}_{SKU} = \frac{\text{Sales in Units}_{SKU}}{365 \text{ Days}} \quad (14.20)$$

Given the Daily Usage$_{SKU}$ and the Target Days of Inventory we can use Eq. (14.21) to compute Target Inventory$_{SKU}$ which is the target number of items a company should have of a particular SKU.

$$\text{Target Inventory}_{SKU} = \text{Daily Usage}_{SKU} \times \text{Target Days of Inventory}_{SKU} \quad (14.21)$$

Excess Inventory is simply the actual inventory minus the target inventory. The value of the excess inventory is the number of units of excess inventory times the unit cost of that inventory. To be conservative in estimating how much cash could be raised by selling off excess inventory, one could discount this amount by 25–50% to allow for brokers fees, obsolesce and damage. Equation (14.22) is an estimate of the amount of cash that can be raised from each SKU by selling off excess inventory (Vance, 2005, pp. 315–316).

$$\text{Amt. Raised}_{SKU} = \sum (\text{Inventory}_{SKU} - \text{Target Inventory}_{SKU}) \times \text{Cost}_{SKU} \times (1 - \text{Discount})$$
$$(14.22)$$

Table 14.1 is an example of what an Inventory Analysis report using this technique might look like.

Table 14.1 Inventory analysis

SKU	Description	Actual days in inventory	Unit cost	Units in inventory	Inventory at cost	Target days in inventory	Target inventory units	Target inventory at cost	Excess inventory value
1392	Circuit Board 8 cm	200	$1.90	18,000	$34,200	15	1,350	$2,565	$31,635
1398	Circuit Board 16 cm	180	$2.80	11,000	$30,800	15	917	$2,567	$28,233
1399	Circuit Board 24 cm	28	$4.00	6,000	$24,000	15	3,214	$12,857	$11,143
1410	Microchip 2200	300	$18.50	22,000	$407,000	30	2,200	$40,700	$366,300
1440	Microchip 2250	150	$32.00	15,000	$480,000	30	3,000	$96,000	$384,000
1444	Microchip 2300	30	$40.00	6,000	$240,000	30	6,000	$240,000	$0
1452	Microchip 2318	80	$48.00	7,000	$336,000	30	2,625	$126,000	$210,000
⋮									
9100	Power supply 300 w	250	$11.00	1,400	$15,400	20	112	$1,232	$14,168
9110	Power supply 500 w	200	$15.00	1,100	$16,500	20	110	$1,650	$14,850
9810	Power supply 800 w	20	$19.00	600	$11,400	20	600	$11,400	$0
9812	Power supply 2400 w	30	$25.00	700	$17,500	20	467	$11,667	$5,833
									$5,066,163
					Less Broker's Discount @ 35%				$1,773,157
					Potential cash from selling excess inventory				$3,293,006

Plant, Property and Equipment

In most companies, significant amounts of cash are locked up in plant, property and equipment (PPE). Cash tied up in non-strategic assets hinder a company's ability to support its core strategies (Whitney, 1996, p. 92). Eliminating unnecessary PPE can generate significant amounts of cash to fund restructuring.

The first step in identifying excess PPE is to examine a company's fixed asset ledger. A fixed asset ledger is simply a list of the company's assets and it is typically used as the basis for calculating depreciation. If the ledger is computerized, as it is in most companies, sort the ledger by net asset value high to low. Examine the high value assets first and ask two questions: (i) have we used this asset in the last 60 days? (ii) Is there a less costly alternative to owning this asset?

Assets that aren't being used in day to day operations on an on-going basis should be sold to raise cash. The truck parked behind the building, the unused computer, the drill press that nobody uses any more should all be sold. There is no point in saving them just in case they might be needed in the future. As time passes their value will decline. They will never be more valuable than they are now. In addition, unused assets are costly in terms of storage, insurance and property taxes. Of course a lawn care company shouldn't sell its equipment each January because it hasn't been used for 60 days, but there are very few such exceptions.

Real estate is an especially high payoff area to examine because companies that have been around for some time often acquire and hold real estate that it no longer needs. Pay special attention to undeveloped land which may not be on the fixed asset ledger because it is a non-depreciable asset. It should, however, be listed in the general ledger. Other high payoff property to sell includes non-revenue producing assets such as airplanes, yachts and corporate owned cars.

As to the second question, is there a cheaper alternative than ownership, there often is. Equipment used only occasionally may be rented. Office space can sometimes be leased cheaper than it can be owned. And sometimes capital can be raised through a sale and lease back of buildings (Vance, 2005, pp. 316–317).

Accounts Payable

When a company sells on credit, it is making a loan to its customer. But when a company buys on credit, its supplier is making a loan to it. If a company buys on credit faster than it pays its bills, accounts payable will grow and suppliers will increase their net loan to the company. Accounts payable represents an important, non-interest bearing source of funds for a company. Some consultants recommend paying bills slowly as a way of forcing suppliers to increase loans to the company.

This approach is foolhardy. It is impossible to force anyone to lend. Stretching payment terms beyond industry norms simply flags the company as a bad customer and credit risk. Ultimately, bad behavior is punished by lower credit ratings and higher interest rates. Pay bills when they are due. On the other hand, if a supplier gives you terms of net 60, pay in 60 days and take advantage of the interest free loan.

Imputed Interest

Companies in trouble often have excessive debt. Interest expense on this debt load drags down net income. Selling off excess assets creates an opportunity to reduce debt and reduce interest expense. Calculating imputed interest provides a means for estimating the income statement impact of reducing a company's debt load.

Imputed interest is net financing costs, usually interest expense less interest income divided by interest bearing liabilities as shown in Eq. (14.23)

$$\text{Imputed Interest} = \frac{\text{Interest Expense} + \text{Other Financing Costs} - \text{Interest Income}}{\text{Interest Bearing Liabilities}}$$

(14.23)

Imputed interest is a rough calculation of the cost of financing interest bearing liabilities. Interest is not paid on all liabilities. For example, interest is not paid on accounts payable, accrued payroll or deferred taxes. So reducing these liabilities will not reduce interest expense. However, interest is paid on a line of credit, bank term loans, bonds, mortgages, credit card interest, and capital leases. Other financing costs include credit card discounts, if the company sells on credit cards, as well as discounts on notes, commercial paper and factored accounts receivable.

Suppose a company has $280,000 interest expense on bank loans and $40,000 interest expense on note discounts; it earns $20,000 per year in interest; and its total interest bearing liabilities are $3,750,000.

$$\text{Imputed interest rate} = \frac{\$280,000 + \$40,000 - \$20,000}{\$3,750,000} = 8\%$$

Identifying excess assets; converting them to cash and paying down debt will reduce the amount of interest paid. Reducing interest payments increases both net income and cash flow. The increase in net income is given by Eq. (14.24).

$$\text{Increase in Net Income} = \text{Imputed Interest Rate}$$
$$\times \text{Net Interest Bearing Debt Paid Down} \qquad (14.24)$$
$$\times (1 - \text{Tax Rate})$$

Suppose a company has $14,000,000 of interest bearing liabilities at an imputed interest rate of 8% and the company's tax rate is 30%. The restructuring team identifies $3,000,000 of unneeded assets which it converts to cash; the cash is used to pay down $2,500,000 of interest bearing debt and $500,000 of accounts payable.

$$\text{Increase in Net Income} = 8\% \times \$2,500,000 \times (1 - 30\%)$$
$$= \$140,000$$

The rational for the tax adjustment is that taxes subsidize interest expense when a company has taxable income. Even though a company might pay a bank $100 in interest payments, the real cost to the company of that interest, if it is in the 30% tax bracket, is only $70. If a company has no taxable income, a $100 interest payment will cost the company $100.[1]

As a company digs itself out from under its debt load and improves its cash management, it might replace an expensive commercial credit company loan with a less expensive bank loan or replace a bank loan with bonds. It may also be able to replace expensive factoring with less expensive alternatives. An imputed interest calculation can help estimate the impact on net income from each of these strategies.

Conclusion

Most companies have significant stores of cash locked up in assets such as accounts receivable, inventory and plant property and equipment. A target level of assets should be estimated using return on assets and asset turnover ratios.

Performance standards should be set for the credit and collections and for inventory management. Performance standards should be supported by specific policies for extending credit, credit applications, credit limits and follow-up. Inventory management goals should be supported by analyses that identify slow moving inventory.

Fixed assets should be analyzed and those not currently being used to generate revenue should be sold. High payoff items to look for include land, buildings, airplanes, automobiles and manufacturing equipment.

Raising cash to support a turnaround cannot just be done in the treasurer's office or in the CFO's conference room. It is necessary to work with credit and collections, people working on the factory floor, and those in the warehouse to squeeze cash from a company's own assets.

Note

1. This assumes a company cannot take a tax loss carry back. Carry backs are limited to 2 years.

References

Vance D (2003) Financial analysis and decision making. McGraw-Hill, New York
Vance D (2005) Raising capital. Springer Science + Business Media, New York
Whitney JO (1996) Strategic renewal for business units. Harv Bus Rev 74(4):84–98, July–Aug

Chapter 15
Emergency Cash Management

Introduction

By the time a new CEO or turnaround consultant is hired, a company is bleeding cash. Cash is the life blood of a company. If a company runs out of cash and cannot make its payroll, defaulting on bonds will look like a minor inconvenience.

Emergency cash management is about stopping the bleeding and finding immediate sources of cash. This means swift, decisive action and shared sacrifice. If a new CEO or turnaround consultant isn't given prompt and unconditional support in doing what it necessary, a company on the edge might collapse entirely.

Emergency Cash Budget

There is a tremendous difference between making a profit and generating cash. How can a company be profitable and run out of cash? It can do it by investing in plant, equipment, growth and acquisitions all of which use cash. But under accounting rules, only a small fraction of these expenditures show up as expenses. Opening new facilities or expanding plant can create an enormous cash drain. For example, the J. Peterman Company, highly successful with its catalogue business expanded into retail outlets, but underestimated the cash drain of opening new facilities (Thierry, 1999). As a result, it ran out of cash and had to file bankruptcy (Brennan, 2000; Peterman, 1999).

Consolidation of Cash

Companies often have dozens of accounts in as many banks. The number of accounts should be reduced to the extent practical at one or a few national banks with branches situated so facilities can deposit cash daily. Cash should then be swept into a central account.

Investments in stocks, bonds, mutual funds, treasury bills and treasury notes should be converted to cash. Other assets that can be converted to cash should be converted to cash.

D.E. Vance, *Corporate Restructuring*, DOI 10.1007/978-3-642-01786-5_15,
© Springer-Verlag Berlin Heidelberg 2009

Daily Cash Report

In an emergency, a company cannot afford to wait until quarter end, or month end or even week end to find out where it stands in terms of cash. A company in trouble must manage cash on a daily basis. Companies receive cash every day in cash sales, checks, wires and remittances from credit card companies. Cash collections should be analyzed to identify day of the week, week of the month and month of the year collection patterns. Collection patterns will help forecast cash available on a day by day, week by week basis.

Cash Disbursement Calendar

Many significant cash disbursements are made on scheduled dates. One of the largest is payroll. Other significant disbursements known in advance include mortgage payments, loan payments, lease payments, bond interest, bond principal, sinking fund payments, pension payments, health insurance payments and tax payments. Put the due date of each of these payments on a calendar along with the amount of each payment. These fixed payments represent disbursement landmarks around which cash must be managed.

Payment Priorities

Cash disbursements must be triaged with the highest priority payments getting the first claim on available cash. The decision of which specific vendors should be paid on any given day, and how much they should be paid should not be left in the hands of accounts payable staff during an emergency. The power to say who gets paid and when should be retained by the turnaround team.

Payroll should have the first claim on cash. Unless payroll is met, people will walk off the job and the company will collapse. In addition, most states impose an absolute requirement on employers to pay employees within a short period of time after work is performed. Further, federal, state and local taxing authorities expect withholding and employer taxes to be remitted promptly. For example, suppose an $800,000 payroll is due on June 7th. It is now June 1. No bills should be paid until $800,000 has been collected. The excess over $800,000 is used to pay other bills.

Bank loans and bond payments should be prioritized next to avoid violation of covenants which place a company in default and may trigger acceleration (a demand for immediate repayment).

Mortgage and lease payments should be prioritized next so that a company can continue to use its facility.

Tax payments, especially, excise and sales taxes should be prioritized next. Tax payments are not generally dischargeable in bankruptcy so it is very important for tax payments to be made on a current basis.

Health insurance and pension payments should be prioritized next to keep faith with the workforce. If the workforce leaves or its morale deteriorates, it will be difficult if not impossible to restructure the company.

The strategy is to accumulate cash until it can meet each of these landmarks; pay the amount due; forecast whether there will be enough cash coming in to meet the next two or three landmarks, and if there is enough cash, then consider other vendors for payment.

A company in trouble, may not be able to pay everyone on a timely basis. Vendors which supply the goods and services needed to make the product or provide a billable service are usually paid next. Suppliers which can hurt the company most are paid after that. For example, companies on the point of suing for non-payment or those whose contracts with the company provide penalties for late payment should be paid next.

Cleaning up (paying) vendors with small balances under $500 or $1,000 greatly reduces the number of creditors calling the company without materially changing the company's cash position. Time freed up not fielding these calls can be used for more critical duties.

Dealing with Collection Agencies

If a supplier turns over a bill to a collection agency, ask the collection agency whether it is empowered to compromise the bill in exchange for prompt payment. The power to compromise allows them to settle the debt for less than the amount owed. For example, if a company owes a supplier $10,000 and the supplier turns this over to a collection agency, the company might ask the collection agency to accept a prompt payment of $9,000 to settle the bill. Often, collection agencies are willing to make such deals. The advantages to the company are that it can satisfy a creditor for a reduced amount and it avoids the hassle of dealing with a collection agency whose stock in trade is persistence.

Halt Spending

It is difficult to bring a moving train to an abrupt halt, but the sooner one applies the brakes, the sooner it will come to rest. Likewise it is difficult to stop a company from bleeding cash, but it is necessary to take immediate and decisive action to stop expenditures at once.

Commitments

All commitments to spend company funds over some threshold should be approved by the turnaround team. This threshold should be set fairly low until cash flow stabilizes. This may seem like a simplistic control, but it is amazing how many needless expenditures a company makes even when it is struggling to meet payroll.

Consultants, Conferences and Other Discretionary Spending

If a company is in danger of not meeting payroll, bank loans or rent payments, it doesn't have money for consultants and conferences. A general order should be issued to halt spending on conferences and consultants. The order should also request department level reports on fees and penalties for canceling prior commitments. There are always people who don't believe the rules apply to them so sometimes one must hit them over the head with a memo to get them to stop spending. If that doesn't work, demotion or termination are always options.

Expansion

Many companies get into trouble because they have an untenable business model and continue to expand that untenable model. Emergency cash management includes halting expansion. Building new stores, leasing new facilities, laying more cable or acquiring more companies must be halted until the turnaround committee can evaluate the company's business model and cash flows. Bringing expansion to a halt in a culture of expansion is often difficult because those involved have a personal stake in its continuation. The directive to halt expansion should be strong, clear and unambiguous.

Labor Costs

Labor is usually one of the biggest expenses and biggest cash outflows at any company. Several things should be done immediately.

Hiring Freeze

Part of weathering a cash crisis must be cutting labor costs. A hiring freeze is an essential first step in cost control. It makes no sense to hire new people, and incur a commitment for their wages, benefits and employer taxes when a company is in the middle of a cash crisis.

Layoffs

Those expected to be laid off should be identified and given notice as soon as possible. Even if those selected for elimination are given notice immediately, it might be 3 months before cash flow improves. Layoff law requires employees be given 60 days notice and even at the end of 60 days the company may owe employees several weeks of vacation.

Executive Sacrifice

Officers, Directors and senior managers should be asked to take a pay cut until the company's fortunes turn. There are several reasons for this, to:

(1) conserve cash
(2) set an example for the workforce and demonstrate that top management is bearing some of the pain of the restructuring which will make the workforce more receptive to doing what is necessary, and
(3) bring home to top management the seriousness of the problem.

I have gotten a company's executives to cut their salaries 40–50% for a period of 120 days. This helped conserve money for a turnaround.[1]

Partial Layoff

A middle ground between losing talent through layoffs and paying full salaries is a partial layoff. A partial layoff cuts an employee's hours and pay proportionately.[2] To ask executives to take a pay cut is one thing, to ask workers and working supervisors to take a pay cut, even temporarily, is difficult. A partial layoff can be implemented immediately unlike a regular layoff.

Suppose a company has 100 workers making $20 per hour. A 20% partial layoff, would reduce their hours from 40 to 32. Gross weekly pay drops from $80,000 (100 × $20 × 40 h/week) to $64,000 (100 × $20 × 32 h/week) for a savings of about $16,000 per week. Between social security tax (6.2%), Medicare (1.45%), FUTA and SUTA (Federal unemployment tax and State unemployment tax estimated at 4% total) and workers compensation insurance (at least 1%), the real cost of labor drops from $90,120 to $72,096 for a savings of about $18,024 per week. In a turnaround, saving $18,000 per week can make the difference between life and death.

To prevent workers from leaving for other jobs and to maintain morale, partial layoffs should be temporary in nature. Workers should have a fairly firm idea of how long the partial layoff will last. If it goes much beyond 6 months, the best workers will probably leave.

Employees on partial layoff should also keep full medical benefits. Otherwise, loss of medical benefits will destroy any goodwill the company hopes to maintain during the restructuring.

Partial layoffs are a useful tool for temporary downturns. If a company needs to permanently contract or is overstaffed, a better approach is a regular layoff.

Held Paychecks

If the cash shortfall is temporary, days versus weeks, paychecks for the top executives might be held in the company vault. This might occur when an expected customer payment arrives a few days late. Since a disproportionate share of pay goes to executives, withholding one executive check is often a more effective way to conserve cash than withholding checks for four or five production workers.

To do this, the consent of each executive should be obtained in person. They should be told that due to a temporary cash shortfall, checks will be held for a specific number of days. Executives must understand the difficult position the company is in. This will not work for those on direct deposit, so if the company is in distress, take executives off direct deposit. Executives who do not consent to have their paychecks withheld, or who do not consent to going off direct deposit clearly do not understand the situation. Such lack of judgment, situational awareness and the need to lead by example probably means they are not a good fit for the management team a company during a turnaround.

Only an executive's net pay can be withheld. Withholding taxes, 401 k contributions and employer wage taxes are automatically remitted by payroll services on payday.

In distressed companies, I have had to go around to all the top executives of a company and say: "I'm sorry; we're going to keep your paycheck in the vault until we have enough cash to cover it." For a company in trouble, this may happen all too often.

No Pay Payday

When cash is low in a law firm, the managing partner goes around to all the other lawyers and says: "I'm sorry there will be no pay this week." Partners and Associates are expected to "suck it up," and keep going. Staff always get paid.

Notes Payable

A longer term strategy is to ask trade creditors to convert accounts payable to a note payable, at interest with a two year payment term. There are three reasons a vendor might do this. First to get interest; second, notes payable can be sold so the trade creditor can get cash immediately and let someone else collect on the note; third, trade notes payable are easier to collect on in court because they resolve all disputes as to the amount owed, whether conforming goods were delivered and they help overcome other defenses a customer might have such as failure of consideration.

Emergency Collection Techniques

Presidential Call

Sometimes a customer just won't pay unless a company raises the visibility of the overdue account. One way to raise visibility is for the president of the company call to request payment. Obviously this is not something a company should do on a regular basis. But, when a company is out of cash, and the customer owes hundreds of thousands, if not millions of dollars, it may be necessary. If possible, the president should call the president of the customer company.

If the president is going to request payment, have him/her request the payment be wire transferred to the company's account. Make sure the president has in front of him or her.

(1) An analysis of the client's account so he or she can speak with authority as to the amount owed, invoice numbers, how long invoices have been open, and any other detail that logically supports demand for payment such as the customer's purchase order numbers, and detailed schedules of work performed.
(2) The company's bank account and other information needed for the customer to wire cash to the company.
(3) All the intelligence developed on accounts payable personnel such as names, phone numbers, times they were contacted and what they promised.

In an emergency situation, where the survival of the company is at stake, everyone should be expected to play their part.

In Person Collection Visit

Sometimes to get a customer to pay, one has to get their attention. One method to do this is to send someone to the customer's office and have them wait all day if necessary for payment. The customer should understand that the person the company sent will return every day until the bill is paid.

(1) This person should be equipped with all the same client account intelligence that would be provided to the president if she or he were to make the collection call.
(2) The person sent should, if possible, be imposing both in title and physical aspect. Make of that what you will.
(3) Call the customer's accounts payable contact and notify them in advance that this person is coming. If the contact says they will be out of the office, ask for their bosses' boss and let them know the person is coming.

I have used this method to great effect, encouraging a reluctant government agency to pay well over $100,000 and a major corporation to hand me a $600,000 check.

Missing Payroll

Sometimes, one needs to give a customer a reason to pay sooner rather than later. One thing that usually has an impact it to tell the customer that the company will miss its payroll if the customer does not pay up. This often has a sobering effect on the client. Only say this if it is true.

Don't be embarrassed at admitting to a customer that the company might miss a payroll. It is much more embarrassing to actually miss a payroll and try to explain it to the company's loyal staff.

Factors

Factors can sometimes provide capital in a short period of time. Even if a company does not have a relationship with a factor, it might be able to begin buying accounts receivable in 10 days to 2 weeks. That is the period of time it takes them to assure themselves that the company and its accounts receivable are legitimate.

Collection Agencies

Collection agencies are effective, but might not be timely enough to help in a cash emergency. Collection agencies will not advance cash against the amount to be collected and then after a debt is collected, only remit at month end, or quarter end, depending on their policy.

Salesperson's Responsibility in Collections

Salespeople are reluctant to get involved in collections for fear of losing the follow up sale. However, the objective isn't to make sales, it is to get paid. At the very least,

(1) commissions shouldn't be paid on uncollected sales, and that makes it in the salesperson's interest to help with collections,
(2) salespeople should provide intelligence as to who the real power brokers are in a client's company so they can be contacted if necessary.

Conclusion

By the time a new CEO or a turnaround consultant is hired a company may be in deep trouble. Its bank has probably cut off credit and may be calling its loans.

Emergency cash management has four elements. (i) Halt cash outflows to the extent possible. Ask top management to take temporary pay cuts and putt workers on partial layoff. (ii) Consolidate cash and analyze cash position daily. (iii) Make extraordinary efforts to collect what is due to the company. (iv) Prioritize cash disbursements, making payments only when absolutely necessary which is different than paying bills as they become due.

Emergency cash procedures should help a company buy enough time for other restructuring efforts to work including improvement in collections, sale of excess inventory, plant, property and equipment and bringing the company's cost structure into line. However, there is no guarantee these procedures will work for every company. Sometimes a company is so far gone by the time a new CEO or turnaround consultant is hired that it must retreat into the protection of Chap. 11 bankruptcy

Notes

1. At Charles Schwab, managers and Vice Presidents are being asked to take a 5% to 25% salary cut Spokesman Glen Mathison said, "We couldn't avoid layoffs but (this action) helps keep layoffs to a minimum." Kansas City Southern Industries adopted a pay-cut plan for middle and senior management. "Workers Cut Pay Cuts Over Pink Slips," Stephanie Armour, USA Today, April 13, 2001, B1.
2. The San Francisco multimedia company 415 Productions asked their workers whether they would prefer to work 4 days a week and take a corresponding pay cut or would they prefer to take a 5% pay-cut. "Workers Cut Pay Cuts Over Pink Slips," Stephanie Armour, USA Today, April 13, 2001, B1.

References

Brennan T (2000) Paul Harris stores files for bankruptcy. The Daily Deal, 17 Oct. www.TheDeal.com. Accessed 1 Apr 2002

Thierry L (1999) Bankruptcy analysis: interview with John Peterman. CNN Financial Network. 1 Oct. Transcript #100103cb.112

Peterman J (1999) The rise and fall of the J. Peterman Company. Harv Bus Rev 77(5):59–66, Sept–Oct

Chapter 16
Bankruptcy

Introduction

Bankruptcy is a powerful weapon for giving a company a fresh start. Bankruptcy can be used to defend against creditors trying to strip a company of assets. It can also be used offensively against customers that file bankruptcy and refuse to pay. Under the right circumstances, bankruptcy law can be used to squeeze concessions from bondholders, banks, customers, suppliers, landlords and unions.

This chapter is limited to corporations. The debt of sole proprietorships and partnerships flows to owners personally. Corporations can only use Chapters 7 and 11 of the bankruptcy code, therefore this discussion is limited to those chapters.

The purpose of this chapter is to demystify bankruptcy and help the new CEO or turnaround consultant understand some of the strategic options that bankruptcy law provides. This discussion will cover the bankruptcy process, where to find bankruptcy law, and how to use bankruptcy.

Background

State law is designed to enforce contracts and help creditors collect money owed to them. The first to sue and execute on his, her or its judgment, is most likely to get paid. Those who wait in hopes that "things will work out," usually get nothing. The race is to the swift.

Federal bankruptcy law, on the other hand has two goals. The first, is to treat all the creditors in a class fairly and the second is to give people and companies a chance for a fresh start. One of the great things about America is that people reinvent themselves all the time. Companies reinvent themselves as well. Bankruptcy also serves a useful economic purpose by releasing unproductive assets back into the economy.

Chapter 7 Liquidation

Chapter 7 of the bankruptcy law is designed for the orderly winding up of a failed company. Essentially, the owner or shareholders as the case may be, tells the court that they cannot make the company work. They give the assets of the company to

D.E. Vance, *Corporate Restructuring*, DOI 10.1007/978-3-642-01786-5_16,
© Springer-Verlag Berlin Heidelberg 2009

the court along with a list of creditors. The court will appoint a trustee to collect and liquidate the company's assets. Then the court will distribute funds to creditors according to a statutory distribution scheme which gives priority to secured lenders court and attorney fees, and then to unsecured creditors of various classes.

At the end of Chap. 7 bankruptcy the court will discharge the company from all liability for unpaid debts and the company will cease to exist (Jordan and Warren, 1985, pp. 22–26). However, if a company owner or shareholder personally guarantees the debts of a company, the bankruptcy of the company will not discharge him or her from liability pursuant to that independent guarantee. Most banks require personal guarantees for small to medium sized businesses. While both individuals and corporations may seek relief under Chap. 7, personal bankruptcy is beyond the scope of this text.

The mechanics of Chapter 7 bankruptcy are:

(1) The petitioner schedules assets and liabilities.
(2) The bankruptcy petition is filed. The petition is simply a form with supporting schedules listing the company's assets and a detailed list of creditors and how much is owed to each.
(3) A trusteeis appointed.
(4) Creditors are notified of bankruptcy by the trustee and invited to file a proof of claim.
(5) The trustee marshals the assets of the estate. This may mean converting assets to cash, voiding preferential or fraudulent transfers, or bringing legal actions against those who owe the estate money. The trustee may abandon assets with minimal value.
(6) Where secured claims are greater than the assets securing them, the trustee may "abandon" the asset to those holding the security interest. The value of the asset "abandoned" reduces the claim of the creditor. The balance is an unsecured claim.
(7) Secured claims are satisfied. Tax liens can qualify as secured liens.
(8) Classes of claims are paid in order. Each class fully paid before the next class takes anything.
(9) The debtor is discharged. This means that legal liability for the company's remaining unpaid debts is forever extinguished. However, a discharge may be denied if a discharge has been granted in a previous bankruptcy in the last 6 months (Epstein, 1985, p. 296).

Since the focus of this text is to resurrect companies not to bury them, the bulk of this chapter will focus on Chapter 11 bankruptcy. Chapter 7 Liquidation is only discussed to provide background.

Chapter 11 Reorganization

Chapter 11 bankruptcy is designed to give a company a chance to reorganize itself. Once a bankruptcy petition is filed, an automatic judicial stay goes into effect which prevents any person or company from collecting any pre-bankruptcy debt, prevents anyone from suing the company and prevents anyone from executing on a judgment against the company.

At the time the petition is filed, a bankruptcy estate is created which is a legal entity separate and distinct from the company and its owners. The bankruptcy estate comes under control of the court which may appoint a trustee to oversee the estate if it finds management is dishonest or incompetent. However, absent such a finding, the court will allow management to reorganize the company.

The bankrupt must file a plan for emerging from bankruptcy. The plan must discuss how much, and when various classes of creditors will be paid. A plan may specify some creditors are paid in full, some partially, and some not at all. If at least one class of impaired creditors agrees to the plan, and the judge believes the plan is fair to all, it will be approved. Once the plan is approved, the company gets a bankruptcy discharge. If the plan calls for paying some class of creditors less than the full value of their claim, those creditors will not be able to collect more than allowed in the plan after the bankruptcy discharge. Not every company qualifies for a discharge. Most do.

Finding Bankruptcy Law and Forms

Bankruptcy law is found at 11 U.S.C. The abbreviation U.S.C. stands for United States Code. The Bankruptcy Code is a collection of Federal laws related to bankruptcy. The 11 refers to Title 11 of the U.S.C., not necessarily the 11th volume of the U.S.C. Any reference librarian will be able to help you find the U.S.C. The Code is divided into sections, denoted by the symbol "§" dealing with different topics. For example 11 U.S.C. §701, is the section of the Bankruptcy Code that deals with Interim Trustees. Bankruptcy forms may be downloaded from: www.uscourts.gov/bkforms/bankruptcy_forms.html#official.

Filing a Bankruptcy Petition

Filing a bankruptcy petition triggers a number of events.

1. It creates an "estate" comprised of all the petitioner's assets. This estate is a separate legal entity, in many respects beyond the control of the debtor.
2. Filing creates an automatic stay of any legal proceedings against the petitioner and or the estate §301, §362. Unlike most areas of the law which requires some kind of adjudication before relief can be granted, bankruptcy law provides that the mere filing of a voluntary petition constitutes an order for relief §301. In many respects, the automatic stay is the most important element of Chapter 11 bankruptcy protection.
3. In a Chapter 11 filing also known as a "debtor in possession" action, the debtor retains control over assets. A trustee may be appointed for cause including dishonesty, incompetence or if it is in the interest of the creditors §1104(b).

Commencement of Bankruptcy

Voluntary Bankruptcy

Generally a bankruptcy begins when a debtor files a petition with the court §301. This is known a "voluntary petition." Insolvency is not a condition for filing bankruptcy (Epstein, 1985, p. 152). Bankruptcy can be filed to avoid unfavorable contracts, leases or labor agreements.

The primary information in the bankruptcy petition is the identification of the debtor, a listing of the debtor's assets and a listing of the creditors and the amount owed to each. A company can file a bankruptcy petition without a lawyer. However, it is always good to have a lawyer look a petition over before filing.

Involuntary Cases

Companies may be forced into bankruptcy "involuntarily" by three or more creditors whose claims aggregate to more than $5,000 or one creditor with a claim of $5,000 or more, if there are less than twelve creditors §303(b). Banks, insurance companies, farmers and charities are protected from involuntary bankruptcy (Epstein, 1985, p. 153).

For the court to order an involuntary bankruptcy, the creditors must show either (i) the debtor is not paying undisputed debts as they become due, or (ii) a guardian or trustee was appointed to take charge of substantially all of the debtors' property within 120 days prior to filing the petition §303(h). There is a presumption that if a guardian or trustee was appointed, the debtor cannot pay his, her or its bills (Epstein, 1987).

Relief does not occur with an involuntary petition until the debtor has had a reasonable time to answer. Thereafter, the court may grant relief §303(h). If a court finds the involuntary bankruptcy petition inappropriate, it may dismiss the case and award the debtor costs, legal fees, and damages §303(i).

Stay of Collection Actions

Filing a voluntary bankruptcy petition automatically stays all collection actions. That means that creditors are restrained, as a matter of law, from taking any action against the creditor or its property §362. The stay applies to both pre and post petition property §362(a)(3, 4).

Examples of prohibited actions include:

(1) commencement of any legal, judicial or administrative process §362(a)(1)
(2) enforcement of a judgment, even if the proceeding commenced prior to the bankruptcy petition §362(a)(2)
(3) any act to obtain possession or control of property of the estate §362(a)(3)
(4) any act to create or perfect a lien against property of the estate §362(a)(4)

(5) any act to collect, assess or recover a claim that arose before filing the petition §362(a)(6)

(6) the setoff of any debt that arose before the petition §362(a)(7).

The stay remains in force until the petitioner is discharged or the case is dismissed because the petitioner failed to perform its duties under bankruptcy law 362(c)(2).

The stay does not apply to certain situations, for example where the property is not part of the estate §362(b). Under certain narrow circumstances, a creditor can petition the court for relief from the stay for cause; for example to protect the property of the estate §362(d)(1).

Relief may also be granted where the debtor has no equity in the property and the property is not required for reorganization §362(d)(2). For example, a company orders a $50,000 truck. The debtor promises to make a $5,000 down payment the day after delivery and finance the balance through the dealership. After delivery, the debtor files for bankruptcy. At that point, the debtor has no equity in the truck since it has not yet made the down payment. If the dealer (creditor) can establish the truck is not necessary to the reorganization, the dealer can reclaim it.

Property of the Estate

The estate includes all property, legal and equitable interests of the debtor as of the commencement of the case, wherever located, and by whomever held §541(a). Property includes cash, accounts receivable, notes receivable, loans due from officers and employees, inventory, plant property and equipment, patents, copyrights, trade marks, trade names, and legal claims against others arising from damages, contracts or claims like the proceeds of an insurance policy.

Non-dischargeable Debts

For corporations, certain debts are not dischargeable in bankruptcy:

(1) taxes and custom duties §523(a)(1)

(2) money, property, services or refinancing obtained under false pretenses or in contemplation of bankruptcy §523(a)(2).

(3) unscheduled debts §523(a)(3)

(4) fraud or larceny while acting in a fiduciary capacity §523(a)(4)

(5) willful or malicious injury to property of another §523(a)(6) and

(6) governmental fines or forfeitures §523(a)(7)

Preferences

Avoidance of Pre-bankruptcy Transfers

Ordinarily, a company may its bills in any order. Suppose Able company owes $100,000 each to Baker and Charlie. Able only has $100,000. It may elect to pay

Baker $100,000 and pay Charlie nothing. However, if Able paid Baker just before filing for bankruptcy, that payment would be called a preference. Since bankruptcy law is designed to treat creditors fairly, the trustee would void the payment to Baker, recovering the $100,000 for the estate. The estate could then pay out $50,000 each to Baker and Charlie, or about 50% of each claim. Any transfer of assets might constitute a preference depending on the circumstances.

When can a transfer be voided? Under the Bankruptcy Act, a transfer can be voided when there is a "preference." A preference occurs when:

(1) there is a benefit to a creditor §542(b)(1),
(2) for an antecedent debt, that is a debt which was pre-existing §542(b)(2). (A purchase for cash would not be payment for an antecedent debt.)
(3) the debtor was insolvent at the time of the transfer §542(b)(3).
(4) the transfer was made within 90 days prior to filing the petition or within 1 year before filing the petition if the transfer was made to an "insider" §542(b)(4). Insiders include relatives and directors of debtors (Epstein, 1985, p. 186). Those associated with a business can be "insiders," as well.
(5) the transfer has the effect of increasing the amount the transferee would receive in a Chapter 7 case.

Allegheny Health System had a representative of Mellon Bank on its board of directors. Allegheny paid down a line of credit that it owed to Mellon bank just before it filed for bankruptcy. This was deemed a preference by the bankruptcy trustee who demanded Mellon disgorge the amount used to pay off its line of credit. If Mellon had merely been Allegheny's banker, it would have probably only had to disgorge payments made within 90 days of Allegheny filing for bankruptcy. But, Mellon was an insider by virtue of the fact that it had a representative on Allegheny's board. Therefore, it had to disgorge payments to it, not made in the ordinary course of business, for up to a year before the bankruptcy filing. Ultimately, Mellon paid $52 million to settle claims by the bankruptcy trustee (Epstein, 2000).

Non-cash Preferences

While a cash payment can be a preference, other things can be preferences as well. For example, if a debtor assigns its accounts receivable to a creditor in lieu of a cash payment, that assignment can be a preference.

Secured Creditors and Preferences

If a debtor gives an unsecured creditor a security interest in property that can be a preference. Why? Claimants with secured interests are paid before unsecured claimants.

The distinction between secured and unsecured creditors raises some interesting situations. A pre-bankruptcy payment to a fully secured creditor would not be considered a preference, whereas a pre-petition payment to an unsecured creditor would be considered a preference (Epstein, 1985, p. 189). The secured creditor is entitled to payment up to either the amount owed to it, or the value of the collateral in which it holds a security interest, which ever is less. The unsecured creditor must stand in line after secured creditors are paid from the assets they have an interest in. Payment to a secured creditor does not change the order of distribution. Giving a secured interest to a previously unsecured creditor has the effect of placing it ahead of other unsecured creditors.

Payments in the Ordinary Course of Business are not Preferences

If payments within 90 days of filing a bankruptcy petition may be voided by the trustee, how does the electric company guard against the chaos of monthly payments being reclaimed by trustees all the time? Payments made in the ordinary course of business may not be avoided by a trustee. Likewise, security interests created in goods used in the ordinary course of business may not be avoided by the trustee §547(c).

This provision also applies to "enabling" loans, that is loans necessary in the ordinary course of businesses §547(c)(3). For example, suppose a company financed a truck for 5 years making regular payments of $500 per month. The payments made just before the company filed for bankruptcy would not be a preference because such payments were made in the ordinary course of business.

Floating Liens

A floating lien is a lien against a class of assets rather than a specific, identifiable asset. For example, the exact make-up of inventory changes all the time as goods are bought and sold. Likewise, the specific balances which make up accounts receivable change all the time as customers pay their bills and sales are made to new customers. A security interest in inventory or accounts receivable does not constitute a new security interest under §547 just because the composition of assets change. However, a preference can be created if a security interest in assets increases within 90 days of the bankruptcy petition date (Epstein, 1995, pp. 200–202).

Set-Off

As a general rule, when two parties owe each other money, one party may set-off one amount against another. For example: Able owes Baker $4,000, and Baker owes Able $1,000. Most states allow Baker to offset the $1,000 debt it owes to Able against the $4,000 Able owes it. The result is that Able now owes Baker $3,000.

If a company owes a bank $500,000 and has a checking account at that bank with a balance of $100,000, the bank may offset the $100,000 against the $500,000. The result is that the company's checking account balance is drawn down to zero, and the bank's loan balance is reduced to $400,000.

In a bankruptcy situation, this looks like a preference. Such a set-off is only allowed to the extent that the bank did not improve its position 90 days prior to filing the petition and the date of the petition §553 (Epstein, 1995, pp. 205–206; Jordan, 1985, pp. 364–377).

If a troubled company owes its bank money, but hasn't filed bankruptcy there is a risk the bank, sensing a problem, may set-off the company's checking account balance against outstanding loans. This could be a disaster if the checking account balance was being accumulated to cover payroll.

Once a bank indicates concern over a company's situation, the company should immediately move its deposits, payroll, and other checking accounts to a bank it doesn't borrow from. This can be done quietly by making deposits to accounts in the new bank and using up the cash in the old bank in the normal course of business. Such a move will prevent the creditor bank from making a surprise offset.

Fraudulent Transfers

A bankruptcy trustee may invalidate a fraudulent transfer. A fraudulent transfer is usually defined as a transfer for less than "reasonable equivalent value." The bankruptcy trustee can only reach back to transfers made within 1 year of filing the petition §548. For example, if a company sells its $500,000 Aspen condo to the president's brother-in-law for $50,000 that would be a fraudulent transfer. The bankruptcy estate would reclaim the condo and the brother-in-law would become an unsecured creditor to the extent of $50,000.

Real Estate – Failure to Timely Record a Lien or Mortgage

A bankruptcy trustee may avoid certain pre-petition transfers that are not timely recorded or perfected. The reason is that a failure to record, or delay in recording can adversely affect other creditors (Epstein, 1995, pp. 221–225).

For example, Bob loans Alice $1 million secured by a mortgage against Alice's factory. Bob fails to record the mortgage at the county court house which keeps a record of deeds and mortgages. Other creditors research Alice's property and find she has a factory with no mortgage lien against it and therefore they are entitled to presume she has a $1 million unencumbered asset. Based on that research, they may extend Alice credit.

Alice files bankruptcy. Bob cannot then file the mortgage setting up a secured claim of $1 million against the factory and thereby step in front of other creditors §547.

Protecting a Company from Bankrupt Customers

Companies in trouble often find their customers are themselves in trouble and have difficulty paying bills when due. When a company gets in trouble, its products become obsolete, quality erodes, deliveries are late, orders are incomplete and customer service deteriorates. When this happens, the company's best customers move on to better suppliers and only customers who can't get credit elsewhere stay with the troubled company. The process of losing the good customers and keeping the bad ones is called adverse selection. The question is what does a company do about it?

Contracts are governed by state law. To standardize commercial transactions, many states joined to draft the Uniform Commercial Code (UCC). While not all states have adopted the UCC most have.

Under the Uniform Commercial Code (UCC) §2-702 a seller may reclaim goods if (i) it was a credit sale, (ii) the buyer was insolvent when the goods were received, and (iii) either there was a written misrepresentation of solvency within 3 months prior to delivery, or the seller makes a demand for reclamation within 10 days of delivery.

The most important defense against customers taking goods and then not paying for them is good credit and collections procedures. The credit application of slow paying and troubled customers should be updated quarterly. The company should ask questions that directly address the criteria for reclamation under UCC §2-702. Examples of such credit application questions are

(1) Is the company now solvent and does it expect to remain solvent in the foreseeable future?

  Yes   No

(2) Are there any factors or circumstances that might cause the company to file bankruptcy in the foreseeable future?

  Yes   No

  If yes explain. _____ _____

If the answer to question (1) is Yes or the answer to question (2) is No and the company files bankruptcy, within 3 months then arguably they have secured credit under false pretenses. That would mean the customer's debt to the company would not be discharged in bankruptcy and the company might also have a right under §2-702 to reclaim goods provided to the customer.

How does bankruptcy law effect reclamation rights granted in state law? Do the goods become part of the estate? Is the vendor left as an unsecured creditor? Generally, reclamation is allowed under §546 (c) if (i) the seller has the right of reclamation under non-bankruptcy law (e.g. the UCC), (ii) the buyer received the goods while insolvent, (iii) the sale is in the ordinary course of business, and (iv) the seller makes a written reclamation demand within 10 days (Epstein, 1995, pp. 242–246).

Order of Payout

There is rarely enough money to pay all claims in a Chapter 7 liquidation. While we are primarily focused on rescuing a company, it is important to understand liquidation priority for a number of reasons. First, not all restructurings succeed. Delays, miss-steps, competition, changing regulations and uncooperative stakeholders can torpedo a turnaround plan. If the worst happens, a Chapter 11 bankruptcy can be converted to a Chapter 7 liquidation so managers and owners should understand what will happen.

Another reason to understand Chapter 7 is that the consequences of liquidation serve as a bargaining chip with uncooperative creditors and shareholders. In a Chapter 7 payout creditors and other stakeholders may get nothing, whereas in a Chapter 11 restructuring they may get some percent of their claim.

Secured Claims

Secured claims are paid first from sale of the assets in which there is a security interest. For example, if a building subject to a mortgage is sold, the mortgage holder is a secured creditor and gets paid first. Banks and auto dealers usually obtain a secured interest equipment or autos by filing a security interest form with the state in which the property is located. If proceeds from sale of the secured asset are insufficient to pay the creditor in full, the creditor becomes an unsecured creditor to the extent of the balance.

Classes of Unsecured Claims

Unsecured creditors are only paid after secured creditors are paid. Classes of unsecured claims are paid in the order specified by statute. All creditors in one class are paid before any of the creditors in the next class are paid. So for example, §507 priority claims will be paid 100% and if there is any money left, allowed, unsecured claims which are timely filed will be paid some percentage of their claim, and if there is not enough money to pay this class in full, lower ranking classes of claims will receive nothing. Classes of claims in payment order are:

(1) §507 priority claims
(2) allowed, unsecured claims which were timely filed.
(3) allowed, unsecured claims which were not timely filed.
(4) fines and punitive damages.
(5) post petition interest on pre-petition claims.

There is rarely enough money to satisfy all classes of creditors in Chapter 7 liquidation (Epstein, 1995, pp. 283–284).

Section 507 Priority Claims

Section 507 priority claims are paid such that all first priority claims are paid before second priority claims are considered. If there is not enough money to cover all claims in a given priority level, those claims share on a pro rata basis.

(1) administrative expenses of the bankruptcy estate §507(a)(1)
(2) claims arising in the ordinary course of business between the time of filing an involuntary petition and the appointment of a trustee, or actual notice to the claimant whichever is earlier §507(a)(2).
(3) allowed, unsecured claims for wages, severance or vacation pay (a) earned within 90 days of the petition and (b) to the extent of $4,000 per employee §507(a)(3).
(4) employee benefits arising from services rendered within 180 days of filing the petition or cessation of business, whichever comes first to the extent of $4,000 times the number of relevant employees less the aggregate amount paid under paragraph 3) above, §507(a)(4).
(5) allowed, unsecured claims of grain producers or fisherman against those purchasing grain or fish to the extent of $4,000 per person §507(a)(5).
(6) unsecured deposits by individuals for goods and services to the extent of $1,800 per person §507(a)(6).
(7) allowed, unsecured tax claims on income, on real property, sales taxes, withheld wage taxes and exercise taxes §507(a)(7) (Epstein, 1995, pp. 285–288).

The bankruptcy courts have the authority to reprioritize certain claims under principals of equitable subordination §510(c). Courts only exercise this power when creditors either contributed to the bankruptcy, or impaired the assets of the estate (Epstein, 1995, p. 290).

Unless otherwise specified, all discussion after this point refers to Chapter 11 reorganization.

Additional Protection for the Bankrupt

Leases and Executory Contracts

An executory contract is a contract unperformed on both sides, and the failure of either party to execute would constitute a material breach sufficient to excuse the other party from performing (Epstein, 1995, p. 292). For example, the company promises to pay $100,000 for 10,000 toasters. The contract is executory if the company has not paid any of the $100,000 and the toasters have not been delivered.

For leases and executory contracts, a bankrupt may:

(1) reject a lease or executory contract
(2) assume and retain a lease or executory contract §365(a) or
(3) assume and assign a lease or executory contract §365(l).

If a lease is rejected, the debtor will no longer have liability for the lease and will no longer be able to use the property. Since this is a breach of the lease, the lessor may have an unsecured claim for future rent. If the lease is accepted, it becomes a first priority administrative expense. If the lease is assigned, the debtor and estate are relieved of any future liability after the date of the assignment. Leases or executory contracts not accepted within 60 days of the order for relief are considered rejected (Epstein, 1995, pp. 285–287). If a debtor contracts with a bank for a line of credit, and then files for bankruptcy, the debtor cannot assign that financing agreement to another §363(c)(2).

Contracts, Covenants and Lease Clauses

Some contracts and bank loan agreements contain provisions that purport to termi-nate agreements, cause forfeitures or modify contracts to the detriment of the debtor if the debtor declares bankruptcy. The Bankruptcy Code nullifies all such provisions (Cowans, 1998, p. 139). For example, a landlord may not use bankruptcy to evict tenants (Epstein, 1995, p. 288). Sometimes a landlord will insert a clause in a lease that says that if the lessee files bankruptcy, the landlord has the right to terminate the lease. Bankruptcy law makes such clauses ineffective. Landlords count on bankrupts not understanding the law and so they send eviction notices hoping the lessee will leave the property.

Retention Bonuses

The importance of executive sacrifice in getting the rank and file to under understand the gravity of a company's situation cannot be overestimated. But, not all executives see the need to sacrifice at a time when facilities are closing and workers are being laid off.

When a company is in trouble, or enters bankruptcy, it sometimes pays executives and managers retention bonuses to stay while a company reorganizes. This results in a situation where those who got a company in trouble are rewarded with additional compensation.

The bankruptcy law which went into effect in October 2005 severely limits such retention bonuses. For example, an executive cannot get a retention bonus unless he or she can demonstrate they have a superior offer from another company. Bonuses are also limited to ten times an average worker's compensation. In addition, judges can reject retention packages when they are not in the best interest of the creditors (Beck, 2005).

Bankruptcy Plan

A bankruptcy plan tells the court how much each class of creditors will be paid, when they will be paid and identifies leases or executory contracts accepted or rejected, as well as modifications to collective bargaining agreements. In addition, the plan may provide for conversion of debt to stock and it may call for the dilu-tion of current stockholder equity. The plan has mandatory provisions §1123(a) and optional provisions §1123(b). The plan may affect the rights of secured and unsecured creditors as well as shareholders (Epstein, 1995, p. 345). Payouts in a Chapter 11 bankruptcy plan need not follow the payout priorities of Chapter 7. In Chapter 11 a debtor in possession may alter the order of payout, pay everyone a little rather than satisfying one class entirely before paying the next class and so forth. However, a bankruptcy plan must be approved by the court so care must be taken to be as fair as possible.

Who May File a Bankruptcy Plan

Section 1121 gives a Chapter 11 debtor a 120 day period of exclusivity during which it is the only one that can file a plan §1121(b). Judges may extend this period of exclusivity for not more than 18 months §1121(d) (Epstein, 1995, p. 344). Since the debtor has the only plan in play for up to twenty two months, it has enormous control over (nervous) creditors. Creditors' options are

(1) accept the debtor's plan,
(2) petition to convert the bankruptcy to a Chapter 7 Liquidation, or
(3) attempt to truncate the period of exclusivity (Epstein, 1995, p. 344).

If the debtor fails to get the requisite number of creditors to approve the plan within the period of exclusivity, any party in interest can file a plan. If a trustee is appointed, he or she may file a plan.

Classes of Creditors

The bankruptcy code segregates claimants into classes with similar characteristics, and treats everyone in that class the same. Sometimes small creditors are given a separate class for administrative convenience (Epstein, 1995, p. 346).

Plan Approval

A class of creditors is said to have approved the plan when more than half the number of claimants, and those representing 2/3 of the amount owed approve the plan, §1126(d) (Epstein, 1995, p. 353).

The Plan then goes before a judge who can approve a plan rejected by creditors or reject a plan approved by creditors. A hearing is held for purposes of obtaining comment on the plan. If at least one class of impaired creditors approves the plan, the judge can confirm the plan (Epstein, 1995, p. 354). A class of creditors is impaired if they receive less than they bargained for.

For example, suppose a debtor defined a class it called raw material suppliers which it owed $20 million. If the plan calls for exchange of this debt for 5 year bonds with a 10% coupon rate, the raw material supplier class is said to have their claim impaired because they expected to be paid shortly after delivery. If the plan is approved by the raw material suppliers and it appears fair on its face to all other creditors, the judge will probably approve it.

On the other hand, suppose the debtor's plan is to pay raw material suppliers only $5 million of the $20 million owed in the form of 50 year bonds bearing 2% interest. The creditors in that class will reject the plan and then have an opportunity at the confirmation hearing to explain why the company should pay the full amount due.

There are usually many classes of creditors. Bond holders may approve a plan which reduces their interest rate from 7.75 to 7.5% making them an impaired class. But the court may reject the plan if it unfairly burdens some other class of creditors.

Once a bankruptcy plan is approved by the court, debts will be paid to the extent specified in the plan. Any debt over the amount approved by the court is forever discharged and the creditors can never seek payment for those debts again.

Prepackaged Bankruptcy

There is a certain element of risk whenever a company enters a judicial proceeding and bankruptcy is no exception. Judicial proceedings are costly, consume management time and attention and tend to drag on for long periods of time, all of which create uncertainty for customers, creditors, employees and investors. The cost, risk, time and expense of bankruptcy can be minimized with a prepackaged bankruptcy. A prepackaged bankruptcy occurs when a debtor:

(1) Prepares the disclosure statement. A disclosure statement provides information to the creditors so that they will have information to decide whether to accept or reject the bankruptcy plan. Usually, a court will hold a hearing after notice to all parties to determine the adequacy of the disclosure (Epstein, 2008).
(2) Pre-selects a creditors committee, and
(3) Negotiates an approved plan with the creditor's committee,
(4) Before the bankruptcy petition is filed.

The authorizing sections of the bankruptcy code include: §1102 that recognizes pre-petition creditor's committees, §1121 that permits a debtor to file a plan of reorganization together with its petition and §1126(b) that provides for solicitation of acceptances prior to bankruptcy (Epstein, 1995, p. 361).

Advantages of a Prepackaged Bankruptcy

The advantages to a prepackaged bankruptcy are that (i) the time a debtor operates in bankruptcy is minimized; (ii) there is less disruption of the debtor's business; and (iii) the debtor has more control over the process (Epstein, 1995, p. 362).

Disadvantages of a Prepackaged Bankruptcy

The disadvantages of a prepackaged bankruptcy are that, until a plan is filed (i) there is no stay of collection efforts; (ii) the company has no ability to reject unfavorable contracts; (iii) there is no halt to accumulation of interest on unsecured debts; and (iv) no ability to obtain funding under the super priority loan provision (Epstein, 1995, p. 362).

Specimen Bankruptcy Plan

Table 16.1 is a simplified version of a prepackaged bankruptcy plan. Depending on the number of bond holders and other classes of creditors and the type and number of equity investors, plans can become quite complex. However, if a plan becomes too complex, the court might read that as trying to take advantage of one class of creditors to the detriment of others.

Conversion of Debt to Equity

Often a company needs to exchange debt for debt or debt for equity. For such an exchange to have an effect, a very high percentage of creditor acceptance is required. Creditors may accept lower interest rates and longer terms if such concessions increase the probability of getting paid. If the company's debt is held by a few large institutions this is not an insurmountable problem. However, if bonds are widely held, a significant number may hold out. The Trust Indenture Act of 1939, §316(b) prohibits the majority of bondholders from changing core provisions such as: principal amount, interest rate and maturity, against the will of the minority bondholders (DiNapoli et al., 1990). A debt exchange offer should contain a provision that accepting the exchange, also constitutes creditor approval in a prepackaged bankruptcy. Since bankruptcy usually only requires two thirds approval, the whole class may be bound (DiNapoli, 1990, p. 121).

Exemption from Securities Laws

Under some circumstances, a company in bankruptcy is exempt from the usual filing and registration requirements of securities laws §1141. The principal use of this provision is to swap debt for equity as part of a plan of reorganization.

Section 363 and Sale of Assets

Troubled companies need to convert assets to cash, and convert them quickly. Outside of the bankruptcy process, there is the possibility that creditors will claim there are liens on the assets sold. Or, ownership of assets may be in dispute. State courts often hold that liens follow assets so that the buyer may find they have purchased assets encumbered by liens. Often bank loan agreements include a blanket

Table 16.1 Astra communications plan of reorganization

Background and summary

Astra Communications has been making solid-state electronic power supplies since 1985. Most recently it has specialized in light weight power supplies and chargers for the telecommunications market. In 2007, it expanded plant and facilities in response to an expected telecommunications boom. However, beginning in late 2008, its principal customers suffered a significant sales decline that resulted in cancellation of planned 2009 orders. The company's sales dropped 40%, and the company was unable to meet cash flow demands.

In May, 2009, the company opened discussions with senior and subordinated bondholders who formed a steering committee to discuss restructuring the company's indebtedness. Effective June 15, 2009, the members of the steering committee entered an agreement pledging their support for a plan of reorganization. Members of the steering committee owned 74% of the senior bonds bearing a coupon rate of 12, and 68% of the subordinated bonds bearing a coupon rate of 14%. The company solicited and received acceptances for a plan of reorganization. In putting together this pre-packaged bankruptcy, the company hopes to shorten the time spent in Chapter 11. On July 15, 2009, the company filed the plan of the reorganization.

Summary of the plan of reorganization

Administrative Expense Claims will be paid in full, in cash, at the later of the effective date, the date the claim is allowed, or such later, mutually agreed date.

Claims that arose in the ordinary course of business after the petition date will be paid in full in the ordinary course of business.

Priority Tax Claims will be paid in full at the effective date, the date the claim is allowed, or at a mutually agreed later date. The debtor reserves the right to pay claims in equal annual payments of principal and interest over a period not to exceed 6 years.

Class 1: Other Priority Claims will be paid in full at the effective date, the date the claim is allowed, or at a mutually agreed later date.

Class 2: Miscellaneous Secured Claims will receive upon reorganization, unless the claimants agree to less favorable treatment, either (i) the legal, equitable and contractual rights of the claim unaltered; (ii) the collateral securing the claim; or (iii) the Debtor will provide such other treatment as will render the claim unimpaired.

Class 3: Bank Claims will receive upon reorganization either: (i) the legal equitable and contractual rights of the claim unaltered; (ii) the collateral securing the claim; or (iii) the Debtor will provide such other treatment as will render the claim unimpaired.

Class 4: Small Vendor Claims, those with accounts payable balances under $1,000, will receive upon reorganization either: (i) the legal, equitable and contractual rights of the claim unaltered; (ii) the collateral securing the claim; or (iii) the debtor will provide such other treatment as will render the claim unimpaired. (Small Vendor claims are a special class of claims carved out by the debtor.)

Class 5: Pre-Petition Management Claims for bonuses and incentive pay will be paid 25% of claims totaling $4 million over a period not to exceed 5 years.

Class 6: Trade Creditors will be paid 80% of pre-petition claims totaling $30 million over a period not to exceed 5 years. Such claims to accrue interest at 6% per year from the date of the bankruptcy discharge. Trade Creditors will be paid 100% of post-petition claims totaling $6 million in the normal course of business, but no longer than 90 days after discharge from bankruptcy.

Class 7: Senior Notes bearing 12% interest have estimated allowed claims of $100 million and Subordinated Notes bearing 14% interest have estimated allowed claims of $60 million. Upon reorganization, senior note holders will receive 60.25 shares of new common stock for each $1,000 of bond principal. Upon reorganization, subordinated note holders will receive 55.65 shares of new common stock for each $1,000 of bond principal.

Table 16.1 (continued)

Upon distribution, this will be equivalent to 95% of the new common stock outstanding. New common stock will have a par value of $0.01, and 20,000,000 shares are authorized. Approximately 10,000,000 shares will be distributed pursuant to the plan. Each share shall have one vote.

Class 8: General Unsecured Claims will receive 70% of their stated value.

Class 9: Old Equity Interest

Estimated Allowed Claims: 10,000 shares outstanding. On the effective date, assuming no old options are exercised prior to the confirmation date, old common stockholders will receive 50 shares of new common stock for each single share of old common stock. This distribution will represent 5% of the new common stock. All old options that have not been exercised as of the effective date will be canceled.

/S/ President & CEO, Astra Communications

lien on all of a companies assets, and have covenants that assets not be sold other than in the ordinary course of business.

Section 363 of the Bankruptcy Code provides that assets can be sold free and clear of liens and other claims. The rationale is that in times of financial distress, the value of a company's assets may deteriorate rapidly. If a buyer has to take the time to verify ownership, or contest liens, it will dramatically discount the value of assets to account for risk.

Creditors are not abandoned in the process. Liens attach to the proceeds of section 363 sales (Cowans, 1998, p. 142). If proceeds are less than the value of the lien then creditors become unsecured creditors to the extent of the deficiency. Therefore, creditors are highly motivated to make sure proceeds are enough to cover liens.

Section 363 Sale Procedures

Section 363 sales can only be made after a bankruptcy petition has been filed. The seller must make a motion to the bankruptcy court listing with particularity (i) the items to be sold, (ii) whether the sale is intended to be free and clear of liens, and (iii) the sale price. As a practical matter, most sellers only make a 363 motion after they have at least one buyer and a price has been established.

Notice must be given to all creditors and parties at interest. The court must approve the sale as in the interest of the creditors. However, courts usually approve sales if there are no opposing motions. Sales in the ordinary course of business, for example a baker selling cookies or an appliance store selling refrigerators needs no prior approval (Cowans, 1998, p. 137). Sale of real estate or the machinery a company uses to make its product are not sales in the ordinary course of business.

Creditors hope that notice of a Section 363 sale will induce other bidders to come forward and over bid the original offer. Sales may be private, or by public auction. A list of the property sold, the price received and the purchaser must be filed with the court, unless impractical (Cowans, 1998, p. 149).

Even though the bankruptcy code provides strong protection to buyers, legal challenges after sales sometimes arise based on questions of (i) title, (ii) notice, (iii) sale procedures, (iv) the qualification of purchasers, or (v) the adequacy of price. Most of these issues are question of fact. To prevent overturning a sale by an appeals court, the sale motion often asks the court to make a finding of fact that the sale was conducted in "good faith" and the five issues listed above have been satisfactorily resolved. A finding of "good faith" requires absence of fraud, collusion, or any attempt to take unfair advantage of other bidders.[1] Appeals courts rarely overturn lower court's "findings of fact (Cowans, 1998, p. 149)."

Who May Buy at a Section 363 Sale

Generally, insiders may not take assets free and clear of liens. Insiders include owners, trustees and anyone who has a fiduciary relationship with the seller or property. This includes board members, employees, and probably the company's lawyers and accountants. The objective is to prevent those with "inside knowledge" of a property from taking advantage of creditors by purchasing assets at less than fair value while cutting off liens.

Sale of the Company or a Major Subsidiary

Sometimes the best thing is to sell substantially all the assets of a company or one of its subsidiaries. This can be done as a §363 sale.

A buyer will usually do substantial due diligence before making a purchase. Due diligence involves substantiating the assets of a company, verifying sales, auditing cost of goods sold, reviewing contracts, searching for hidden liabilities, investigating patents, inspecting employment contracts and payroll registers, inquiring about key customers and suppliers, and a number of other procedures. Due diligence is expensive and time consuming.

Break-Up Fees, Overbid and Sale Procedures

A buyer may make a bid conditional on the seller including certain terms, conditions and bid procedures in their §363 sale motion.

A break-up fee, also called the "topping fee," is designed to compensate the buyer who conducts the initial due diligence in the event than another buyer overbids them. The theory behind authorizing a break-up fee it that the initial buyer is the one who brought attention to the assets of the estate and provided a floor for the value of the assets. The break-up fee should approximate the cost of due diligence (Drinkman, 1998).

Buyers often ask the sale motion include minimum overbid procedures. This prevents bids from rising in insignificant increments. An aggressive buyer might request that all they have to do is match any overbid, rather than going to the next bid level (Drinkman, 1998, p. 13).

For example, a buyer offers to purchase all the assets of a company for $10 million. Their offer is contingent on the §363 sale motion including a break-up fee of $800,000, a minimum first overbid of $1 million and subsequent overbids in increments of $500,000. In the interests of the creditors, the court may authorize a sale for $10 million, a break-up fee of $400,000 and a first minimum overbid of $500,000 with subsequent overbids of $250,000.

Bidder Qualifications – Financial Capacity

Not all bids are created equal. Some bidders offer an all cash deal for assets, others offer notes, and others offer stock. Therefore, the initial buyer may ask the seller to include standards for qualifying other bidders in the §363 sale motion. Qualifications might require bidders to make an "earnest money" deposit or make a showing of the financial ability to close on the sale (Drinkman, 1998, p. 13).

Other Legal Considerations – Forum Shopping

The Bankruptcy Code vests substantial discretion in the bankruptcy judge. That discretion can affect things like a court's willingness to approve break-up fees, qualify other bidders, or approve sale motions.

Some courts are reluctant to approve sale of all the assets of a company under §363 because they fear that loss of the substantive and procedural protections afforded to creditors by bankruptcy proceedings. On the other hand, a Chapter 11 debtor might not be stable enough to survive a reorganization. A company may run out of money, or assets may deteriorate as the reorganization unfolds (Drinkman, 1998, p. 14). Over time, judges develop a track record predictive of whether they will facilitate, or oppose a prompt sale. Picking the "best" judge is called forum shopping.

Collective Bargaining Agreements

A union contract is a collective bargaining agreement. A debtor in possession or trustee may reject a collective bargaining agreement under certain circumstances, §1113. After filing the bankruptcy petition, and before filing an application with the court to reject the collective bargaining agreement, the debtor must make a proposal to an authorized representative of the collective bargaining unit based on the most complete and reliable information available. Enough information must be provided for the representative to evaluate the impact of the proposal on wages and benefits. There is also a requirement that all creditors be treated fairly and equitably. The debtor must meet, at reasonable times, to confer with labor's representative, and make a good faith effort to reach a mutually satisfactory set of modifications.

If, after those steps have been taken, and the debtor and union are unable to reach an agreement, the debtor may petition the court to reject the union contract. The debtor must provide notice of a hearing on its petition to reject the contract.

The court will approve the application for rejection if it finds (i) the debtor has, prior to the hearing, made a proposal that fulfills the above conditions, (ii) the authorized representative of the employees has rejected the proposal, and (iii) the equities clearly favor rejection of the collective bargaining agreement.

For the equities to favor rejection of the collective bargaining agreement, the company (debtor) should have some documented, quantitative evidence that the collective bargaining agreement provides pay, benefits, pension, and work rules that are outside the norms of the industry. The company should propose to a set of pay, benefit, pension and work rules which the court can compare to those of other companies to determine whether the proposal is fair to the employees as well as creditors.

To gain approval, the court will probably need a showing that the proposed changes to the union contract will substantially improve the probability of returning the company to solvency. The perception of fairness to employees will be enhanced if the company can show shared sacrifice. This means management should give up pay and privileges as well as union members.

Several airlines have recently emerged from bankruptcy after a reduction in union pay and benefits. Auto companies and their suppliers are negotiating reductions in pay and benefits with unions as well. But caution is advised.

A demoralized work force is an unproductive work force. Costs may include increased accidents and sick time, failure to follow through on assignments, doing the absolute minimum required to maintain one's job and poor customer service. Northwest Airlines emerged from bankruptcy after cutting pilots salaries by 40%. Afterward, a significant number of their pilots called in sick causing cancellation of hundreds of flights at a time when the company was trying to rebuild its relations with the flying public (Gustafson, 2007). Another legacy airline, UAL was still struggling with a demoralized staff and poor customer service 17 months after leaving a bankruptcy in which union members were asked to take substantial pay and benefits cuts (Carey, 2007).

Conclusion

Bankruptcy provides a powerful toolkit for restructuring a company. The most important tool is the automatic stay of collection and legal actions against the company.

A Chapter 7 bankruptcy is used to wind up a company's affairs in an orderly manner. The assets of a company are sold and its creditors paid according to a statutory priority scheme. A company ceases to exist after Chapter 7.

A Chapter 11 bankruptcy is designed to give a company the opportunity to reorganize free of collection or other legal actions against it. Once bankruptcy is filed, the assets of the company become part of a bankruptcy estate which is under the control of the court. Unless there is a showing of fraud or incompetence the debtor is allowed to manage the bankruptcy estate. Not every Chapter 11 reorganization is successful and some are converted to Chapter 7.

The primary concern of the bankruptcy law is that creditors be treated fairly. A bankruptcy trustee, or debtor can void preferential or fraudulent transfers of assets prior to bankruptcy. A debtor can affirm, reject or assign executory contracts and leases. Contracts or leases that purport to impose penalties when a company files bankruptcy are void as a matter of law.

Bankruptcy begins when a company files a bankruptcy petition or it is forced into bankruptcy by creditors after notice and a hearing. Bankruptcy terminates after the court approves a bankruptcy plan. Usually the debtor company files the plan, but if it does not, creditors can file a plan. The plan determines who will get paid, what amount, and when. If one class of impaired creditors approves the plan, the judge may approve it. When the plan is approved the company is discharged and any debt beyond that which will be paid under the plan is forever discharged and uncollectible.

Assets from a bankruptcy estate can be sold free and clear of any liens provided the procedures in §363 are followed. These procedures require notice of what is to be sold, at what price and allows creditors to challenge sales. The procedure allows sales of the whole company or individual assets. Public notice allows new buyers to bid against one another to get the best result for creditors.

Bankruptcy law can also be used to void a collective bargaining agreement if the union fails to agree to reasonable modifications and the company can show the modifications are reasonable, necessary, and in the best interests of the creditors. But, the tactic of voiding collective bargaining agreements can have a demoralizing effect on the workforce, so this strategy should be used with caution, if at all.

Note

1. In re: Rock Industries Machinery Corporation, 572 F.2d.1195, 1198 (7th Cir.1978).

References

Beck R (2005) New law limits retention bonuses. Phila Inq, C5, 10 Aug
Carey S (2007) United struggles to navigate new course. Corporate focus section. Wall St J, 29 June
Cowans D (1998) Bankruptcy law and practice, 7th edn. Lexis Publishing Co., Charlottesville, NC
DiNapoli D, Sigoloff S, Cushman R (1990) Handbook of workouts and turnarounds, 5th edn. Irwin, Homewood, IL, pp 118–119

Drinkman D (1998) Buying assets out of bankruptcy: procedural hurdles to bargain bonanza. Bus Credit 100(9):12–15, Oct

Epstein D (1985) Debtor-creditor law, 3rd edn. West Publishing Co. St. Paul, MN

Epstein D (1987) Bankruptcy code, rules & official forms, Law Edition, – West Publishing Company, St. Paul, MN, p 39

Epstein D (1995) Bankruptcy and other debtor-creditor laws, 5th edn. West Publishing Company, St. Paul, MN

Epstein D (2000) Mellon, banks agree to pay $52 million to settle suit. Dateline Pittsburgh. The Associated Press State & Local Wire, Business News Section, 9 Dec

Epstein D (2008) Bernstein's dictionary of bankruptcy terminology. Bernstein Law Firm, P.C. Suite 2200 Gulf Tower, Pittsburgh, PA 15219

Gustafson S (2007) Northwest airlines: pilot absenteeism key in flight cancellations. The Associated Press, Detroit, 27 June 2007, 6:36 p.m. EDT

Jordan RL, Warren WD (1985) Bankruptcy. The Foundation Press, Mineola, NY

Chapter 17
Execution

Introduction

All the good intentions in the world weigh less than a single act of kindness. Likewise, all the restructuring theories in the world weigh less a simple plan, well executed. The difference between average companies and great ones is execution. A company that expects and demands great execution year after year will get it. A company that only demands great execution sporadically or not at all will not get great execution (Stewart and O'Brien, 2005, p. 106).

Talking about restructuring; knowing what must be done; and having equations to model it, are different than executing a restructuring plan. Execution is where most companies fail. A Harvard study indicated that large companies only achieve about 63% of their strategic goals every year and a third of companies achieve less than 50% of plan (Mankins and Steele, 2005). An AMA study indicated only 3% of CEOs said their companies were very successful at implementing strategy and 62% said their ability to execute was moderate or worse (Mankins and Steele, 2007). In another survey, companies estimated that 60% of planned productivity gains were lost due to failure to execute (Neiman and Thomson, 2004, p. 17).

A reasonable question to ask is whether the execution failed or the plan was unrealistic, sometimes both. Often management doesn't have enough information to know. So if management does not know what went wrong, there is no way to take corrective action. As a result, management often resorts to slogans like "work smarter not harder," or "do more with less," or implements show policies that fail to solve real problems.

This chapter discusses a number of proven techniques for improving execution including (i) having executable plans, (ii) prioritizing tasks, (iii) establishing time-lines, (iv) measuring and monitoring, (v) building a culture of success, (vi) management development, (vii) rewarding achievement and punishing failure.

Execution Shortfalls

Why does execution fall short so often? Table 17.1 lists the eleven most widely cited reasons for execution failure in a study of companies with sales over $500 million (Mankins and Steele, 2005, p. 66).

D.E. Vance, *Corporate Restructuring*, DOI 10.1007/978-3-642-01786-5_17,
© Springer-Verlag Berlin Heidelberg 2009

Table 17.1 Reasons for execution failure

Reason	Percent
Inadequate or unavailable resources	20.3
Poorly communicated strategy	14.1
Action plan not clear	12.2
No accountability	11.1
Organizational silos and cultural failure	10.0
Inadequate performance monitoring	8.1
Inadequate consequences for failure	8.1
Poor senior leadership	7.0
Uncommitted leadership	5.1
Unproven or inadequate strategy	1.9
Other, including inadequate skills	2.1
	100.0

A company will never have enough resources to do everything, so one issue is how well a company can match plans and limited resources. A common problem is that organizational boundaries result in misallocated resources as each department fights to maintain and expand its budget (Sorensen, 2003, p. 48). This and other reasons for failure are avoidable and can be overcome with discipline and strong leadership.

This study also found less than 15% of companies routinely compared actual results to strategic plans (Mankins and Steele, 2005, p. 68). Unless a company systematically analyzes variances from plan, it is difficult to tell whether the plans were unrealistic, or whether there was poor execution.

An analysis of why CEOs fail ranks lack of execution a substantial reason for failure in 70% of cases (Charan and Colvin, 1999). Many factors contribute to execution failure. One of the most insidious is a culture of underperformance. When there is a gap between performance and goals year after year, with few consequences, management learns to expect a performance shortfall (Mankins and Steele, 2005, p. 68). Other factors that contribute to the performance gap include poorly formulated plans, misapplied resources, breakdowns in communication and limited accountability (Mankins and Steele, 2005, p. 67).

On the other hand, there are many examples of excellent performance and the key is identifying the practices that drove that performance. Combining good execution practices with mistake avoidance provides a systematic framework for outstanding execution.

The Plan

Both restructuring and strategic plans have certain elements in common. They outline broad goals, and set directions for reaching those goals. They assign responsibilities and allocate resources. Unfortunately, many companies spend a significant amount of time every year developing a plan, put it in a nice cover, approve it, stamp it, and put it on a shelf. It rarely sees the light of day after approval.

Plans suffer from other maladies as well. First, they represent compromises between corporate which always wants more, and divisions which want to set targets low so that bonuses will flow. Second, budgets revolve around what top management wants to hear rather than what is realistic. For example, some executives' idea of planning is to tweak excel spread sheets until a certain profit number appears. Profit doesn't come from spreadsheets. It comes from meeting customer needs. Third, budgets are used to allocate resources which constrain strategy. The reverse should be happening. Strategy should be developed, and then budgets should be used to communicate resource allocations. If strategy doesn't drive budgets, budgets will drive non-strategic behavior (Sorensen, 2003, pp. 45, 48) Managers desperate to "make the numbers" may take on business or cut costs that seems to help in the short run but damages the business in the long run (Whitney, 1996, p. 92).

On the other hand, good plans drive execution (Mankins and Steele, 2005, p. 68). Good plans are executable, set priorities, assign responsibility and have monitoring built into them.

Executable Plan

Strategic plans are often too vague to execute. Companies frequently confuse a mission statement with a strategic plan. A strategic plan has several characteristics. One is that it sets specific goals. If the goals are to sell as much as possible and cut costs as much as possible and make customers as happy as possible, the company has no plan. These goals are unexecutable because they are not specific.

Executable plans must be realistic. Unrealistic plans cause people to shut down rather than to stretch. Executable plans must be adequately funded and staffed with good people. This involves setting priorities to allocate limited resources. Executable plans should also be customer specific. Customers aren't generic and to treat them that way is to miss significant opportunities to improve upon execution (Sorensen, 2003, p. 45).

Plans should be simple, concrete and measurable (Mankins and Steele, 2005, p. 69). If the strategic goal is to grow revenue by 20% everyone should know it. Another strategic plan goal might be to increase gross margin by 5% or to enter a particular market. Each of these high level goals can then be deconstructed into the specific steps that have to be executed at each level of the organization. Table 17.2 provides an example of a very high level strategic plan.

Each of these goals can be further broken down into executable steps that can be assigned as goals for lower level employees. One extremely important thing to note is that the CEO cannot be excused from performance of his or her goals by saying the Vice President of Marketing did not meet his or her goals. The CEO is responsible for meeting goals no matter what. Likewise the Vice President of Marketing is responsible for meeting his or her goals no matter what. Each person in authority must take responsibility for the performance of those acting under them and to a significant extent for those in other departments that support their effort. No excuses (Stewart and O'Brien, 2005, p. 106).

Table 17.2 Strategic plan

The plan for the CEO for 2xxx is to:
(i)   *Improve customer relations to the point where repeat sales increase 40%.*
      Q1 Analyze what must be done, Q2 Implement improvements, Q3 Measure results and
      refine improvements, Q4 Measure results to goal.
(ii) *Cut overhead by 20%*
      Q1 Determine target headcount and identify specific individuals to be terminated. Q2
      Begin termination process. Identify overhead expenses which can be eliminated
      including consulting contracts. Q3 Terminate non-essential contracts. Q4 Measure
      overhead reduction results.
(iii) *Increase gross margin 5%.*
      Q1 Identify low performing products for elimination and eliminate same. Q2 Identify
      manufacturing processes which can be improved and improve them. Q3 Review all
      suppliers, eliminate those with poor quality or service, look for new suppliers, and
      develop relationships consistent with low price, quality and service. Q4 Measure
      results to goal.
(iv) *Increase return on invested capital by reducing the company's assets 20%.*
      Q1 Set targets for accounts receivable, inventory and plant property and equipment.
      Identify excess plant property and equipment and sell it.
      Q2 Strengthen credit and collection procedures; identify excess inventory and sell it.
      Q3 Cut off credit to slow accounts and deliver balances to collection agencies. Q4
      Measure results.

The goals of the Vice President of Marketing for 2xxx is to:

Improve customer relations to the point where repeat sales increases 40%.
Q1 Interview lost and existing customers and analyze customer complaint files, determine
   the top ten reasons customers are lost, don't make frequent repeat purchases or do not
   satisfy all their needs for product from this company. Prepare a report for the CEO and
   board. Design a customer intelligence system to track who customers are, where they
   are, when they buy, and what they buy. The system should have a way to track repeat
   sales. Design a system to track sales on a daily, weekly and monthly basis by product
   for the current year and prior year to the extent the data is available.
Q2 Implement a solution to eight of the top ten reasons that customers do not make a repeat
   purchase. Reduce order processing time 50%. Increase on-time deliveries 30%.
   Implement the customer intelligence system. Implement the system to track sales on a
   daily, weekly and monthly basis.
Q3 Implement a customer focused sales, marketing, and order processing team. Retrain
   customer sales and support team. Implement routine customer service surveys. Measure
   results to repeat sales goal.
Q4 Implement a data mining program to forecast when customers might need to make a
   purchase and make sure sales and marketing people make offers during or slightly
   before the buying window is open. Measure results to repeat sales goal.

The notations Q1, Q2, Q3 and Q4 indicate the quarter a plan element is to be complete.

Priorities

A hallmark of successful plans is that they set priorities. Unfortunately, there is a
tendency to have a laundry list of priorities and such a laundry list simply dissipates
the company's energy. A company must focus on initiatives that are clear, specific
and few. The first few priorities selected should have the greatest impact on bottom

line results and growth (Neiman and Thomson, 2004, p. 18). No new initiatives should be introduced until the old initiatives become deeply embedded in the company's culture. Jack Welsh, as CEO of GE, only launched five major initiatives in 18 years (Charan and Colvin, 1999).

Other successful companies focus on just three to five goals every year. For a company in restructuring the goals might be to (i) focus on the customer, this includes improving customer service, delivery times, product quality, and talking to former customers about why they left the company, (ii) cutting overhead, overhead is the great killer of companies, (iii) reducing cost of goods sold which is the same as saying increasing gross margin, and (iv) increasing return on invested capital by minimizing the assets the company uses. In subsequent years, the goals might be to introduce new products, take on additional quality control initiatives, and expand into new territories.

Clarity and Communication

There must be absolute clarity as to the company's goals and priorities and those goals must be repeated over and over again. Dell, for example, repeats its standard of performance in presentation after presentation so there is no mistake about what the company wants. To reinforce the message, rewards followed good performance and punishment followed bad performance (Stewart and O'Brien, 2005, p. 105). At UPS managers meet with their employees for exactly three minutes every day to make sure everyone knows the goals and priorities for the day (Kaihla et al., 2006).

The habit of clarity of communication must be ingrained at a deeply cultural level. For example, one practice of successful CEOs is to write down what everyone promised to do and when they promised to complete it at the end of every meeting and read the list back to everyone to make sure they were on board, and then to send them a follow up note afterwards (Charan and Colvin, 1999).

Responsibility

Clarity of expectations as to what each employee must do, backed with the knowledge that he or she will be held accountable is the most effective way to drive profit improvement. This goal alignment was responsible for doubling one company's division's profits in a single year (Layman, 2005, p. 27).

As strategic goals are deconstructed into sub-tasks, each sub-task must be assigned to a specific individual who will be responsible for completing task goals. Responsibility must be backed up by accountability which means that sub-task results must be objectively measurable. At Dell, every level of management has three to five sub-tasks to perform or goals to meet in support of higher level goals (Stewart and O'Brien, 2005, p. 105). Great CEOs always hold people accountable for meeting their commitments (Charan and Colvin, 1999).

Rewards must be aligned with responsibility otherwise rewards will drive non-strategic behavior. If bonuses are given just for making it through the year, rather than for hitting specific numerical goals, effort will be focused on survival versus execution. The key to keeping good people is to learn how to measure and reward them (Bhide, 1986, p. 62).

Of course the argument against detailed plans with specific steps is that it limits flexibility. The argument for detailed plans is that when everyone knows what he or she should do, and what they will be measured on, they are more likely to execute well. In the balance between the principal of flexibility and specific steps of execution, remember that execution pays the rent, not principals.

Time Frames and Sense of Urgency

One of the reasons companies fail to execute is indecisiveness. Quick action on problems is imperative. When Lou Gerstner was hired to restructure IBM he focused on execution, decisiveness and simplifying the organization for speed (Charan and Colvin, 1999). Dell believes that a company requires a sense of urgency in every thing it does. The notion of investing in the future can become a trap. The future is this afternoon and this evening (Stewart and O'Brien, 2005, p. 105). Much of the success of Silicon Valley companies is attributed to their view that there is no time for committees, meetings and task forces. They have to get things done and products to market (Charan and Colvin, 1999). What counts most in good execution is vigor and nimbleness, or what one might call hustle (Bhide, 1986, p. 59).

Contingencies

Life never unfolds exactly as planned. However, many executives and managers are linear thinkers and set about to achieve goals in a step one, step two, step three fashion. When something goes awry with step two it brings them to a halt. A good manager will always have in his or her pocket two or three ways to complete step two so that his or her ultimate commitment and goals can be met.

Contingency planning should not take the form of padding budgets or time estimates. Contingency planning should be about alternative courses of action. The more credible alternatives one has to reach a commitment, the more likely one is to reach it. Adapt. Improvise. Overcome.

A Culture of Success

It is difficult to instill a culture of success in an underperforming company with a demoralized workforce, but it can be done. Failing to meet goals one year increases the likelihood that goals will be missed the next year. The expectation of failure can become the norm. A culture of success can also become the norm. The transition from a culture of failure to a culture of success is usually painful, but it can be done.

Success begets success. One way to change the culture is to focus on a number of short interval projects, those which can be completed in 60–100 days. Select projects with a high payoff, and for which the payoff can be quantitatively measured. For example, an electronics firm set and met the goal of reducing the time from order to installed service by 80% (Neiman and Thomson, 2004, p. 18). A credit card company set and met the goal of replacing lost cards in 2 days and reduced customer billing query time from 16 days to 10 days (Bhide, 1986, p. 64). The demonstration of a clear impact on profitability will begin to turn the culture. When a CEO who executes well brings habits into a company where they didn't exist, attitudes begin to change in subtle ways. People are more prepared for meetings and begin to focus on closing the plan-performance gap. They begin to realize that commitment is everything (Charan and Colvin, 1999).

Successfully completing significant short interval projects gives people a sense of the possibilities, but not everyone is likely to have the skill or desire to follow through on every task. Those who can't or won't meet their goals must go. The first people cut under a regime that insists on success will be shocked, but those who remain will get the message, and will find ways to improve performance. Dell's no excuses policy is a model for the kind of success based culture a company should aspire to (Stewart and O'Brien, 2005, p. 105).

Measurement and Monitoring

Accountability must be designed into execution. Accountability requires measurable goals and a systematic means to collect and analyze progress toward goals (Stewart and O'Brien, 2005, p. 105).

Key Performance Indicators

Everything that can be measured should be measured is an overstatement, but not by much. Everything that contributes to the company's overall goals should be measured, not just at a financial level by at a non-financial level as well. For example, quality costs money, inventory costs money and time costs money, so measures of quality, inventory and time are critical to a company making its profit goals (Stewart and O'Brien, 2005, p. 105).

If a retailer's goal is to grow sales, then it should measure sales by store; sales per square foot per store; sales this year compared to last year; sales per square foot per dollar of rent to determine the payoff for renting premium space; sales per dollar of assets invested in plant property and equipment; sales per dollar of inventory investment; the number of customers visiting stores; the conversion rate which is the number of visitors that actually make a purchase; the average purchase; the contribution on the average purchase; and so forth. At the level of the store manager, key performance indicators will drive him or her to get more customers to the store; focus on customers likely to purchase; stock more attractive merchandise; offer more impulse buy items; spawn high contribution sales through better product selection and placement; train sales staff to up sell and suggest accessories to go with purchases.

Every industry has a key set of metrics or performance indicators. In auto manufacturing, it might be the number of labor hours it takes to assemble a vehicle; the clock time to assemble a vehicle; absenteeism; overtime; on the job injuries; percentage of vehicles that pass final inspection; warranty claims in the first 90 days; unsold inventory; inventory in dealerships; or contribution per vehicle. When restructuring a company it is important to understand how each of these industry metrics contributes to the company's goals. Measure performance and hold people accountable for meeting expectations.

Dell tracts things like generating leads and increasing margin (Stewart and O'Brien, 2005, p. 107). Hewlett Packard tracks more than a dozen variables across its business units including things like real estate cost per square foot and operating expenses as a percent of gross margin. They also benchmark themselves against their competitors' (Kaihla et al., 2006). Other companies tract things like sales from new products and the number of new products introduced.

Trade journals are one place to find industry specific metrics. The financial literature is another source. As writers grapple to compare companies and sort out the good, the bad and the hopeless, they often report on, or develop interesting metrics. Company specific metrics can be developed through an understanding of all the sub-activities that roll up to financial performance. Regular contact with line workers and first line managers might help identify such metrics.

The best metrics are those captured as a byproduct of operations rather than as separate tasks that require staff to fill out forms or make computer entries they wouldn't ordinarily make. For example, most of the metrics discussed for retail stores can be gleaned from computerized inventory, accounts payable, budget and sales data.

Annual or even quarterly reports are not useful for execution management because they are not timely. Many successful companies like Dow Chemical and Boeing measure performance on a weekly basis which forces everyone to "live the details of execution (Mankins and Steele, 2005, p. 72)." Some companies measure key metrics like sales and production on a daily basis. Dell, for example, monitors order activity in real time and if fewer than expected orders come in by 10:00 AM, they run a special on their website by 10:15 (Stewart and O'Brien, 2005, p. 105). Great CEOs are always hungry for details that can help improve performance (Charan and Colvin, 1999). But, lower level managers need this kind of feedback as well so they can constantly adjust tactics to meet their commitments.

There is an unfortunate tendency in many underperforming companies to keep information secret. This isn't healthy. A better approach is to make everyone's metrics available to everyone else so they can see where they are. No one wants to be the last one around the track or even in the last half of the pack, so making performance measures widely available can stimulate performance (Stewart and O'Brien, 2005, p. 105).

Management by Walking Around

Monitoring also means the CEO or turnaround consultant must routinely talk to workers, first line managers and customers (Charan and Colvin, 1999). Bloomberg's new headquarters takes this idea to a whole new level by placing the CEO in a glass office in the middle of a floor of sales and customer service agents. This gives him an unprecedented and real time view of what is going on (Kaihla et al., 2006). Home Depot's board members are expected to visit a dozen stores a year and report on customer service, merchandise selection, store appearance and a number of other variables (Kaihla et al., 2006).

This is sometimes called management by walking around and it can be useful in collecting intangible information about morale, operations, and the market place. It also helps provide context to the numbers. Sometimes management by walking around can identify trends, good or bad, before they are reflected in the numbers. And sometimes management by walking around generates ideas for new and more relevant measures of performance.

People Development

Unless a company has the right people, with the right skills and the right attitude, it will not be able to execute its plan. GE's philosophy is people first, strategy second (Charan and Colvin, 1999). The idea is that if one has the right people, people who can execute well, they will achieve good results even if the strategy is inadequate. In fact, there are some who say that strategy confers a temporary advantage at best and that true competitive advantage comes from superior execution (Bhide, 1986, p. 62).

Selection

Selection of the right people for leadership positions is challenging. Barkley's Capital, for example makes it their policy to hire only "A" players. Therefore, top management takes responsibility for all hiring. Executives also vet each others hires to keep raising the bar (Mankins and Steele, 2005, p. 72). Anyone can look good on paper or behave well in an interview. One advantage to promoting internally is that internal candidates have a track record that is easier to evaluate than that of a new hire. Dell, for example has shifted from 75% new hires for leadership positions to 70% internal promotions (Stewart and O'Brien, 2005, p. 106).

Southwest Airlines begins the interview process with a candidate's first contact with the company and documents the candidate's interaction with every Southwest employee they meet, from reservationists, if they are flying in for an interview, to secretaries, to flight attendants and human resource staff. They also ask candidates to give speeches about themselves and watch the reaction of the other candidates. If candidates are bored by other candidates' speeches, they are probably not the people-people Southwest wants. The company credits this screening process for both superior execution and one of the lowest employee turnover rates in the airline industry (Kaihla et al., 2006).

Investment banking is an industry in which the hustle and drive of individual employees makes or breaks a firm. Therefore, it is rare for any professional to be hired without an interview with one or more of a firm's managing directors (Bhide, 1986, p. 64).

All this screening takes a substantial commitment by senior executives and responsibility for good hires cannot be delegated to human resources or lower level managers.

Training, Coaching, Nurturing

It is rare that anyone is born with all the skills, training and viewpoint necessary to drive a company to success. In an underperforming company, most managers will need training to build habits of discipline and execution. Building habits, which is a deeply ingrained philosophy and method of operation, is far different than sending someone to a seminar. Live experience as well as coaching is required to build habits and discipline (Neiman and Thomson, 2004, p. 18). Building the habits leading to successful execution requires the application of principals on a consistent basis. The reason most trendy approaches like TQM, Zero Based Budgeting, or others fail is not because of any inherent flaw in their approach, but in the fact that they are not consistently applied.

Executives and managers who don't understand profit and loss are in trouble (Stewart and O'Brien, 2005, p. 106). If they don't understand how all the elements of a business work together to produce a profit they can't help build a superior company. Top commercial banks understand this and invest in rigorous training. Some investment banks put their professional recruits through a year long training program that is equivalent to a top MBA (Bhide, 1986, p. 64).

GE has a school for developing it managers throughout their careers at Crotonville, New York. Jack Welsh regularly gave lectures there and met informally with future general managers to listen to their complaints about bureaucracy and management indecisiveness, and at the same time provided one-on one coaching. Jack Welsh also ran what he called " work-out" meetings in which managers met in open forums to argue, discuss and debate the best way to meet performance objectives (Abetti, 2006, p. 78).

In addition to building skilled, focused leaders, training and education has other benefits. For example, when managers believe a company is interested in their professional development, they tend to be more dedicated and loyal to the company which results in better execution and reduced turnover (Stewart and O'Brien, 2005, p. 106).

Occasionally a company finds itself with managers or executives that act inappropriately, resist change, abuse other employees, or lack commitment to goals. These people don't need retraining; they need elimination. Companies should be in the behavior selection business, not the behavior modification business.

Conclusion

Transforming an under-performing company into an exceptional company requires good execution. Good execution begins with an executable plan, that is a plan with defined goals, dates certain for performance, and clear responsibility. One of the hallmarks of a good plan is that it sets priorities. Long lists of plan goals dissipate energy. Shorts lists focus attention. Performance to goals must be measured at short intervals so that corrective action can be taken. Strategy should drive performance not budgets. If meeting budget is the goal, that goal will drive unstrategic behavior.

A CEO may inherit a company with a culture of underperformance; where results are either never compared to plan or results routinely fall short of plan. Changing that sort of culture will be painful, but it can be done. One way to change the culture is to focus on short interval projects with measurable results. The success of these projects is the first step in changing the culture. This must be followed by the consistent application of discipline in setting and achieving goals.

Performance to goals and rewards must be aligned. Commitment to meeting goals must be the highest virtue. Those who make commitments should be rewarded, those who don't, can't or won't must be pushed aside.

Measurement and monitoring are two of the keys to good execution. Everything that affects a company's performance should be monitored. This includes both financial measures like contribution margin and non-financial measures like the number of leads generated or the number of new customers. Performance should be transparent across all divisions so that everyone can see where they stand. This encourages superior performance. Secrecy is the enemy of good execution.

Management by walking around is another important source of information. Many aspects of a business cannot be adequately captured by performance measures and management by walking around can provide context to the numbers. Management by walking around can also help identify emerging trends for which measures have not yet been developed. This technique involves regular contact with front line workers, first line supervisors and customers.

No CEO can run a company alone and he or she must have good people to drive performance. Companies must select people on a number of criteria including drive, commitment to company goals, technical skills, willingness to be a team player and leadership. Not everyone possesses these qualities.

Training, coaching and nurturing are important tools for management development. They can help build technical skills, help people understand how various aspects of the company work together to drive performance and provide direction. However, companies should be in the behavior selection business not the behavior modification business. People who can't, won't or don't commit to company goals or people who can't, won't or don't want to be team players should be eliminated. Warnings rarely affect behavior so those who don't meet the company's criteria should be eliminated sooner rather than later.

In summary, good execution is probably the most important element driving excellent performance, more important than strategy, market position or a number of other factors. Good executions starts with well thought out and specific plans and well defined responsibility and continues with prompt and detailed measurement and accountability applied on a consistent basis.

References

Abetti PA (2006) Case study: Jack Welsh's creative revolutionary transformation of general electric and the Thermidorean Reaction (1981–2004). Creat Innov 15(1):74–84, Blackwell Publishing

Bhide A (1986) Hustle as strategy. Harv Bus Rev 64(5):59–65, Sept–Oct

Charan R, Colvin G (1999) Why CEOs fail. Fortune 139(12):68–72 Cvr, 21 June

Kaihla, P, Baltatzis P, Collingwood H, Copeland M, Finn B, Hamner S, Jacobson D, Nachtigal J, Schonfeld E, Sloan P, Thomas O (2006) Best kept secrets of the world's best companies. Business 2.0 7(3):82–96, Apr

Layman S (2005) Strategic goal alignment at CMP technologies. Strateg HR Rev 4(4):24–27, May–June

Mankins MC, Steele R (2005) Turning great strategy into great performance. Harv Bus Rev 83(7–8):65–72, Jul–Aug

Mankins MC, Steele R (2007) Increasing margins. Contractor's business management report, published by the Institute of Management & Administration. May, p 15. Also see: The keys to strategy execution. AMA/HRI Survey available at www.amanet.org/research

Neiman RA, Thomson H (2004) Execution plain and simple. Can Manag 17–19, Fall

Sorensen D (2003) The value market: creating profitable growth thorough consistent strategy execution. Strateg Finan, July pp 43–49

Stewart TA, O'Brien L (2005) Execution without excuses. Harv Bus Rev 83(3):102–111, Mar

Whitney JO (1996) Strategic renewal for business units. Harv Bus Rev 74(4):84–98, July–Aug

Appendix A
Restructuring Timeline

Introduction

Two things always in short supply are time and money. A restructuring timeline should help a new CEO or turnaround team get up to speed as quickly as possible and begin implementing reforms without delay.

Every company is different and the circumstances of each troubled or underperforming company are different. The timeline discussed in this appendix may have to be amended, re-sequenced or abandoned depending on circumstances. Never the less this timeline provides a useful starting point.

A new CEO or turnaround team probably has less than a hundred days to take action before the Board or others begin to question whether they selected the right person for the job. Those hundred days are precious and a timeline should help make the most of them.

The following sample turnaround plan timeline is phrased in terms of tasks and weeks. These plan tasks should cover all the improvements recommended in the restructuring plan and a substantial number of the sub-tasks. The tasks in a real plan might take a dozen pages.

D.E. Vance, *Corporate Restructuring*, DOI 10.1007/978-3-642-01786-5_BM2,
© Springer-Verlag Berlin Heidelberg 2009

Turnaround Timeline

Plan Begin and Plan End are weeks from the beginning of the restructuring.

Task no.	Description	Plan begin	Plan end	Actual end
1	Preliminary interviews of top executives and outside accountants to get overview of company.	1	3	
2	Meet with Board of Directors and get them to detail turnaround expectations. If possible, get them to quantify expectations. Form Turnaround Committee.	1	2	
3	Obtain cash flow projections.	1	2	
4	Implement temporary hiring freeze and freeze on new contracts over $10,000 per year. Halt new expansion until it can be reviewed.	2	3	
5	Hire three financial / management consultants to work on the turnaround team and recruit four company managers to work on the turnaround team full time.	2	4	
6	Perform a comprehensive ratio analysis of the company and its best ten competitors. Establish industry norms.	3	5	
7	Centralize cash collections, disbursements and cash management. Establish daily cash collections forecasting. Establish calendar of major cash disbursements.	3	8	
8	Implement headcount management system	3	6	
9	Evaluate divisions for disposal or restructuring	3	8	
10	Rank employees throughout the company	4	8	
11	Reverse engineer the company in terms expected sales, target profit, target COGS and target overhead.	5	6	
12	Set target headcount by division, at corporate and for the company as a whole.	6	7	
13	Hire an investment bank to advise on disposal of underperforming divisions.	9	12	
14	Develop a schedule of headcount reductions detailed to the level of specific individuals and propose same to the Turnaround Committee for approval	9	12	
15	Notify those who will be eliminated via headcount reduction and take other steps necessary to comply with layoff law.	13	13	
	o			
	o			
	o			

Index